SIEGE OF JERUS

The Middle English Texts Series is designed for classroom use. Its goal is to make available to teachers and students texts that occupy an important place in the literary and cultural canon but have not been readily available in student editions. The series does not include those authors, such as Chaucer, Langland, or Malory, whose English works are normally in print in good student editions. The focus is, instead, upon Middle English literature adjacent to those authors that teachers need in compiling the syllabuses they wish to teach. The editions maintain the linguistic integrity of the original work but within the parameters of modern reading conventions. The texts are printed in the modern alphabet and follow the practices of modern capitalization, word formation, and punctuation. Manuscript abbreviations are silently expanded, and *u/v* and *j/i* spellings are regularized according to modern orthography. Yogh (ȝ) is transcribed as *g*, *gh*, *y*, or *s*, according to the sound in Modern English spelling to which it corresponds; thorn (þ) and eth (ð) are transcribed as *th*. Distinction between the second person pronoun and the definite article is made by spelling the one *thee* and the other *the*, and final *-e* that receives full syllabic value is accented (e.g., *charité*). Hard words, difficult phrases, and unusual idioms are glossed on the page, either in the right margin or at the foot of the page. Explanatory and textual notes appear at the end of the text, often along with a glossary. The editions include short introductions on the history of the work, its merits and points of topical interest, and brief working bibliographies.

SIEGE OF JERUSALEM

Edited by
Michael Livingston

Published for TEAMS
(The Consortium for the Teaching of the Middle Ages)
in Association with the University of Rochester

by

MEDIEVAL INSTITUTE PUBLICATIONS
Kalamazoo, Michigan
2004

Library of Congress Cataloging-in-Publication Data

Siege of Jerusalem (Middle English poem)
 Siege of Jerusalem / edited by Michael Livingston.
     p. cm -- (Middle English texts)
 "Published for TEAMS (The Consortium for the Teaching of the Middle Ages) in
association with the University of Rochester."
 Text in Middle English; commentary in English.
 Includes bibliographical references.
 ISBN 1-58044-090-8 (paperbound : alk. paper)
1. Jerusalem--History--Siege, 70 A.D.--Poetry. I. Livingston, Michael, 1975- II. Western
Michigan University. Medieval Institute Publications. III. Consortium for the Teaching
of the Middle Ages. IV. Title. V. Middle English texts (Kalamazoo, Mich.)
 PR2065.S5 2004
 821'.1--dc22

                                                    2004030188

ISBN 1-58044-090-8

CONTENTS

In Memoriam
Otto Gründler
(1928–2004)

 ## ACKNOWLEDGMENTS

Just as this volume was undergoing a final read-through at the Middle English Texts Series, the long-promised edition of *Siege of Jerusalem* by Ralph Hanna and David Lawton was published. For its timely appearance I am very grateful, as I was able to pull my volume temporarily in order to account for their findings and thereby produce a better edition than would have otherwise been possible. I am, as a result, doubly indebted to their work: not only was their scholarship a welcome and supportive addition to my own work, but no doubt the combination of our two editions will help to stir interest in this remarkable but neglected poem. To David goes treble thanks, for he agreed to read this volume pre-publication and made a number of helpful suggestions to improve it.

For the opportunity to engage in the editing of this work, I must express my deepest gratitude to Russell A. Peck, General Editor of the Series. In addition to being a remarkably intelligent man, he is one of the kindest that I have known. His input at all stages of the project has no doubt led to the production of a better text than I could have ever produced on my own.

Thanks are owed to my many colleagues at the Series for their aid in bringing this project to fruition. Particular mention should be made of Thomas G. Hahn, who gave the volume a final reading just prior to its going to the press; he made a handful of excellent suggestions for glosses and notes, as well as catching a few formatting errors and embarrassing typos. Patricia Hollahan, Julie Scrivener, and the staff of Medieval Institute Publications gave the manuscript a final read-through and formatting check, then sent the edition to the printer. We all owe thanks to the National Endowment for the Humanities for its continuing support of the Series.

As if it needs to be said, any and all mistakes that remain in the text at this point are despite the efforts of Russell, David, Tom, and everyone else who read the text prior to publication.

Lastly, I would like to acknowledge and thank my wife, Sherry, for her patience during my interlude with *Siege*. She went to bed alone on too many nights so that I could complete the latest stage of this work. I'm not sure whether she considered this a good or a bad thing, but I hope that it is the latter. Thanks for putting up with me.

This volume has been dedicated to the memory of Otto Gründler, former Director of the Medieval Institute at Western Michigan University. Though I arrived too late to know him as the Director, during my years at the Institute I was fortunate to know him as a warm and generous man whose door was always open and whose mind was always extraordinarily sharp. Such men are too rare.

And after sixty-two weeks Christ shall be slain: and the people that shall deny him shall not be his. And a people, with their leader, that shall come, shall destroy the city, and the sanctuary: and the end thereof shall be waste, and after the end of the war the appointed desolation. (Daniel 9:26)

For the days shall come upon thee: and thy enemies shall cast a trench about thee and compass thee round and straiten thee on every side . . . (Luke 19:43)[1]

A recent critic, Roger Nicholson, summed up the feelings of many when he observed: "to admit to interest in the Middle English alliterative *Siege of Jerusalem* seems like confessing a secret guilt, or at least like committing an act of critical indecorum, since this alliterative romance is indisputably scandalous."[2] The poem is, after all, one that Ralph Hanna famously labeled as "the chocolate-covered tarantula of the alliterative movement . . . . so offensive as to exist on the suppressed margins of critical attention, unaccompanied by commentary."[3] David Lawton, though less rhetorical in his feelings, amusingly refers to *Siege* as a poem that "even its editors cannot love."[4] Nicholson explains the modern reader's dilemma succinctly:

Viewed one way, it [*Siege*] mars the reputation of medieval chivalric literature; viewed another, it stains the good name of medieval piety. It seems ruined by rank anti-Semitism; since it transgresses ethically, it also must fail as literature. In short, its grossness is so palpable that it seems to merit the critical invisibility that has been its textual fate for most of its post-medieval existence.[5]

Nicholson quite rightly goes on to refute some of these attitudes, and the rising interest in the poem among scholars — if quantity of publication is evidence of renewed interest — might indicate a shifting tide in favor of the poem's study. It is possible that *Siege of Jerusalem* may at last be getting the critical attention that it has been missing. Still, though critical studies of the poem are appearing with more frequency, Nicholson's hesitancy to confess his "secret guilt" is understandable: it is simply difficult for twenty-first-century readers to like the poem.

---

[1] This and all subsequent quotations from the Bible are from the Douay-Rheims translation as revised in 1749–52 by Richard Challoner.

[2] Nicholson, "Haunted Itineraries," p. 447.

[3] Hanna, "Contextualising *The Siege of Jerusalem*," p. 109.

[4] Lawton, "Titus Goes Hunting and Hawking," p. 105. Lawton refers, of course, to his own work (with Hanna) in editing the poem: *Siege of Jerusalem*, ed. Hanna and Lawton.

[5] Nicholson, "Haunted Itineraries," p. 447.

The alliterative *Siege of Jerusalem* dates from the end of the fourteenth century, depicting the historical destruction of the Second Temple in AD 70 by the Roman generals (and future emperors) Titus and Vespasian. The poem is extraordinarily graphic in its depiction of this event — at times bordering on what Dorothy Everett calls a "ghoulish relish for the horrible,"[6] combined with what A. C. Spearing describes as a deep anti-Semitic strain that leads to "horrible delight in the suffering of the Jews."[7] Such features of the poem have helped to marginalize it from the more "happy" literary canon of the period. These twin problems of violence and intolerance understandably make modern readers uneasy. But the poem has merits both as a literary undertaking and as a significant historical document that warrant careful consideration. Indeed, as Bonnie Millar has argued in the only full-length study of *Siege* yet available, most current views of the poem are grossly inadequate in that they fail to account for the poem's "physical, literary and historical contexts in order to assess how the poet has handled his material in an innovative and perceptive manner."[8] One might argue, then, that critics have the proverbial mirror turned around: the marginalization of *Siege of Jerusalem* in this politically correct world says far more about us as readers, and our own difficulties in coping with such charged topics, than it does about medieval perspectives on the material in question. As an artifact of late-medieval England, *Siege of Jerusalem* provides a remarkable document on the brutality of siege warfare that was on the minds of Englishmen in the so-called interim period of the Hundred Years' War; and it exposes as well numerous crises within the Christian Church, particularly the increasing economic uses of crusader politics.[9]

HISTORY OF THE TEMPLE

In January of 588 BC, Nebuchadrezzar, the king of Babylon, invaded Judah and began to assault Jerusalem (Jeremias 21:2, 7; 32:1–2; 34:1; 37). In August of the following year, on the ninth of Av according to Rabbinic tradition, the Babylonians took control of Jerusalem, and Solomon's Temple, the great edifice built by the son of King David to house the Ark of the Covenant (1 Kings 5–8; 2 Chronicles 1–6), was destroyed. The Babylonian Captivity of Israel began. For the next fifty years, the Jewish people were a people in exile. It was only after the king of Persia, Cyrus the Great, defeated the Babylonians in 539 that the Jews were allowed to return to Judaea and to begin the reconstruction of the Temple. The Second Temple was completed in 516 and, for a time, things were relatively quiet. Jerusalem came under the control of Alexander the Great shortly after he conquered the Persians in 334, and Judaea passed into the hands of the Ptolemies during the breakup of Alexander's empire following his death, but little direct action was taken against the Jews or the Second Temple. Then, in 200 BC, a minor empire of Syrian Greeks called the Seleucids forced the Ptolemies out of Judaea and took control of the region. The Jews were uneasy under the Gentile authority of the Seleucids, who worked hard to Hellenize them in the interest of consolidating their rule and maintaining order. Matters took a distinct turn for the worse in 169 when Antiochus IV Epiphanes, the king of the Seleucids, looted the Second Temple,

---

[6] Everett, *Essays on Middle English Literature*, p. 59.

[7] Spearing, *Readings in Medieval Poetry*, p. 172.

[8] Millar, *Siege of Jerusalem*, p. 9.

[9] For more on the late fourteenth-century historical background to the poem, see pp. 24–30, below.

an act that resulted in the deaths of a number of Jews who stood against him. A year later, Antiochus forbade Jews to practice many of their religious rites, including circumcision (1 Maccabees 1:41–51). He threatened to execute anyone found in possession of the Torah, and in 167 built an altar on the Temple Mount that was probably dedicated to Zeus. Many Jews were dismayed at this act of desecration, viewing the pagan sacrifices as an "abomination unto desolation" (Daniel 11:31). The resistance of the Jews soon grew into all-out guerilla warfare under the leadership of Judas Maccabeus (Judas "the hammerer"), who, after a series of brilliant military victories, managed to achieve religious freedom from the Seleucids. He then set himself the task of purifying the Second Temple. Exactly three years after Antiochus had begun pagan sacrifices at the Temple, on 25 Kislev, 164 BC, the Second Temple was rededicated — an achievement that is celebrated annually with the feast of Hanukkah.[10]

One hundred years later, in 63 BC, the Jewish state came to an end when Rome entered Jerusalem and the city was peacefully handed over to Pompey. In 41, the Romans appointed Herod the Great as tetrarch of Galilee, and he was named king of Judaea in the following year. Herod the Great undertook a massive and widespread building program in Jerusalem, and the culmination of this project was the restoration of the Second Temple beginning in 20 BC. Herod's restoration — which amounted to almost an entire rebuilding, such that the restored Temple is sometimes called "Herod's Temple" — doubled the size of the Temple complex and left little of the original structure intact. Matthew 2 places the birth of Jesus just prior to the death of Herod around 4 BC.

Following the death of Herod the Great, Emperor Augustus divided the kingdom (which had grown to near the size of Solomon and David's) between three of Herod's sons: Herod Antipas (Galilee and Peraea), Philip (Decapolis and the provinces north to Damascus), and Herod Archelaus (Judaea and Samaria). Archelaus proved to be a particularly poor leader, and so angered both his Jews and Samaritans that Augustus was forced to depose him in AD 6, replacing him with a series of Roman procurators. This practice was followed by Augustus' successor to the Roman throne, Tiberius, who continued to rule Judaea through procurators including, from 26 to 36, Pontius Pilate. It was during the rule of Pilate that Jesus of Nazareth began a ministry of preaching that called for a kingdom of God to replace the kingdom of the Caesars; His preaching was viewed as sedition by the Roman authorities, and it is very likely that Pilate sentenced Jesus to execution by crucifixion on this charge.[11] According to the Christian gospels, which were composed some decades after His death (and probably after the historical destruction of the Second Temple in 70), Jesus prophesied before His Crucifixion that the Second Temple would be destroyed.

With the exception of the brief rule of the Jewish vassal king Herod Agrippa I from 41 to 44, Jerusalem continued to be ruled by Roman procurators who kept control via the might and power of the Roman military. The Jews grew increasingly frustrated with Roman rule, however, as the procurators — often some of the worst officials in the empire due to

---

[10] For this brief history, I am particularly indebted to Josephus' *Wars of the Jews* and *Antiquities of the Jews* in *The Works of Flavius Josephus*, trans. Whiston; the brief presentation provided by Wright in *Vengeance of Our Lord*; Rhoads, *Israel in Revolution*; and the still-unsurpassed study of the fall of Jerusalem, Furneaux's *Roman Siege of Jerusalem*.

[11] Since Jesus was a native of Galilee, Pilate is reported in one gospel to have given Herod Antipas the option of dealing with the matter, an offer that Herod declined (Luke 23:6–16). Antipas makes several other appearances in the New Testament, including ordering the beheading of John the Baptist at a feast (Matthew 14:6–12).

the undesirability of the Judaean post — grew increasingly violent against them. Stephen K. Wright (p. 3) summarizes the conditions that led to the First Jewish Revolt:

> The widespread discontent with Roman rule was compounded by the frustrations of the impoverished lower classes, who suspected wealthy native landowners of maintaining their own privileged positions by accommodating themselves to the interests of their idolatrous, polytheistic rulers. The incompetence and cultural insensitivity of the procurators did nothing to relieve these economic and political pressures. On the contrary, a dismal history of injustices and unpopular administrative decisions only served to provoke sporadic protests ranging from minor disturbances to full-scale urban riots. The situation exploded into outright rebellion in 66 AD when the procurator Gessius Florus confiscated a share of the Temple treasury and responded to the outrage of the citizens by allowing two cohorts to plunder the city. A violent mob attacked the troops dispatched by Gessius, drove them from the streets, and eventually overran the Roman garrison in the city. Within weeks the rebellion spread throughout all of Palestine.

The emperor Nero (r. 54–68) responded to the uprising by sending an army almost sixty thousand strong against Judaea under the command of Vespasian and his son Titus. The Romans first attacked Galilee in Syria and met with a number of successes. The town of Jotapata, however, under the direction of the Jewish leader Flavius Josephus (to whose account we owe much of our information about the details of the First Jewish Revolt) held firm. Vespasian set a siege upon the city and, despite the often-ingenious stratagems of Josephus, the town fell in 67. Titus, meanwhile, took the towns of Jaffa, Gamala (which also required a brief siege), and Gischala. After putting down the revolt in Galilee, the Romans moved on Judaea, sweeping toward Jerusalem. Joppa, Jamnia, Azotus, Emmaus, and Caphartobas fell in the south, followed in the north by Coreae, Gadara, Gerasa, and Jericho in 68.[12]

Nero, meanwhile, died, and a series of men (Galba, Otho, and Vitellius) rose to the throne of Rome after his death only to be quickly murdered in turn. By 69, the throne had fallen to Vespasian, who returned to Rome in order to fill the imperial vacancy, leaving the Roman armies in the control of his son, Titus. With Jericho and the lands to the north of the Dead Sea secured, Titus and the Roman armies laid siege to Jerusalem in 70.[13] Titus had four legions at his disposal: the Tenth Legion had moved from Jericho to the Mount of Olives; the Twelfth Legion had come from Caesarea and encamped west of the city; the Fifth and Fifteenth Legions had come from the north and completed the surrounding of the city. The Jewish forces were under the command of two feuding leaders: Simon, son of Gioras (bar-Giora), and John of Gischala. Josephus, who had been taken prisoner by the Romans after the fall of Jotapata only to become one of Titus' close friends and perhaps advisor, accompanied the Romans and was an eyewitness to the siege. After breaching the third and second walls of the city but failing to take the Fortress Antonia that protected the Second Temple itself, Titus encompassed Jerusalem in a massive circumvallation that was, according to

---

[12] It is perhaps of interest to note here that it was probably during the Roman attacks on Jericho that the Essenes at Qumran hid the Dead Sea Scrolls in caves just outside their community. This community seems to have been subsequently destroyed by the Tenth Legion as it marched from the area of Jericho to Jerusalem.

[13] It is difficult to ascertain with accuracy the total number of forces engaged in the fight, but it was certainly staggering. In his succinct retelling of the siege (complete with a map showing the movements of the Roman forces), Davis estimates 70,000 Roman men against a total of 23,400 fighting Jews; see *Besieged*, pp. 35–39.

Josephus, almost eight kilometers (five miles) long, and that was built in only three days (*Wars of the Jews* 5.12.1–3). The siege lasted six months, during which time a terrible famine was inflicted upon the people of the town. Josephus describes this and other horrors most graphically, including an account of a woman so taken with hunger that she killed, cooked, and consumed her own son (*Wars of the Jews* 5.10–6.5). The Fortress Antonia was taken by Titus on 22 July 70, and many Jews barricaded themselves in the Second Temple. On 5 August, the temple was burned with the Jews still inside (this may or may not have been an accident), and the Roman soldiers carried out a campaign of slaughter along the entire east ridge. According to the Jewish calendar, this destruction of the Second Temple took place on the ninth of Av, the same date on which Solomon's Temple was destroyed 657 years earlier. The remaining Jews made a desperate last stand in Herod's Palace in the Upper City, but the end was inevitable. The Lower City was burned at the beginning of September, and by the end of the month all resistance ended when Titus' men assaulted Herod's Palace and took the Upper City. Titus ordered the Second Temple razed to the ground, and ultimately only a portion of the western retaining wall of the Temple Mount — known today as the Western Wall and regarded as one of Judaism's most holy sites — survived the destruction. Suetonius numbered the Jewish dead at 600,000, while Josephus gives the number 1.1 million; even if those numbers reflect, as many historians surmise, "the casualties inflicted on all Jews in the entire campaign and not just in the siege," either number is difficult to fathom.[14] Most of those Jews who were not executed were carried off as slaves, and the Tenth Legion was thereafter quartered in Jerusalem; only three years later, the tragic fall of Masada marked the end of Jewish resistance until the Bar-Cochba Revolt in 132 (a rebellion prompted by Hadrian's construction of a temple to Jupiter on the site of the Second Temple).[15] On returning to Rome, Titus held a triumphal procession in which he displayed the golden menorah looted from the Temple as a trophy. The Arch of Titus in Rome was built to commemorate the triumph; on one of its panels is carved in high relief the scene of his soldiers carrying the menorah.

THE VENGEANCE OF OUR LORD TRADITION

The siege and destruction of Jerusalem by Titus and Vespasian was a popular subject for medieval writers. This was particularly true of Christian writers who used the destruction of Jerusalem as what Wright (p. 6) has called "a new interpretation of the Church's own history, nature and mission":

---

[14] Davis, *Besieged*, p. 39. Most medieval writers, probably basing their accounts ultimately on Josephus, accept the number of dead as 1.1 million. See, for example, any of the versions of *Mandeville's Travels* that briefly sum up the destruction of Solomon's Temple (and therefore of Jerusalem) in their account of Jerusalem; in the so-called Defective Version recently edited by Seymour it appears on p. 33.

[15] As Wright notes, the failure of the Bar-Cochba Revolt in 135 led to "the virtual extinction of Judaism in Jerusalem and southern Palestine, and spelled the end of Jewish national independence until the creation of the modern state of Israel" (*Vengeance of Our Lord*, p. 4). For a brief overview on the further lasting effects of the fall of Jerusalem on both the history of Judaism (not least of which is the move toward rabbinical Judaism following the establishment of the Jamnia school by Johanan ben Zakkai) and the development of Christianity as it moved toward a Gentile-oriented ministry, see Wright, *Vengeance of Our Lord*, pp. 4–6. The latter issue is discussed in more detail in Brandon, *Fall of Jerusalem and the Christian Church*, and Conzelmann, *History of Primitive Christianity*.

In a sense, the bitter separation of Church and Synagogue can be traced to the destruction of Jerusalem, since for the latter it resulted in renewed obedience to the Torah, while for the former it became a sign of the rejection of the old Israel and the birth of a new Christian empire in Rome. In the Christian imagination, the destruction of Jerusalem was finally removed from its secular context altogether and came to stand for nothing less than the ultimate triumph of Ecclesia over Synagoga, a symbol of the Western Church's repudiation of its own Jewish heritage.

This movement from Synagogue to Church, revealing the strength of the Christian faith and what was deemed to be its natural place in history, accounts for much of the story's popularity in the Middle Ages. In addition, however, Malcolm Hebron makes a convincing argument that part of the story's popularity may be due to the various generic elements already present in the story:

> The material provided a combination of legend, miracle, history, and Roman chivalry, as well as opportunities for vivid description of siege warfare in the East; the triumph of Western Christendom in the form of the Roman army must have provided a pleasing contrast to the present situation in the Holy Land at a time when the recapture of Jerusalem was still the dream of monarchs. While the combination of the religious and the chivalric, crusading elements in the story of the siege and the events leading up to it contributed to its popularity, the matter of Jerusalem also contains deeper resonances concerning the pattern of history. The romances, like those on Troy, tend to concentrate on action rather than reflection, but the ways in which the historical event is recreated bear traces of a wider context of ideas concerning destiny and salvation which give the episode a special significance.
> As an image of history, the siege of Jerusalem contrasts with that of Troy. Where the fall of Troy illustrates a Boethian model of history as a cycle of rise and fall of power and fortune, the destruction of Jerusalem by the Roman emperors Titus and Vespasian illustrates the separate, Augustinian conception of history as a succession of great events which reveal part of the divine scheme of things. The siege of Troy is a warning against human vanity and folly, while that of Jerusalem reveals the will and power of God. Where Troy is a tragic fall of power and pride, Jerusalem even in its tribulations is seen as a sign of the triumphal march of destiny.[16]

This great "triumphal march of destiny," through which the superiority and inevitability of the Christian faith was evidently played out in the historical events of the destruction, lent itself to the accretion of legendary materials, especially those of a religious nature. That is, the destruction of Jerusalem came to symbolize the failure of the Old Law of the Jews and the triumph of the New Law of the Christians. Because one of the first conclusions that Christian writers drew from the fall of Jerusalem was that the Jews were punished for their rejection (and, as the accusation grew in popularity, their perceived murder) of Jesus, medieval writers and subsequent critics have referred to the various works of poetry, prose, and drama that came to represent the story in this way as the Vengeance of Our Lord tradition, a description drawn from one of the primary Latin sources, *Vindicta salvatoris*.[17]

---

[16] Hebron, *Medieval Siege*, p. 112.

[17] This brief overview of the literary history of the destruction of Jerusalem is based primarily on that found in Hebron, *Medieval Siege*, pp. 113–17. An additional overview can be found in *The Middle English Prose Translation of Roger d'Argenteuil's Bible en François*, ed. Moe, pp. 22–28.

One of the first accretions to the basic history was that of the story of St. Veronica and her Vernicle, a cloth (usually a veil) that bore an image of the face of Jesus and had the ability to cure the sick. St. Veronica appears with her veil in Eusebius' *Ecclesiastical History*, but her story grew in popularity after it was combined with the life of Pontius Pilate in the fourth-century *Acta Pilati*. Around the year 600, St. Veronica's story is attached to Josephus' story of the fall of Jerusalem in *Cura sanitatis Tiberii*. Around the year 700, the healing of an ill Titus by the Vernicle (and his subsequent conversion) is incorporated into *Vindicta salvatoris*, along with the explicit portrayal of the siege as vengeance for the Crucifixion. The eleventh-century *De Pylato* names Vespasian as the miraculously healed leader of the siege. Jacobus de Voragine's *Legenda aurea* added the detail of a number of portents of the destruction. The accreted tradition then appears in Old French in the twelfth-century *La Venjance Nostre Seigneur*, probably in direct connection with the Crusades against the Muslims in the East.

As Alvin E. Ford has pointed out, the fourteenth and fifteenth centuries were witness to a flurry of texts in the Vengeance of Our Lord tradition: "Verse versions, prose versions, *chansons de geste*, mystery plays, book-length documents and one-page résumés, all attest to the widespread diffusion of the apocryphal *Vengeance of Our Lord* throughout the medieval Christian world." Of Old and Middle French prose versions alone, Ford identifies fifty-four (and counting) manuscripts, "representing nine independent but interrelated traditions," the primary works being *La Vengeance de Nostre-Seigneur* and Roger d'Argenteuil's *Bible en François*.[18] Wright, studying the representation of Jerusalem's destruction in medieval drama, comments (p. 1) on the surprising popularity of the story in drama during this same period:

> From their first appearance in the mid-fourteenth century until as late as 1622, plays of the destruction of Jerusalem are known to have been performed in six different languages (German, French, Italian, Spanish, English, and Latin) to the delight of audiences in dozens of communities scattered across the Continent. Indeed, French performance records indicate that, over the course of more than two centuries, only the story of Christ's Passion was staged more frequently than the Vengeance of Our Lord. By the late sixteenth century, dramatizations of the siege of Jerusalem, most of which required from two to four days to perform, had spread from their earliest homes in Thuringia and Burgundy to the Tirol, Savoy, the Italian Briançonnais, Switzerland, England, and Castile.

Even within the relatively small corpus of late Middle English poetry, we have at least four extant poems that focus primarily on the Vengeance of Our Lord: the alliterative poem of *Siege of Jerusalem* here edited, two versions (one short, one long) of the rhyming-couplet *Titus and Vespasian*,[19] and a translation of Roger d'Argenteuil's *Bible en François*.[20]

---

[18] *La Vengeance de Nostre-Seigneur*, ed. Ford, 2.1. The oldest French version in verse survives in at least nine full manuscripts (as well as a set of fragments) and is edited by Gryting as *La Venjance Nostre Seigneur*.

[19] The longer version, *Titus and Vespasian*, has been edited by Herbert. Morey provides a succinct summary of the work in his *Book and Verse*, pp. 228–31. A fifteenth-century prose redaction of the same version, *Siege of Jerusalem in Prose*, has been edited by Kurvinen. At least three prints of *The Dystruccyon of Iherusalem*, a prose retelling in this same tradition, have survived from the early years of the sixteenth century, testifying to the continued popularity of the theme; see Pollard and Redgrave's *Short-Title Catalogue*, items 14517–19.

[20] In addition, there are a number of other poems, like those centered on Joseph of Arimathea (who was said in some traditions to have been freed from prison in Jerusalem by the conquering

DATE AND PROVENANCE OF THE POEM

Firm dates are hard to come by in the Middle Ages, and the difficulties grow near to impossibilities when one is dealing with literary texts. Few works survive in autograph manuscripts, meaning that almost everything we have is a copy at least one remove from the author's hand. Multiple manuscript copies tend to compound the problem. Nine manuscripts containing parts or the whole of *Siege of Jerusalem* have survived.[21] None of them are in the poet's own hand, and it is quite likely that none are even in his precise dialect. The best we can hope for in dating the poem, therefore, is to build a case of circumstantial evidence that, if true, allows us to give a narrow range of dates in which the poem was probably written. The first step in such a task is to examine the nine surviving manuscripts of the poem, of which only four are entirely complete:[22]

- *Manuscript A*
(British Library, MS Additional 31042, fols. 50r–66r)
Copied s. xv med., by Robert Thornton of East Newton, northern Yorkshire.
Fragmentary: lacks lines 293–369, on a lost leaf after fol. 53.

- *Manuscript C*
(British Library, MS Cotton Caligula A.ii, part I, fols. 111r–125r)
Copied s. xv$^{3/4}$, in the East Midlands, perhaps the edges of East Anglia.
Fragmentary: lacks lines 167–248, on a lost leaf after fol. 112.

- *Manuscript D*
(London, Lambeth Palace Library, MS 491, part I, fols. 206r–227v)
Copied s. xv$^{1/4}$, by a London professional scribe who uses the forms of the Rayleigh, Essex, area (*LALME* LP 6030).

- *Manuscript E*
(San Marino, Huntington Library, MS HM 128, fols. 205r–216r)
Copied s. xv in., in extreme southern Warwickshire (*LALME* LP 6910, a dialect similar to that of a second scribe in the volume, LP 8040).

Romans) or on Christ's harrowing of Hell, that are tangentially related to events or personae within the tradition or that make reference to the destruction of Jerusalem at the hands of Titus and Vespasian; many of these works are rooted in apocryphal sources like *The Gospel of Nicodemus*. Quite a few Passion narratives also make reference to the destruction, with some actually devoting some length to retelling the whole of the Vengeance narrative (*Metrical Life of Christ*, for example, does so in almost four hundred lines). See Morey, *Book and Verse*, pp. 118–19, 226–31, 237–49, and 252–56.

[21] The most thorough discussion of the manuscripts is that found in Hanna and Lawton's edition of the poem, pp. xiii–xxvii; the more specific relationships between the poems are discussed on pp. lv–lxix.

[22] This listing is based on that given by Hanna, *Pursuing History*, pp. 83–84, emended by Hanna and Lawton's most recent findings in *Siege of Jerusalem*. The line numbering presented here, therefore, does not precisely match that of the earlier edition of Kölbing and Day.

- *Manuscript Ex*
(Exeter, Devon Record Office, MS 2507, a binding fragment)
Copied s. xv², in the North Midlands.
Fragmentary: contains portions of lines 985–1017, 1106–23, 1196, 1125–38.

- *Manuscript L*
(Bodleian Library, MS Laud Misc. 656, fols. 1v–19r)
Copied s. xiv ex., in northwest Oxfordshire.

- *Manuscript P*
(Princeton University Library, MS Taylor Medieval 11, fols. 104vb–110vb)
Copied s. xiv ex., with ex libris possibly of St. Mary's Abbey [OSA], Bolton, extreme western Yorkshire (*LALME* LP 598).
Fragmentary: ends at line 1143, and mostly illegible after line 1055 (fol. 110v).

- *Manuscript U*
(Cambridge University Library, MS Mm.v.14, fols. 187r–206v)
Copied s. xv^{1/4}, by the London scribe Richard Frampton.

- *Manuscript V*
(British Library, MS Cotton Vespasian E.xvi, fols. 70r–75v)
Copied s. xv med., in the East Midlands (*LALME* LP 553)
Fragmentary: begins at line 966.

Following the work of previous editors and scholars, Ralph Hanna has established a plausible stemma for the dissemination of the poem, a series of relationships intended to reveal how the manuscripts relate to one another. He concludes that the surviving copies fall into three groups: L (deriving from the hypothesized manuscript *alpha*), PAVEx (deriving from manuscript *gamma*), and UDEC (deriving from manuscript *delta*).[23] Figure 1 illustrates these basic relationships.[24] Of the surviving manuscripts, then, L stands alone both as the oldest fairly complete copy and the most unique: the remaining manuscripts share enough features to be considered to be part of the same family (both *gamma* and *delta* manuscripts deriving from the shared manuscript *beta*).

Of these many manuscripts, the incomplete P is actually the closest artifact of the poem's original dialect, which is generally identified as in the far west of Yorkshire; Hanna submits Sawley, Whalley, or Bolton as possible locations for the poem's composition.[25] Elisa Narin van Court argues for Bolton on the basis that it alone is home to an Augustinian abbey — a necessary requirement, she feels, due to the poem's inability to condemn the Jews outright.[26]

---

[23] Hanna does note, however, that after line 621 copy C seems to derive information both from the UDEC examplar and that of PAVEx.

[24] This diagram is based on that found in Hanna, *Pursuing History*, p. 91 (and reproduced in Hanna and Lawton's edition, p. lxvii). I have simplified the diagram somewhat by collapsing the holograph text and archetype text under the single heading "Original Text."

[25] Hanna, "Contextualising," pp. 114–16.

[26] As Millar summarizes: "the ambiguous attitude to the Jews in the text, at times advocating violence towards them and on other occasions encouraging sympathy for their plight, displays evidence

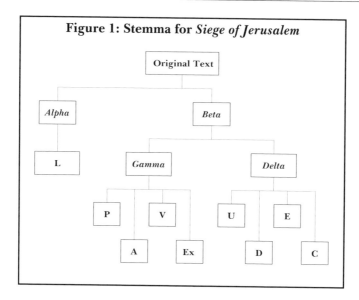

Figure 1: Stemma for *Siege of Jerusalem*

While the necessity of Augustinian provenance cannot be proven, Bolton Abbey in Craven remains the most likely location for the poem's origin, a conclusion also reached by Hanna and Lawton in their edition of *Siege*.[27] The oldest of the manuscripts seems to date from the very end of the fourteenth century, so we must begin with the assumption that the *terminus ad quem*, the latest time that the poem could have been composed, is in the late 1390s.[28] Determining an initial *ad quem* in this way is generally straightforward; determining the *terminus a quo*, the earliest date that the poem could have been composed, is more difficult.

Though *Siege of Jerusalem* relies on five primary works for its basic plotting and details — *Vindicta salvatoris*, Roger d'Argenteuil's *Bible en François*, Ranulf Higden's *Polychronicon*, Jacobus de Voragine's *Legenda aurea*, and Josephus' *Wars of the Jews*[29] — the poet also operates within an alliterative tradition of poetry in which poets freely borrowed phrases and even entire lines and sets of lines from either a common stock of alliterative material or directly from each other's work.[30] As a result, it has long been thought possible to provide

---

for the influence of Augustinian historical writing, such as the chronicle of William of Newburgh, which was on the whole tolerant of Jews, although it disapproved of their religious beliefs." See Millar, *Siege of Jerusalem*, p. 10, and Van Court, "*Siege of Jerusalem* and Augustinian Historians," pp. 227–48.

[27] Using *LALME* overlays of isoglosses (often referred to as the Benskin Fit Method), Hanna and Lawton found that the authorial dialect seems to be that of the Barnoldswick-Earby area of western Yorkshire (*Siege of Jerusalem*, ed. Hanna and Lawton, pp. xxvii–xxxv). They further theorize a connection to the Clifford family that, although it must remain speculative, is rather intriguing as the sixth lord Clifford was a knight of the King's Chamber under Richard II (see pp. lii–lv).

[28] In addition, it seems that the composer of the couplet *Titus and Vespasian* may have utilized *Siege*; the earliest manuscript of that poem also appears to date from around the year 1400.

[29] More detailed discussion of the poem's sources is given below, pp. 21–23.

[30] In addition to *Destruction of Troy* here discussed, Oakden (*Alliterative Poetry in Middle English*, pp. 99–102) calls attention to possible connections with *Wars of Alexander* (see also note 35, below), *Sir Gawain and the Green Knight*, *Patience*, *Purity*, *Parlement of the Thre Ages*, and *Wynnere and Wastoure*; as we will see, one can certainly add *Alliterative Morte Arthure* to this list, and perhaps even *Awntyrs of*

a *terminus a quo* for *Siege* based on its supposed borrowing from other works of the alliterative tradition. In particular, *Siege* has often been thought to echo the alliterative *Destruction of Troy*, a translation of Guido delle Colonne's Latin work, *Historia destructionis Troiae*. As first noted by George Neilson at the turn of the twentieth century, the correspondences between these works are quite numerous.[31] And, while many of these borrowings might well be thought to be due to a common "word-hoard" (to borrow a kenning from the Anglo-Saxons), one sequence in particular stands out in perhaps showing a more direct relationship between the two texts:

> By that was the day don: dymmed the skyes,
> Merked montayns   and mores aboute,   *Darkened; moors*
> Foules fallen to fote   and here fethres rysten,
> The nyght-wacche to the walle   and waytes to blowe.[32]
>
> Bryght fures aboute betyn   abrode in the oste;   *fires; army (host)*
> The kyng and his consail   carpen togedre,   *speak together*
> Chosen chyventayns out   and chiden no more,   *Choose chieftains; quarrel*
> Bot charged the chek-wecche   and to chambre wenten,   *check-watch*
>
> Kynges and knyghtes,   to cacchen hem reste.   *to get their rest*

Compare these lines from *Siege of Jerusalem* with the following passage, from the beginning of the seventeenth book of *Destruction of Troy*, concerning the falling of night after the third great battle outside the walls of Troy and the coming together of a council of Greeks in Agamemnon's tent in which they will plan the death of Hector:

> When the day ouer drogh, & the derk entrid,
> The sternes full stithly starond o lofte;
> All merknet the mountens & mores aboute;
> The ffowles þere fethers foldyn to gedur.
> Nightwacche for to wake, waites to blow;
> Tore fyres in the tenttes, tendlis olofte;
> All the gret of the grekes gedrit hom somyn.
> Kinges & knightes clennest of wit,
> Dukes & derffe Erles droghen to counsell . . . (*Destruction*, lines 7348–56)[33]

Arthur. I have noted most of these various echoes in the notes to this volume. This wide range of works covers most of the breadth of the Alliterative Revival. One must be careful, however, about reading too much into these echoes. As Waldron ("Oral-Formulaic Technique") and others have shown, the very nature of alliterative poetry lends itself to echoes of convention and formulae. Turville-Petre states the matter quite bluntly: "verbal parallels are a very uncertain guide to establishing relationships between alliterative poems" (*Alliterative Revival*, p. 29).

[31] Neilson, "*Huchown*," pp. 282–88. Neilson attempted to use such borrowings to establish common authorship between numerous poems of the alliterative revival, though subsequent generations of scholars have largely abandoned such theses.

[32] Lines 731–32: *Birds fall to their feet and their feathers shake out. / The night-watch [goes] to the wall and waits to sound [the alarm]*

[33] As a text for *Destruction of Troy*, I have used the Early English Text Society edition edited by Panton and Donaldson: "*Gest Hystoriale*" *of the Destruction of Troy*.

As Mary Hamel points out, such a lengthy "sequence of ideas and images, of word choices and collocations, over passages of nine lines each seems irrefutable evidence of a relationship of dependence."[34] In other words, the similarities here cannot be attributed to coincidental borrowing from a common stock of alliterative material but instead argue persuasively that one poet knew the other poet's work.[35] The question then becomes one of chronology: which poet wrote first?

Most previous scholars have held that the *Siege*-poet is the one doing the borrowing in the present case since, as Hamel states the matter: "while there is no other known source for the *Siege* lines, the *Troy* passage is an elaboration in the poet's typical style of a few lines in his source, Guido's *Historia*."[36] The composition of *Destruction of Troy* is, as a result, generally assumed to be a solid *terminus a quo* for the composition of *Siege of Jerusalem*. And since critics are fairly certain that *Destruction of Troy* borrows from Chaucer's *Troilus and Criseyde*, and Chaucer's poem is generally accepted to have been composed between 1382 and 1385,[37] a *terminus a quo* for *Siege of Jerusalem* would thus be, at a minimum, these dates. Allowing for the dissemination of the poems prior to their influence on other poets, the date range for *Siege* posited by Mabel Day and Eugen Kölbing in their edition of the poem has been thought to remain accurate: the poem was composed in the last decade of the fourteenth century, between 1390 and 1400.[38]

Yet in their recent edition of *Siege*, Hanna and Lawton cast doubt on this long-held sequence, stating that since

> Most modern opinion would, of course, date the completion of Chaucer's poem *c*.1385–86. Placing [*Destruction of Troy*], the longest of all the poems in the alliterative corpus, after this date yet early enough to allow its dissemination, the collection of sources for and the composition of *The Siege*, and the dissemination of both the visible *Siege* manuscripts and their archetypes before the 1390s, for us stretches probability considerably.[39]

---

[34] *Morte Arthure*, ed. Hamel, p. 55.

[35] Neilson notes an additional thirty-one lines as echoing *Destruction of Troy*, astutely pointing out that most of the echoes in *Destruction of Troy* are from the siege and subsequent destruction of Tenedos. He also hears echoes of eighteen lines from *Wars of Alexander* in *Siege* (mostly from *Wars'* account of the siege of Tyre), and I have noted a number of these, as well. Let me be clear, however, in voicing my hesitancy to acknowledge them all as evident signs of direct influence.

[36] *Morte Arthure*, ed. Hamel, p. 55. In their edition of *Siege*, however, Hanna and Lawton have observed that this position is more tenuous than it might seem on first glance since portions of *Destruction of Troy* are best explained by reliance on *Siege*; see *Siege of Jerusalem*, ed. Hanna and Lawton, p. xxxvn10.

[37] An excellent synopsis of the dating of *Troilus* is provided in Stephen A. Barney's explanatory notes to the poem in *The Riverside Chaucer*, pp. 1020–21. Hamel summarizes the extended sequential dating of *Siege* in her edition of *Alliterative Morte Arthure* (*Morte Arthure*, pp. 53–58), a poem that either is borrowed by or borrows from *Siege*. In addition to the correspondences between *Troilus* and *Troy* originally noted by Skeat (*The Complete Works of Geoffrey Chaucer*, 2.lxvi), Hamel cites, as particularly representative of these arguments, Benson's "A Chaucerian Allusion and the Date of the Alliterative 'Destruction of Troy,'" and Sundwall's "*Destruction of Troy*, Chaucer's *Troilus and Criseyde*, and Lydgate's *Troy Book*," pp. 313–15.

[38] *Siege of Jerusalem*, ed. Kölbing and Day, p. xxix.

[39] *Siege of Jerusalem*, ed. Hanna and Lawton, p. xxxvii.

Their solution is to place *Siege* before *Troilus and Criseyde* and to brand the author of *Destruction of Troy* as the borrower. The closest we might get to a certain *terminus a quo*, then, would be the publication of Higden's *Polychronicon*, itself written in various stages between 1327 and c. 1360.[40] In concluding their discussion of authorial dialect, Hanna and Lawton theorize that a compositional date for *Siege* "during the 1370s or 1380s would seem an appropriate conservative inference."[41] In addition to providing a far more plausible chronology for the dissemination of the texts involved, such a date provides a clearer relationship between *Siege* and *Alliterative Morte Arthure*, which is discussed in further detail below. I would argue, then, that Hanna and Lawton's dating of *Siege* makes good sense: the poem was composed sometime in the 1370s or 1380s, probably at Bolton Abbey in Craven.

OVERVIEW OF THE POEM

Placed against the historical and contextual background of the Vengeance of Our Lord tradition, the basic path of *Siege of Jerusalem* is simple enough to follow. The poem begins with an account of the crucifixion of Christ at the hands of Pontius Pilate, an act that Christ waits forty years to avenge (lines 1–24). Already in these opening lines, the poet pulls no punches regarding the violence of his subject matter. The realistically drawn mockery of Christ at the hands of his tormenters is poignantly graphic; the description of Christ's blood running like rain upon the street (line 12) certainly provides an indication of the violence that is to come in the narrative. After the brutal abuse of Christ, the poem moves forward in time to focus on Gascony, where a vassal of the Emperor Nero, Titus of Rome, is afflicted with a cancer of the lip that causes him great pain and renders him unable even to open his mouth. In Rome his father, Vespasian, also suffers from grotesque illness: not only is he a victim of leprosy, but a hive of wasps has bred in his nose (lines 25–44).

The poem next shifts to a messenger named Nathan, who has been sent to Nero by Cestius Gallia of Syria to report that the Jews will no longer pay tribute to Rome. On his way across the Mediterranean Sea, a terrible storm blows Nathan into Bordeaux, where he is taken before Titus. Nathan tells Titus of Christ's mission, miracles, and death, including the story of Veronica's veil, a cloth bearing the image of Christ that has miraculous healing powers. Titus grieves over the death of Christ and is immediately healed of his illness (lines 45–188). Titus is summarily baptized, and he vows to take vengeance for Christ's Passion. Titus travels to Rome and tells his father, Vespasian, the tale. St. Peter, in turn, confirms the account of Veronica's veil, and twenty knights are dispatched to bring Veronica and her Vernicle to Rome where she gives the veil to St. Peter. The Vernicle cures Vespasian of his illness and is subsequently displayed in the church as a relic (lines 189–264).

The Emperor Nero, meanwhile, has grown incensed that tribute from the East has ceased, and he summons his barons to prepare for war. Titus and Vespasian are chosen to lead the attack on Judaea. The poet clearly points out that theirs is a just war with both political (cessation of tribute) and religious (vengeance for Christ's death) motivations. The ships are loaded with men, weapons, and supplies, and Titus and Vespasian set off with a good wind at their backs. The setting of the poem then shifts to Judaea (lines 265–96).

The poet conflates the historical battle for Judaea into a few preliminary lines concerning the devastation of Syria, followed by the retreat of the remaining Jews to Jerusalem

---

[40] Gransden, *Historical Writing in England II*, p. 44.

[41] *Siege of Jerusalem*, ed. Hanna and Lawton, p. xxxv.

(lines 297–324). The primary purpose of these battles is to set the stage for the siege proper that constitutes the heart of the poem. The conflict begins with the swapping of insults between Vespasian and the leaders of Jerusalem, which culminates in the decision to meet in battle in the valley of Josaphat outside the walls of the city (lines 325–88). The poet explains the preparations for the impending battle on both sides with a careful eye to details, such as the setting of the watch during the night, the guard whose detail is to protect the tents and train, and the outpouring of the exotic army of the Jews, replete with camels and elephants bearing fortifications upon their backs. The two armies clash in a tour-de-force of violence conveyed in energetic alliterative verse. The battle results in a resounding victory for the Roman forces and a terrible defeat for the Jews, who retreat back into the city leaving their dead behind (lines 389–636). The captured high priests of the Jews, including Caiaphas (who is said to have manipulated the death of Christ), are executed most horribly. The few other prisoners taken by Titus and Vespasian are summarily killed, the bodies of the dead are plundered, and a drawn-out siege begins with the circumvallation of the city (lines 637–896).

Meanwhile, in Rome, the wickedness of Nero results finally in his suicide (lines 897–920). Emperors subsequently come and go in rapid succession while the siege of Jerusalem continues unabated. Eventually, the crown falls to Vespasian, who must return to Rome in order to fulfill his destiny (lines 921–64). At a council of the Roman leaders, Titus is given full control of the Roman armies in his father's absence. Vespasian leaves, and Titus' happiness at seeing his father made emperor causes him to take ill. The Roman doctors cannot find a cure, and Titus is only healed when a leader of the Jews, Josephus, agrees to treat him. Josephus refuses any reward for his assistance (lines 965–1066).

The siege continues: the people of Jerusalem suffer under miserable living conditions, including a terrible famine in which they resort to eating the leather of their shoes and shields (lines 1067–80). Their woeful state is exemplified by the story of a mother, Marie, who grows so mad with hunger that she cooks and cannibalizes her own child (lines 1081–1100). The Jews kill all of their non-combatants in an effort to preserve their provisions, but eventually they are forced to submit for terms. Titus refuses to accept any treaty, his wrath at their earlier rebukes still strong. The Jews react by tunneling under the walls that the Romans have erected and ambushing Titus in an unsuccessful surprise attack that only manages to multiply the dead (lines 1101–32). News of the deplorable conditions within Jerusalem comes to Titus, and he subsequently offers a new settlement to the city. But this time it is the leaders of the Jews who refuse; the famine worsens, and the Jewish dead are thrown over the walls because there is no more room for burial within the town (lines 1133–56).

His offer of peace rebuffed, Titus swears to vanquish the Jews once and for all and, after he breaches the walls, Jerusalem is taken and sacked. The Second Temple is destroyed. The Romans sow the ground with salt and leave no stone standing upon another (lines 1157–1296). Pontius Pilate is found and brought before Titus, who acts as judge against the Jews. Those Jews left alive are sold thirty to a penny, and Pilate is imprisoned in Vienne, a town in the Rhone valley, where he eventually commits suicide (lines 1297–1334). *Siege of Jerusalem* ends with the triumphant, treasure-laden return of Titus to Rome (lines 1335–40).

INITIAL CRITICAL ISSUES: GENRE, JEWS, AND VIOLENCE

As one can see from this brief sketch of the poem's plot, determining the genre of *Siege of Jerusalem* is not easy. Its subject matter (the destruction of the Second Temple) would seem to place it as a history, while the dramatic presentation of the conversion narratives seems most appropriate to hagiography. The lengthy descriptions of battle, on the other hand, look more akin to the conventions of romance or epic. Given these generic distinctions, critics have long had difficulty placing the poem, a fact clearly evident in Lillian Herlands Hornstein's attempt to solve the problem by splitting the difference between two genres, categorizing *Siege of Jerusalem*, along with *Richard Coer de Lyon*, *Titus and Vespasian*, *Three Kings' Sons*, and John Barbour's *Bruce*, as "romance treatments of historical themes."[42] A few years later, Gisela Guddat-Figge placed the poem "in the border area between romance, legend and historiography,"[43] while Derek Pearsall placed it alongside *Alliterative Morte Arthure*, *Destruction of Troy*, and the *Alexander* poems as historical epics.[44] Even manuscript contexts, so often helpful in determining intended (if not actual) genre, do little to solve the debate, since the poem is affiliated with historical, legendary, and religious narratives in the surviving record. In the face of so much uncertainty, we are probably best to follow the lead of Bonnie Millar, who argues that the poet of *Siege of Jerusalem* "is essentially stretching the limitations of genre by presenting historical and religious subject-matter through the medium of romance," a statement that effectively answers the question of genre by denying the existence of an adequate, applicable category for the poem. *Siege of Jerusalem* is historical in its setting, religious in its convictions, and romantic in its conventions. It is also topical, given the late fourteenth-century concerns over a just war.[45] And it is quite possible that part of the popularity of the story of the fall of Jerusalem in the Middle Ages was due to this complexity of generic elements. *Siege of Jerusalem*, perhaps as much as any other work in the tradition, uses and blends material from all of these traditions to produce a chronicle-like poem that functions within several audience-oriented contexts.

Beyond matters of genre, the most problematic issue for modern audiences is the role of the Jews within the poem, an issue greatly complicated by the apparent popularity of *Siege of Jerusalem*. The poem survives in nine manuscripts,[46] "significantly more," Nicholson points out, "than *The Destruction of Troy*, or *The Wars of Alexander*, or indeed any other alliterative poem of substance, except for *Piers Plowman*," a fact that many critics have regarded as quite scandalous:

> If we find this poem perverse in its approval of imperial genocide — the Roman destruction of Jerusalem in 70 AD — then we would seem forced by the evidence of its appearance in so many manuscripts to conclude it reports another story than that which it tells, the ugly tale of an entire culture's prejudice. . . . [The poem] can all too easily be read as symptomatic of a larger cultural condition. No medieval verity, after all, is better attested or more abject than Christian revulsion against Jews, viciously displayed in pogroms and expulsions that show Europe becoming, in R. I. Moore's suggestive phrase, a "persecuting society."[47]

Yet, as Nicholson goes on to argue, regarding the poem as rote anti-Semitism is short-sighted. Within its political and religious parameters, the Jews were clearly the enemy in the

---

[42] Hornstein, "Miscellaneous Romances," 1.158.

[43] Guddat-Figge, *Catalogue of the Manuscripts Containing Middle English Romances*, p. 41.

[44] Pearsall, *Old English and Middle English Poetry*, p. 153.

[45] For more information on the historical contexts of the poem, see pp. 24–30, below.

[46] On the textual history of the poem, see pp. 8–13, above.

[47] Nicholson, "Haunted Itineraries," p. 448.

historical war of AD 70, but the poet places much of the guilt in the war at the feet of the Jewish leaders — it is the leadership of Jerusalem, after all, who refused to pay tribute, who put the people in jeopardy of war, and who refused to surrender the city. The poet is unflinching in casting blame at the Jewish priests for the death of Christ, though this charge also is somewhat mitigated by Pontius Pilate's role in the matter. The poet shows sympathy for the masses of people incarcerated by the siege, being slaughtered as non-essentials by their own leaders as well as suffering the brutalities of the Romans, and, most piteously, being betrayed by each other as they vie for food and water. Even the depravity of the Jewish woman cooking her own child over a fire in the midst of the famine is undercut by the "wode hunger" (line 1093) that forced her hand: in modern legal terminology, Marie is said to be not guilty by reason of insanity. Clearly there is more at work in the poem than what Hamel has called "a repugnant brand of anti-Semitism."[48] As Millar states the matter:

> The poet appears to be suggesting that spiritual blindness and failure to stand up for the Christian faith is not to be tolerated. This is not the fault of the Jewish people, who merely follow their tyrannical leaders with misgiving, suffering greatly in the process. Although the poet is by no means in favour of Judaism, he can at least make a distinction among Jews, seeing some as victims and some as villains. Furthermore, the Jewish leaders are not the only evil characters in the poem; there are others such as Nero. Not all Romans are good, nor are all Jews wicked.[49]

It is the poet's interest in historical contexts and the brutalities of warfare that alleviates much of the poet's anti-Semitism: the Jews cannot be inherently evil any more than the Romans can be inherently good. In fact, as Christine Chism has pointed out, "the poem is absolutely clear that the Christians are the ones responsible for visiting upon the Jews every crime that the Jews had ever been accused of practicing upon Christians, from the eating of babies to the poisoning of wells."[50] Indeed, on several basic points the *Siege*-poet is no more anti-Jewish than Josephus in *Wars of the Jews*, a work that ultimately lies behind historical components of the sources of *Siege of Jerusalem*. Both writers record many of the same events, even if the *Siege*-poet regards the Jews as "faithles folke" (lines 485, 496, 513, 597) while Josephus regards them as kin. That the poet wishes to compose a poem in which the triumph of Christianity over Judaism is clear — indeed, as we will see, it is one of the structural principles behind the composition of the poem — but this is not, in our sense of the word, anti-Semitism. Nicholson points out that it was during the fourteenth and fifteenth centuries that Europe "struggled ferociously over the boundaries between its constituent parts and came under intense pressure to establish its own larger geographical limits." Against this backdrop, a poem like *Siege of Jerusalem* "might well have been the palliation of a set of political anxieties, the Jew being part of the problem, but equally part of a narrative resolution."[51] This perspective amounts to anti-Semitism not as an end to itself, but as a means to an end, as a political and poetical instrument. The Jews in *Siege of Jerusalem*, when seen in this way, might represent the margins of a Europe seeking the stability of boundaries

[48] Hamel, "*Siege of Jerusalem* as a Crusading Poem," p. 178.

[49] Millar, *Siege of Jerusalem*, p. 53.

[50] Chism, "*Siege of Jerusalem*: Liquidating Assets," p. 319.

[51] Nicholson, "Haunted Itineraries," p. 449.

(Nicholson's view). Sympathetically and paradoxically, the Jews in the poem could be seen in the more positive light of their roles as witnesses, an Augustinian perspective argued by van Court. Most of these interpretations work on the fundamental assumption that what the poet means by "Jew" is, in fact, a Jew. But this is open to debate, as we cannot be certain what the poet, or his audience, would have understood by "Jew" since Jews had supposedly been expelled from England in 1290 and were not allowed to reenter officially until their re-admission after Manasseh Ben-Israel's negotiations with Oliver Cromwell in 1655; historians are still unsure what this expulsion meant in practical terms.[52] It might mean that the Jews were, for the late Middle Ages, a true "other," and that the *Siege*-poet had no direct contact with Jews. His "Jews" might then be interpreted to signify any number of marginal threats to orthodoxy. Thus, as Hanna has argued in "Contextualising *The Siege of Jerusalem*," they may act as symbols for any community of unbelievers or heretics, including the Lollards. According to Hamel, the Jews in the poem can act more specifically as placeholders for the Muslims — the war against the Jews becoming nothing more than a thinly veiled call to crusading ideals. And Chism admits to having "a more sinister reading of the poem's acknowledgment of Christian brutality"[53] when she argues that the poem transforms the Jews into little more than placeholders for economic profit, negotiating the "essential contradiction between destroying the Jews and exploiting them."[54] Elsewhere, Chism highlights the "internationality" of the poem, moving "between Jerusalem, Marseilles, and Rome — exoticizing Judaism and demonizing pagan Rome as . . . Christian Romans face and obliterate two different forefathers and rivals for power, the Jews and the pagan Roman emperors."[55]

Quite evidently, the role of the Jews in the poem is by no means a simple issue, and this is especially true given the cultural uncertainties of England in relation to the worlds across the Channel in the last decades of the fourteenth century as the Great Schism festered the old wounds of the Hundred Years' War and gave rise to crusades called against fellow Christians as often as they were against the "heathen" of the Holy Land.[56]

The role of violence in the story has concerned many readers of this poem. Chism, for example, writes that "even in a genre where battle eviscerations are more or less de rigueur, *The Siege of Jerusalem* has the dubious distinction of being the most gratuitously and imaginatively vicious poem of the Alliterative Revival."[57] She and others have noted such grisly details as the Romans setting spears to tear out the guts of the Jews' elephants so that their "Rappis rispen forth" ("Entrails break forth" — line 571), the description of a man struck in such a way that the "gretter pese of the panne" ("largest part of his brain" — line 827) was flung a furlong across the battlefield, the death of a pregnant woman whose body was so smashed by a stone from a catapult that her unborn child flew from her body over the walls (lines 829–32), or the fate of Sabinus, a man whose brain bursts from his nostrils when he is given a particularly hideous blow to the top of the head (lines 1202–04). There is much exaggeration here, of course, but it is a morbid, visceral exaggeration, and it is in keeping

---

[52] See, for example, Lawton, "Sacrilege and Theatricality," 293.

[53] Chism, "*Siege of Jerusalem*: Liquidating Assets," p. 319n26.

[54] Chism, "*Siege of Jerusalem*: Liquidating Assets," p. 309 and *passim*. These ideas are also revisited in the course of her discussion of *Siege* in her book *Alliterative Revivals*.

[55] Chism, *Alliterative Revivals*, pp. 11–12.

[56] For more on the late fourteenth-century background of the poem, see pp. 24–30, below.

[57] Chism, "*Siege of Jerusalem*: Liquidating Assets," p. 317.

with romance rhetoric, where the popping of Saracen heads "als dose hayle-stones / Abowtte one the gras" in *Sir Perceval of Galles* (lines 1191–92) has an unsettling, but oddly comic, effect.[58] Yet we must also remind ourselves that even such horrid exaggerations are based on the very real violence of an age of siege warfare, brutal executions, piking, public eviscerations, and numerous other means of death that were no doubt experienced within the lifetimes of those living in the Middle Ages. As but one example, Hamel notes that the Roman soldiers' disemboweling of captive Jews in order to find the treasures that they have swallowed is not only a detail that ultimately derives from Josephus' writings,[59] but also reflects a similar event described by Fulcher of Chartres after the fall of Jerusalem in 1099.

The poet is likewise not shy about turning his poetry to descriptions of violence on a larger scale, violence both natural and manmade. Note, for example, his description of the storm that blew Nathan off-course and into the haven of Bordeaux (lines 53–64):[60]

Nathan toward Nero nome on his way	*went*
Over the Grekys grounde myd the grym ythes,	*amid the fierce waves*
An heye setteth the sayl over the salt water,	*On high set the sail*
And with a dromound on the deep dryveth on swythe.[61]	
The wolcon wanned anon and the water skeweth,	*sky waned; grew dark*
Cloudes clateren on loude as they cleve wolde.[62]	
The racke myd a rede wynde roos on the myddel	*storm; red wind rose*
And sone sette on the se out of the south syde.	*soon set upon the sea*
Hit blewe on the brode se, bolned up harde;	*swelled*
Nathannys nave anon on the north dryveth,	*Nathan's ship soon*
So the wedour and the wynd on the water metyn	
That alle hurtled on an hepe that the helm gemyd.[63]	

Compare this passage with the following, a report of the retreat of the Jews and the subsequent aftermath of the first day's battle before the walls of Jerusalem (lines 597–608):

Anon the feythles folke fayleden herte,	*failed [in their] hearts*
Tourned toward the toun and Tytus hem after:	*Titus [came] after them*
Fele of the fals ferde in the felde lefte,	*Many; army; field [were] left*
An hundred in here helmes myd his honde one.	*helms with his hand alone*

---

[58] *Sir Perceval of Galles*, ed. Braswell, p. 39. Many of these gory details, we might add, are in the poet's sources; such is the case, for example, for the baby borne over the walls and the skull flung across the battlefield, both of which derive ultimately from Josephus' account of the siege of Jotapata in *Wars of the Jews* 3.7.23.

[59] Josephus reports that two thousand Jews were thus torn open in a single night (*Wars of the Jews* 5.13.4); noted by Hamel, "*Siege of Jerusalem* as a Crusading Poem," p. 183.

[60] On the storm as a topos of Middle English poetry, see Jacobs, "Alliterative Storms." Jacobs is less than favorable in comparing this particular description with its brethren, saying that it is "technically less impressive, and its irrelevance to the story makes it appear doubly perfunctory" (p. 713).

[61] *And with a drumond (a large ship) on the deep drives on quickly*

[62] *The clouds thundered loudly as [if] they would break apart*

[63] Lines 63–64: *The weather and the wind so meet on the water / That [he] who governed the helm was hurtled into a heap*

The fals Jewes in the felde fallen so thicke	*fall*
As hail froward Heven, hepe over other;	*from; heaping over each other*
So was the bent over-brad, blody by-runne,	*field covered over*
With ded bodies aboute alle the brod vale.	*broad valley*

Myght no stede doun stap bot on stele wede,	*steed; step; steel clothing*
Or on burne, other on beste, or on bright scheldes;	*man, or on beast*
So myche was the multitude that on the molde lafte	*high; number; earth*
Ther so many were mart; merevail were ellis.	*dead*

Both passages stage the drama through fine attention to minutiae: the thundering clouds, the protective hatches of Nathan's ship, the ground running red with the blood of the fallen, and the corpses of man and beast so thick that a horse could not find solid earth without stepping upon them. The poet does not revel in the horrible images that he describes. He is simply aware of them as a source for making the matter more real to his audience. The unflinching eye of the poet clarifies the drama, bringing it to life by the visceral reality of what is described in narrow, carefully chosen details. They are grim details, certainly, and very likely they are details that we may not wish to see, but they are true to the historical character of the poem itself and to the historical realities of the poet's own surrounds. The composer of *Siege of Jerusalem*, despite all of his efforts to make a coherent history of the actual siege, cannot know the reality of a first-century siege in Judaea. What the poet instead provides us with is the reality of a late-medieval siege in Europe.[64] And, to paraphrase Sherman, war is, and always has been, Hell.

Beyond noting the historical realities of life and death at a late-medieval siege, however, we must always bear in mind the poem's literary contexts and cultural concerns in addressing the role of violence in the poem. The description of Christ's Passion, for example, a moment of violence at the very heart of Christianity, is told with a brevity and clarity that is startling in both in the iconography and humanizing imagery given to Christ's tormentors and their brutality. But it is also conventional:

A pyler pyght was doun upon the playn erthe,[65]	
His body bonden therto, and beten with scourgis.	*bound; beaten*
Whyppes of quyrboyle by-wente His white sides	*pliable leather beset*
Til He al on rede blode ran, as rayn in the strete.[66]	

Suth stoked Hym on a stole with styf mannes hondis,	
Blyndfelled Hym as a be and boffetis Hym raghte:[67]	
"Gif thou be prophete of pris, prophecie!" they sayde,	*If; prophet of worth*
"Whiche berne here aboute bolled Thee laste?" (lines 9–16)	*man; struck You*

The details of the buffeting and the scourging from whips crafted of leather have a historicizing effect, albeit within the iconographic representations of the several stages of the

---

[64] Similar siege tactics appear in *Alliterative Morte Arthure*, though Sutton notes that the siege warfare depicted there is archaic compared to late fourteenth-century military practices; see "Mordred's End."

[65] *A pillar was set upon the flat ground*

[66] *Until His whole body ran red with blood, as rain [does] upon the street*

[67] Lines 13–14: *Then [they] struck Him upon a stool with stiff men's hands, / Blindfolded Him as a bee and gave Him blows*

Passion of Christ. The pathos of the scene is heightened by the blood falling like "rayn in the strete," an image at once familiar and shocking. The brutality of the event is cemented in our minds as the tormentors roughly set Christ upon a stool, blindfold Him, and beat Him with their fists. The mockery of their rhetorical questions make us, the audience, accomplices to the mockery as the tormentors ask Him, since He is said to be a prophet, to tell them who last struck Him. The scene is built of graphic violence, but it is a conventional account that would be almost universally familiar during the Middle Ages: medieval drama commits whole plays to the torment of Christ. In addition to plays on the Crucifixion, the Towneley[68] and the York[69] cycles include separate plays on both the buffeting (*Coliphizachio*) and the scourging (*Flagellacio*) of Christ, and the events also appear in the Chester Mystery Cycle.[70] The buffeting in the Towneley Cycle, one of the plays of the Wakefield Master, provides the details of Christ being placed on a stool and then blindfolded prior to his beating:

> *1 Tortor.* Now sen he is blynfeld, I fall to begyn;
>   And thus was I counseld the mastry to wyn.   *[Striking Jesus.*
> *2 Tortor.* Nay, wrang has thou teld; thus shuld thou com in.   *[Striking him.*
> *Froward.* I stode and beheld — thou towchid not the skyn / Bot fowll.
> *1 Tortor.* How will thou I do?
> *2 Tortor.* On this manere, lo!   *[Striking again.*
> *Froward.* Yei, that was well gone to; / Ther start vp a cowll.
> *1 Tortor.* Thus shall we hym refe all his fonde talys.   *[Striking again.*
> *2 Tortor.* Ther is noght in thi nefe, or els thi hart falys.
> *Froward.* I can my hand vphefe and knop out the skalys.
> *1 Tortor.* Godys forbot ye lefe, bot set in youre nalys / On raw.
>   Sit vp and prophecy —   *[To Jesus, as they strike in turn.*
> *Froward.* Bot make vs no ly —
> *2 Tortor.* Who smote the last?
> *1 Tortor.*   Was it I?
> *Froward.* He wote not, I traw.[71]

From another literary perspective, we might note the grim portrayal of the scourging in *Cursor Mundi*:

> To a pillour they hym bond
> and with scorges hym swong
> ffro the hed to the fote
> ouer alle the blode out-sprong
> They Crownyd hym þo with sharpe thorne   *[then]*
> that thorogh his hed throng.[72]   *[pierced]*

---

[68] Plays 21 and 22, *Towneley Plays*, ed. England, pp. 228–57.

[69] Plays 29 ("The Bowers and Flecchers") and 33 ("The Tyllemakers") in *York Plays*, ed. Smith, pp. 254–69 and 320–36.

[70] Play 16 ("The Fletchers, Bowiers, Cowpers, and Stringers Playe") in *Chester Mystery Cycle*, ed. Lumiansky and Mills, 1.284–303.

[71] *Coliphizachio*, lines 397–414, in *Wakefield Pageants*, ed. Cawley.

[72] From the Fairfax version of *Cursor Mundi*, ed. Morris, lines 16433–38.

We can see a number of the details from *Siege of Jerusalem* between these two examples: the stool and the echoed taunting in the work of the Wakefield Master, and the pillar and out-springing of blood in *Cursor Mundi*. The cumulative effect of such brutalities set the stage in the popular imagination for a just retaliation by the God of Judgment. Thus, to accuse the *Siege*-poet as having a particular morbid sensibility would be doubly remiss: not only would such an accusation ignore the historical realities of violence, but it would also ignore the larger literary milieu in which *Siege of Jerusalem* is situated. In addition, we must not set aside the fact that the poet's sources were unflinching in providing some of the more grue-some details — even the mother's cannibalism of her own son — and that the poet is likewise unflinching in utilizing such source material.

SOURCES FOR THE POEM

Siege of Jerusalem is, in the main, a compilation from three primary sources: *Vindicta salvatoris* (the basis for lines 1–200 and 1297–1340), Roger d'Argenteuil's *Bible en François* (for lines 201–788), and Ranulf Higden's *Polychronicon* (for lines 789–1296).[73] Jacobus de Voragine's *Legenda aurea* represents a fourth source, used to add details such as the wasps in Vespasian's nose (lines 33–36), his rule of Galatia (line 39), Titus' illness at the siege and subsequent healing by Josephus (lines 1027–66), and the details of Nero's villainy and sui-cide (lines 903–20).[74] The fifth and final known source for the outlines of *Siege* is Josephus' *Wars of the Jews*, only recently identified by Hanna and Lawton, a text utilized for various details throughout the course of the poem.[75] The poet's selective use of these sources says much about his goals in the composition of *Siege of Jerusalem*: "to convey the value of reso-lute faith and of actively fighting for God,"[76] to affirm the divine justice of the destruction of Jerusalem and the ascension of Christianity over Judaism, and to chronicle the historical realities (as he understood them) of the destruction of Jerusalem.

The first two hundred lines of the poem, aside from some extended descriptions (the description of the storm, for example), are an almost verbatim translation of the Latin *Vin-dicta salvatoris*, a text detailing the medieval legend of St. Veronica and the Vernicle (the veil with Christ's image upon it) along with the destruction of the Temple.[77] Even within this strict framework, however, the poet makes changes. As Eugen Kölbing and Mabel Day note in the introduction to their edition of the poem, the phrase "zelatus a Tiberio" from the open-ing line of *Vindicta salvatoris*[78] is altered by the poet, who apparently knows that Tiberius

---

[73] For this summary and much of what follows, I am indebted to both Millar's excellent discussion of the sources in her study of the poem (*Siege of Jerusalem*, pp. 42–75) and the introduction of the poem by Mabel Day for the EETS edition; see *Siege of Jerusalem*, ed. Kölbing and Day, pp. xv–xxxi.

[74] See Millar, *Siege of Jerusalem*, pp. 70–73; *Siege of Jerusalem*, ed. Kölbing and Day, p. xx.

[75] As Hanna and Lawton point out, the poet probably knew Josephus through the translation by Rufinus of Aquileia; see pp. xl–lii.

[76] Millar, *The Siege of Jerusalem*, p. 56, speaking on the poet's adaptation of *Vindicta salvatoris*.

[77] There are two primary recensions of the Latin *Vindicta salvatoris*. Millar (*Siege of Jerusalem*, pp. 50–51) concluded that a manuscript copy based on version B must have been used as the poet's exem-plar since the poem omits the character of Volosian.

[78] Kölbing and Day kindly provide the initial portion of *Vindicta salvatoris* as Appendix II in their edition (*Siege of Jerusalem*, pp. 83–85), a practice followed by Hanna and Lawton, who reedited the

(r. 14–37) cannot have any connection whatsoever with the events of AD 70; his role in the narrative ends with the Crucifixion of Christ. In addition, Nathan's mission to Rome is not to give a pledge of support, as stated in *Vindicta salvatoris*, but to inform Nero that the Jews are henceforth refusing to pay tribute to the emperor. This change, too, is made in the interest of historical accuracy. Both the Crucifixion of Christ and the storm that drives Nathan to Titus are given far more detailed presentations in *Siege of Jerusalem* than they have in the poet's source. This interest in historicity, Millar points out, illustrates the poet's desire "to provide his readers and listeners with a Christian history, not a doctrinal work or religious propaganda arousing hatred of the Jews, but a measured account of what happened."[79] Beyond this basic need to provide an accurate account of the events, however, Millar does note the poet's interest in the doctrinal significance of his narratives. In particular, the poet of *Siege of Jerusalem* seems intrigued by *Vindicta salvatoris'* representation of Titus' miraculous cure, faithful conversion, and validating baptism — so much so, in fact, that he essentially duplicates the cure-conversion narrative for Vespasian, despite the fact that in his primary sources the latter is only converted.[80] The poet depicts the converted as taking the sacrament of baptism immediately upon conversion, whereas *Vindicta salvatoris* claims that the two men wait until their arrival in the Holy Land to take the sacrament. The importance of this difference, it seems, is to show not only the primacy of the sacraments as fundamental to right faith, but also that Titus and Vespasian are both fully Christian prior to their departure for Jerusalem. The poet's interest in these doctrinal points goes far toward explaining the role of St. Veronica, who garners only passing notice in *Siege of Jerusalem* despite her central role in *Vindicta salvatoris*. Since Veronica is already a Christian and "thus does not need to be converted or baptized,"[81] she is of little interest to the poet beyond her historical role as the owner of the Vernicle.

Beginning at line 201 and lasting through the speech of Vespasian that ends at line 788, the primary source of the poem shifts from *Vindicta salvatoris* to Roger d'Argenteuil's *Bible en François*.[82] This shift in source material helps to explain the backgrounding of Titus, as he is mentioned only once in the French poem. The poet's dual emphasis of history and theology is made clear as he highlights the political maneuverings that lead to the siege — Nero's anger at losing tribute and the appointment of Titus and Vespasian to lead the armies — as well as the religious rationale for joining the fight:

Latin text for their Appendix B (pp. 159–63). The relevant line here is: "In diebus imperii Tiberii Cesaris, tetrarcha [Herodes], sub Poncio [Pilato] Iude traditus fuit Dominus zelatus a Tiberio."

[79] Millar, *Siege of Jerusalem*, p. 55. This is not to say, however, that religious issues do not lie behind the presentation of the poem.

[80] Millar, *Siege of Jerusalem*, p. 52.

[81] Millar, *Siege of Jerusalem*, p. 53.

[82] More specifically, *Bible en François* is the primary source behind lines 201–64 and 325–788, since much of the intervening material is either original to the poet (though still loosely based on the accumulated legends) or from Josephus (see *Siege of Jerusalem*, ed. Hanna and Lawton, p. xlvi). See Moe, "French Source of *The Siege of Jerusalem*." Interestingly, Hanna and Lawton have subsequently observed that "the only known copy of Roger's *Bible en François* produced in England (unknown to Moe) survives and is a Bolton book" (p. lii). This manuscript is now held in the Bodleian Library as MS Fairfax 24. For a very succinct summary of the Middle English translation of Roger's work, see Morey, *Book and Verse*, pp. 118–19.

Now is, Bethleem, thy bost   y-broght to an ende;   *boast*
Jerusalem and Jerico,   for-juggyd wrecchys,   *condemned wretches*
Schal never kyng of your kynde   with croune be ynoyntid,   *lineage; anointed*
Ne Jewe, for Jhesu sake,   jouke in you more. (lines 301–04)   *Nor; rest; again*

As Millar rightly notes, the *Siege*-poet derives his four Jewish tyrants — Caiaphas, Pontius Pilate, John, and Simon — from *Bible en François*, though he has opted to modify the role of Pilate.[83] Whereas Pilate "surrenders and disassociates himself from the crucifixion of Christ" in *Bible en François*, he "remains a villain, a false figure of authority" in *Siege of Jerusalem*.[84] Indeed, the poet will later return to *Vindicta salvatoris* to incorporate the fate of Pilate, and his desire for unity of narrative necessitates an emphasis on Pilate as a collaborator with the Jews and their leadership. Pilate's authority is as wicked as the rest of the Jewish leaders; right authority rests in the hands of Titus and Vespasian as servants of God.

The central portion of the narrative, comprising almost forty percent of the poem's length (lines 789 to 1296) and detailing the action of the siege itself, is derived from Ranulf Higden's famous text, *Polychronicon*.[85] Higden's account of the story is, in turn, ultimately based on the eyewitness account of Josephus recorded in *Wars of the Jews*,[86] an account that the *Siege*-poet also appears to have utilized directly.[87] And although Josephan echoes are to be found throughout the text, the unusually high number located in this central part of the poem has the look of fact-checking: it appears that the poet, surely conscious of Higden's reliance on Josephus, has gone back to the original source to supplement and confirm his text. But regardless of why or how the poet has accessed Josephus' text, one cannot deny the influence in light of the preponderance of facts.[88]

For the final stage of his history, the poet returns once more to *Vindicta salvatoris*, recounting the selling of the remaining Jews into slavery, the imprisonment and subsequent suicide of Pontius Pilate, and the return of Titus to Rome (lines 1297–1340). The incorporation of Pilate's suicide effectively frames the poet's narrative: vengeance for Christ's death must, perhaps by definition, begin and end with Pontius Pilate. Beyond this, however, the poet's interest in the story of Pilate shows quite clearly the wickedness of those who actively and knowingly oppose the Christian faith. And the poet's interest in revealing the primacy of Divine Providence in history, as we shall see, is a structural principle in the construction of the poem. But before entering into a discussion of the poem's intricate architecture, we must examine the immediate historical contexts in which the poem was written and disseminated.

---

[83] Millar, *Siege of Jerusalem*, pp. 58–59.

[84] Millar, *Siege of Jerusalem*, p. 59.

[85] Kölbing and Day provide the relevant passage of Higden as Appendix III of their edition (pp. 86–89); Hanna and Lawton re-edit the passage and provide it as Appendix B in theirs (pp. 164–69). For general information about Higden, see Taylor, *"Universal Chronicle" of Ranulf Higden*.

[86] In addition, Higden appears to have relied heavily on the account of Hegesippus, but Hegesippus' account is also a recasting of Josephus. For a succinct but detailed account of Josephus' work and its journey into the hands of Higden, see Millar, *Siege of Jerusalem*, pp. 60–69.

[87] See *Siege of Jerusalem*, ed. Hanna and Lawton, pp. xl–lii. The fact that the *Siege*-poet directly utilized Josephus stands against the conclusions of earlier critics such as Millar, who opined (*Siege of Jerusalem*, p. 69) that "there is no good reason to think that the poet used *The Jewish War*."

[88] Hanna and Lawton identify over thirty Josephan echoes.

THE END OF THE FOURTEENTH CENTURY: THE IDEA OF JUST WAR

Edward III, the man whose claim on the French throne through his mother Isabella effectively began the Hundred Years' War, died on 21 June 1377, and the young Richard II, son of the late Black Prince, was crowned the following day. Two years earlier, in 1375, France and England had signed the Truce of Bruges. The year 1376 had even seen some government reforms introduced during the so-called Good Parliament. Things, one might say, were looking up for Englishmen. Early historians even labeled the period from Edward III's death to the ascension of Henry V in 1413 as the "interim" period of the Hundred Years' War, probably on the assumption that a lack of massive invasions and great battles indicated, to borrow lines from the poet C. Day Lewis that are often applied to the 1930s, a calm "no man's land . . . / Between two fires."[89] But this interim period of the Hundred Years' War, like the 1930s between two world wars, was far from quiet. The war between England and France was not over, it was merely smoldering, and England was about to fall into massive internal turmoil. It is worth recalling some of the primary political and social events of this period in English history, as it was probably in the first two decades of Richard II's reign that *Siege of Jerusalem* was written.[90]

In 1378, the Great Schism began as rival popes ruled in Rome and Avignon, a situation that would last until 1417. Predictably, the French supported the papacy at Avignon while the English took every opportunity to support the interests of the papacy at Rome. These underlying hostilities came close to the breaking point in 1380, when the French besieged the English at Chateauneuf-de-Randon. The English repelled the French, and the French commander, Bertrand du Guesclin, lost his life. While the action did not formally break the Truce of Bruges, it was certainly a sign of continued strain and the fact that the relationship between the two powers had resolved into what we might consider a "cold war" mentality. And all was not well at home in England, either. This same year saw the king direct Simon Sudbury, the archbishop of Canterbury and chancellor of England, to institute the third poll tax in four years: a flat tax of one shilling on every individual over the age of fifteen. The lower classes, still reeling from the massive losses sustained in the Black Death, the conscription calls in the Hundred Years' War, and the two previous poll taxes, resisted the levy, and resistance turned to outright rebellion in the form of the Peasants' Revolt in 1381. Peasants from Kent and Essex entered London through Aldgate (where Chaucer was then living) and burnt John of Gaunt's palace, the Savoy. They then beheaded Sudbury. The fourteen-year-old Richard II rode out to meet the rampaging mob at Smithfield, proclaimed himself the leader of the rebellion, promised consideration for the rebel's interests, and, after the killing of one of their leaders, Wat Tyler, by William Walworth, the people dispersed.

In 1382, the "Earthquake Council" at Blackfriars condemned John Wyclif and many of his teachings. It was the second condemnation in two years for Wyclif, who continued to speak out against various orthodox Catholic doctrines and against the abuses of power and

---

[89] C. Day Lewis (1904–72), "The Conflict," lines 31–32. The line provides the title, for example, of Large's examination of what W. H. Auden called the "low dishonest decade" ("September 1, 1939," line 5): *Between Two Fires*.

[90] For some of what follows I am indebted to the broad outline provided by Dean in the introduction to his useful collection of Middle English literature about Richard's reign in *Medieval English Political Writings*.

privilege within the organization of the church itself. Wyclif's teachings spread through all classes of society and represented a source of social unrest in England for years to come. This same year, the French invaded Flanders and, after seizing control of the country, forced it to submit to Avignon. The following year, in 1383, Hugh Despenser, the bishop of Norwich, campaigned for an expedition against Flanders and the heretical followers of Avignon (though it was no doubt far more of a political attack on the French than it was a religious attack against heretics). Pope Urban VI, however, sensing an opportunity, granted Despenser's campaign the status of a crusade, meaning that financing could be procured through the collection of alms and the selling of indulgences. Henry Knighton's chronicle reports the dissatisfaction of the English people with the subsequent rapacious campaign for financing:

> The bishop [Despenser] had raised an incalculable and unbelievably large sum of money, in gold and silver, and in jewels, necklaces, rings, dishes, plate, spoons, and other ornaments, and especially from ladies and other women, for it was said that one lady gave him £100, and others likewise, some more, and some less.
>
> And it was believed that very many gave more than they could afford, in order to secure the benefit of absolution for themselves and their devoted friends. And thus that hidden treasure of the kingdom which is in the hands of women was put at risk.[91]

The expedition was a complete disaster, and Despenser returned in shame only to be reprimanded by Richard, who claimed that royal approval for the expedition had been revoked before it set sail.[92] Regardless of Richard's claim that he had no hand in Despenser's dirty work, the abysmal failure of the crusade only served to fuel attacks on the king: in 1384 both John of Gaunt and Thomas of Woodstock spoke against the king in Parliament.[93]

The English and French had, of course, joined opposite sides in the war between Portugal and Castile, and on 14 August 1385 the English aided the Portuguese forces in a victory at the Battle of Aljubarrota, securing independence for Portugal. English opposition to Castile was furthered by John of Gaunt's claim to the throne of Castile through his wife, Constance, though no doubt any opportunity to oppose the French was considered a good one. In 1386, Gaunt ultimately joined with the king of Portugal in conducting a crusade against Castile that Adam Usk likened to Despenser's greedy expedition, which concluded with equally disastrous results: "he lost many English nobles — virtually the bloom of the nation's chivalric youth."[94]

---

[91] Knighton, *Knighton's Chronicle, 1337–1396*, ed. and trans. Martin, p. 325. That the crusade was moderately successful until the siege of Ypres is perhaps also relevant to the composition of *Siege of Jerusalem* (depending, of course, on the dating of *Siege*). One of the details provided by Knighton is that Despenser "had installed a great siege tower with a trebuchet" at Ypres (p. 327), a detail perhaps echoed in the siege tower at Jerusalem. If the poet is, indeed, hoping to make referral to Despenser's failures at Ypres, the point would be to further emphasize the illegitimacy of such current crusading practices.

[92] See Aston, "Impeachment of Bishop Despenser."

[93] On the Norwich Crusade, and the political situations under Richard II, see Perroy, *L'Angleterre et le Grand Schisme d'Occident*. That the Norwich Crusade stuck in the minds of the English people is perhaps best shown in the fact that in the General Prologue to *The Canterbury Tales* Chaucer's Squire is described as having taken part in the expedition (*CT* I[A]85–88).

[94] Usk, *Chronicle of Adam Usk, 1377–1421*, ed. and trans. Given-Wilson, p. 15. Other chronicle accounts useful to this period are *Historia Anglicana* 2.84–104 and *Westminster Chronicle* 34–46.

At the naval battle of Margate on 24 March 1387, the English defeated a combined French and Castilian fleet. Later that same year, the battle of Radcot Bridge saw nobles, in effect, take on the king in open arms when they attacked one of Richard's most trusted councillors, Robert de Vere. The "Merciless" Parliament convened the following year and the Lord Appellants executed many of the king's supporters. Richard declared himself full monarch in 1390, abolished the regency, and began to press his own interests more forcefully. His egotism was made most abundantly clear in his 1392 conflict with the city of London, at the conclusion of which he forced the city leaders to submit to him publicly in a pageant of spectacle that had the air of both a second coronation and Christ's Palm Sunday entry into Jerusalem.[95]

In an effort to create a lasting peace with France, Richard married Isabella, the eight-year-old daughter of the king of France in 1395. The relationship between the two countries seemed amiable enough to Philippe de Mézières that he wrote Richard and urged him to join with the king of France in a crusade against the Turks to recapture Jerusalem.[96] Richard did not accept the invitation, and it was left to Sigismund of Hungary and John of Burgundy to lead a crusade to try and recapture the Holy Land. On 25 September 1396 their invasion ended disastrously at Nicopolis. This failure is widely regarded as the final gasp of crusading momentum aimed at Jerusalem.[97]

Back in England, Richard lashed out against the Appellants in 1397, and the same year even found John Holland, Richard's half-brother and earl of Huntington, negotiating with the Roman pope, Boniface IX, to conduct a crusade against Avignon. Richard exiled John of Gaunt's son, Henry Bolingbroke, in 1398. And it was only a matter of months after the death of John of Gaunt in 1399 that Bolingbroke returned to popular acclaim and took the crown as Henry IV. The deposed king was murdered on 17 February 1400.

Between 1370 and 1400, against this background of violence and religious controversy both at home and abroad, *Siege of Jerusalem* was written and initially circulated. And, if the manuscript record is any indication, it found a wide audience within a relatively short amount of time; the poem, we might say, struck a chord (or some number of chords) with its readers. Richard II, of course, looms large over the latter portion of these years, a king who

> saw the principal object of his government as the establishment of what he called "peace"
> — unity, in other words — in his realm. And, following Giles [of Rome's *De regimine prin-*

[95] For more information about this event, and an eyewitness account of it, see Maidstone, *Concordia*, ed. Carlson.

[96] Mézières, *Letter to King Richard II*, ed. and trans. Coopland. It is perhaps of note that Philippe asks Richard to follow in the footsteps of Titus' actions at the siege of Jerusalem (pp. 16–17 [English] and 89–90 [French]). See Hamel, "*Siege of Jerusalem* as a Crusading Poem," pp. 187–88, for more discussion of Philippe's letter and our poem.

[97] See Palmer, *England, France and Christendom, 1377–99*, p. 205. Hamel argues that this event might actually represent the *terminus ad quem* for *Siege* because the poem is favorable to the "longer range English-French project against Jerusalem" ("*Siege of Jerusalem* as a Crusading Poem," p. 189). But, as Tipton has pointed out, the English participation in the crusade was quite slim, indeed, as their role "was passive rather than active" ("English at Nicopolis," p. 538). Additionally, as we will see, *Siege of Jerusalem* is not necessarily pro-crusade. In fact, it may be just as anti-crusade as *Siege off Melayne* or *Alliterative Morte Arthure*, the latter of which almost surely borrowed from the present poem (see p. 29n113, below).

cipium], he believed that he could only achieve this if he, the king, was strong and his subjects were obedient to his will. . . . Unity — that is, peace — was incompatible with dissent; what the king required was unquestioning acceptance of his rule and submission to his will.[98]

Though Richard saw peace in absolutism, many of his countrymen sought peace of another sort. The Peasants' Revolt in 1381 brought the ideas of true social reform to the forefront of both political and literary argumentation,[99] and the final decades of the fourteenth century, in that briefest of respites from the terrible loss of life that arose from the pitched battles and the inevitable sieges of the massive, drawn-out campaigns in France, gave rise to writings about the nature of peace and what, if anything, constituted a just war. As John Barnie and George R. Keiser have both pointed out, the 1370s had seen an impatience among Englishmen for the lack of military successes in France,[100] and this impatience grew during the 1380s into "direct criticism of the war in and of itself,"[101] such as Knighton's already-noted displeasure with the Bishop's Crusade and Usk's disappointment with Gaunt's crusade in Castile. This disenchantment increased as the years of this chaotic period passed, so that by the 1390s anti-war-in-France sentiments had given way to a number of irenic arguments in literature, building on the foundations of mid-fourteenth-century texts like *Wynnere and Wastoure*.[102] One of the strongest of these peacemaking voices, perhaps, is that of John Gower, who completes his first recension of *Confessio Amantis* around 1390, writing again and again within its lines on the evils of war and the crusades.[103]

The only just war, Gower argues, is that fought in defense of one's country, not for purposes of greed or of vainglory.[104] In the last years of the century, Gower also writes his last poem, "In Praise of Peace," in which he implores the new king, Henry IV, to avoid the horrors of war altogether. Chaucer probably adapts his Tale of Melibee in the later 1380s,

---

[98] Saul, *Richard II*, pp. 250 and 388. Compare the Prologue to Gower's *Confessio Amantis*, lines 141–56.

[99] See, for example, Peck, "Social Conscience and the Poets."

[100] See Barnie, *War in Medieval Society*, pp. 14–31, and Keiser, "Edward III and the Alliterative *Morte Arthure*," pp. 48–51. The findings of these historians run counter to those of earlier critics like Matthews, who argued that, because of the anti-war sentiments espoused by his work, the poet of *Alliterative Morte Arthure* "may have composed his work soon after 1375, when the piled-up misfortunes of John of Gaunt had added Pelion to the Ossa of Edward's failures in France and when the ordinary Englishman was weary of the tragic futility of his rulers' imperial conquerings" (*Tragedy of Arthur*, p. 192). But it was not their rulers' war itself that was troublesome in the 1370s. As Hamel states the matter, it was "their failure to gain *further* military successes in spite of the great expensiveness of the war" (*Morte Arthure*, ed. Hamel, p. 57).

[101] *Morte Arthure*, ed. Hamel, p. 57, who goes on to note that "most of the writings that Matthews himself quotes [in arguing for anti-war literature in the 1370s] . . . date not from the 1370's but from the period 1390–1425." See note 100, above. Similar conclusions are drawn by Finlayson, "*Morte Arthure*: The Date and a Source for the Contemporary References."

[102] On the anti-war nature of *Wynnere and Wastoure*, a poem critical of Edward III's continental wars that may have been written as early as the 1350s (though more likely in the 1360s), see Stillwell, "*Wynnere and Wastoure* and the Hundred Years' War."

[103] See, for example, *Confessio Amantis* 3.2251–2362, and 3.2485–2515.

[104] See *Confessio Amantis* 7.3594–3626.

with its strong argument against war — so easy to begin but so hard to stop.[105] Indeed, the notion of peace, and perhaps even of pacifism, is a major theme of *The Canterbury Tales* as a whole.[106] Reexamination of war was, we might say, in the air; R. F. Yeager points out that "on all sides of Chaucer and Gower, and apparently swelling during their lifetimes, there is . . . a contrary voice, often raised to question, even denounce, the legitimacy of war and the military class."[107] And in these reexaminations of just war, as Yeager has pointed out, it was St. Augustine who provided the ultimate basis for discussions.[108] In a letter to Boniface, for example, Augustine argues that a just war is the correction of the sinful by God, whose only aim is to bring about peace:

> Peace should be the object of your desire; war should be waged only as a necessity, and waged only that God may by it deliver men from the necessity and preserve them in peace. For peace is not sought in order to promote the kindling of war, but war is waged in order that peace may be obtained. Therefore, even in waging war, cherish the spirit of a peacemaker, that, by conquering those whom you attack, you may lead them back to the advantages of peace; for our Lord says: "Blessed are the peacemakers; for they shall be called children of God" [Matthew 5:9].[109]

In *The City of God*, Augustine sides even more forcefully with peace:

> But, say they, the wise man will wage just wars. As if he would not all the rather lament the necessity of just wars, if he remembers that he is a man; for if they were not just he would not wage them, and would therefore be delivered from all wars. . . . Let every one, then, who thinks with pain on all these great evils, so horrible, so ruthless, acknowledge that this is misery. And if any one either endures or thinks of them without mental pain, this is a more miserable plight still, for he thinks himself happy because he has lost human feeling.[110]

Against this background of questions concerning just war, critics have long understood that certain alliterative poems, like *Alliterative Morte Arthure*, appear to take a peacemaking position,[111] but that the contemporary *Siege of Jerusalem* might well be similarly themed has

---

[105] On Melibee as an advice to Richard poem, with Dame Prudence as a figure for Anne of Bohemia as a counselor to Richard on behalf of peace, see Stillwell, "Political Meaning of Chaucer's Tale of Melibee." Similarly, Scattergood, in "Chaucer and the French War," links Melibee and Sir Thopas as anti-war tracts situated at the heart of Chaucer's *Canterbury Tales*.

[106] A case for the pacifism of both Chaucer and Gower is made by Yeager in "*Pax Poetica*." Barnie calls Gower "a man of peace but not a pacifist" (*War in Medieval Society*, p. 122). For a more recent investigation into Chaucer's opinions on the matter, see Pratt, *Chaucer and War*.

[107] Yeager, "*Pax Poetica*," p. 133. A similar point is made by Barnie (*War and Medieval Society*, p. 131), who ties Chaucer's decision to enter into such debates to "the political and social turmoil of the 1380s and 90s."

[108] See Yeager, "*Pax Poetica*," pp. 101–03. A good overview of medieval opinion on the nature of and proper rationale for "Just War" can be found in Keen, *Laws of War*, pp. 63–133.

[109] Augustine, Letter 189.6, in Schaff, *Select Library*, 1.554.

[110] Augustine, *The City of God* 19.8.7, in Schaff, *Select Library*, 2.405.

[111] That the *Alliterative Morte Arthure* is built around anti-war sentiments was first argued by Peck in "Willfulness and Wonders." Hamel's critical edition of the poem seems to take the poet's irenic goal

thus far escaped critical attention.[112] Like the gritty violence of *Alliterative Morte Arthure*, the gore in *Siege* is perhaps best read as a grim awareness of the terrible realities of war, not as a bloodthirsty and berserk cry for further bloodshed. The poem chronicles a historical war, and it is this historical quality that must stand out: the poem not only has resonances of the bloodshed that battle inevitably brings, but it also is, in a very literal sense, *history*. That is to say, the war is over. The vengeance of Jesus has been accomplished. The *Siege*-poet's answer to the social-political-religious question of whether there is such a thing as a just war is that there was one: Titus and Vespasian's vengeance for the death of Christ. It was commissioned, one might say, by Christ Himself, sanctioned by God through Peter (who was, unquestionably, a pope), executed by God's chosen representatives on Earth, and finished. Christ was avenged. Further efforts to avenge Christ are unnecessary and could only have ulterior motives behind them. That the poem is a call to action and to crusade, then, seems to be a claim that is far less sustainable than its opposite: a call to peace and to remembrance. We know, at least, that one reader of *Siege*, the anonymous poet behind *Alliterative Morte Arthure*,[113] astutely used the historical nature of the vengeance tradition to undermine Arthur's growing tyranny and further the irenic goals of his poem: the extent of Arthur's disconnection from his proper goals is most resolutely underscored by his desire to go to the Holy Land, "over the grete se with good men of armes / To revenge the Renk that on the Rood died!"[114] But the vengeance of Christ has already taken place. Arthur's actions, therefore, drive home his vanity and greed, since man should never appoint what God has determined.[115] Like Gower, then, the *Siege*-poet would appear to be in line with the notions of just war expressed by St. Augustine. The destruction of Jerusalem was a just war: a divine justice, a punishment for the death of Christ that prepares for the peace of His Second Coming. Other wars — the

---

almost as a given, but see especially pp. 34–58. Turville-Petre discusses the problem of just when Arthur becomes "unjust" in *Alliterative Revival*, pp. 102–03.

[112] The entirely opposite conclusion has been reached, however, by Hamel ("*Siege of Jerusalem* as a Crusading Poem"), who regards *Siege of Jerusalem* as a call to arms in the midst of crusading fervor prior to the disaster at Nicopolis.

[113] The interrelationship of these poems is problematic. Benson's 1398–1402 dating of *Alliterative Morte Arthure* would surely make *Siege* the source, yet other theories place composition of *Alliterative Morte Arthure* as early as 1350 (for a discussion of the matter, see *Morte Arthure*, ed. Hamel, pp. 53–58). That the *Alliterative Morte Arthure* uses *Siege*, however, would help to explain a number of verbal echoes of *Siege* within its lines (Oakden [*Alliterative Poetry in Middle English*, p. 100] records five occasions; I have included all of these in the Explanatory Notes), as well as a few oddities such as the swearing of Arthur upon the Vernicle when it should be a peacock, Lucius' golden dragon standard that should be Arthur's, and the mention of a fight in the valley of Josaphat (for a rather lengthy catalog of possible influences, see Neilson, "*Huchown*," pp. 297–300). Adding complexity to an already complicated problem, it is even conceivable that *Siege* and *Alliterative Morte Arthure* might have been composed by the same poet, with *Siege* coming first: the two works bear a remarkable number of similarities not only in language but also in structure, technique, geographical origin, and theme. If *Alliterative Morte Arthure* does, indeed, utilize *Siege*, we might plausibly assign a pre-1380s date to the earlier poem since concerns over the dangers and advisability of costly continental campaigns — thought by many critics to be the primary purpose for *Alliterative Morte Arthure*'s composition — would argue for a 1380–90 date to the Arthurian poem.

[114] *Alliterative Morte Arthure*, lines 3216–17. Compare lines 521–22 of the present text.

[115] See Peck's "Willfulness and Wonders."

wars in France, for example, or Despenser's crusade against Flanders, or the wars on the Iberian peninsula — are not acts of God, but of man, executed for what often amounted to very mortal, rapacious ends. The *Siege*-poet condemns such actions as un-just wars by providing a chronicle of what he believed to be a just war ordained by God.

Eustache Deschamps, whom Carter Lindberg has called "the leading pessimist in a depressed age," described the latter half of the fourteenth century in which he lived as an "age of tears, of envy, of torment, . . . [an] age of decline nigh to the end."[116] The description is doubly appropriate for a discussion of *Siege of Jerusalem*. Despite the fact that the historical background against which the poem was written was a "dark" time of what the *Siege*-poet considered injustice, the notion that the downward spiral of society would end, finally and inevitably, was never absent from his mind.

THE STRUCTURE OF THE POEM: ARCHITECTURE OF DIVINE PROVIDENCE

We have seen that the poet behind the construction of *Siege of Jerusalem* utilized a wide range of sources to create his poem. He also utilized, one might say, a wide variety of generic forms. But the poem is not a mere pastiche of preceding materials randomly strewn together. The material was carefully chosen and ordered in such a way as to make sense as history; it was for this reason that the poet changed the order of some events, or omitted certain details from his retelling that may not have properly meshed with the story as told in other portions of his source material. That is, the poet *constructed* his poem in the most literal sense: he built his poem around a structure that, although clad in the veil of the poetic form, clearly sustains focus on what he regards as the architecture of history.

As Figure 2 shows, the structure of *Siege of Jerusalem* is relatively simple and straightforward, yet at the same time quite involved (or perhaps I should say convoluted): the second half of the poem parallels in reverse the events of the first half, a hysteron proteron structure that is remarkably similar to that of *Alliterative Morte Arthure*.[117] As Hebron has pointed out, the story of the destruction of Jerusalem reflects an Augustinian concept of history as "a succession of great events which reveal part of the divine scheme of things."[118] This historiographical model, a self-reflexive, uni-directional scheme of time in which Divine Providence, represented by the Church (which has qualities of both the City of God and the City of Man) presses mankind invariably and inexorably toward the apocalyptic arrival of the New Jerusalem, stands against that of the older Greek and Roman models in which history (like Boethius' wheel of fortune), always turned back upon itself "as infinite variations on the theme of a constant human nature."[119] In Augustine's time scheme the past is finished, left behind in the inevitable march of time toward the end of time. According to this overarching scheme divine history, the avenging of Christ was a necessary step to prepare for the Second Coming — just as the death of Christ was necessary to set the stage for redemption — but it is a step that was completed by the actions of Titus and Vespasian. This

---

[116] Cited by Lindberg, *European Reformations*, p. 24.

[117] On the hysteron proteron structure of *Alliterative Morte Arthure*, see Peck, "Willfulness and Wonders." I am indebted to Peck's hypothesis for my discovery of a similar application to *Siege*.

[118] Hebron, *Medieval Siege*, p. 112. In this regard, he carefully sets the destruction of Jerusalem against the fall of Troy, whose course of action is clearly Boethian in its cyclical nature.

[119] Breisach, *Historiography*, p. 78.

Figure 2: Structure of *Siege of Jerusalem*

First visitation of Christ
. Pontius Pilate
. . Christ sold for 30 pennies
. . . Crucifixion
. . . . Titus and Vespasian ill
. . . . . Nathan driven to Bordeaux
. . . . . . Story of Christ, conversion of Titus
. . . . Veronica and the healing of Vespasian
. . . . Vespasian healed, oaths to avenge Christ
. . . . Nero orders assault
. . . . Events in Judaea
. . . . Roman council
. . . . Vespasian's standard
. . . . Battle in the valley of Josaphat
. . . . Vespasian's speech
. . . . Slaughter of Jews, Caiaphas captured
. . . . Assault 1: Jerusalem surrounded
. . . . Caiaphas executed
. . . . Vespasian's arming
. . . . Assault 2
. . . . Vespasian's wounding
. . . . Roman council
. . . . Events in Rome
. . . . Nero commits suicide
. . . . Vespasian crowned, Titus' oath to avenge Christ
. . . . Josephus and the healing of Titus
. . . . . . Story of Marie, pseudo-conversion of Jews
. . . . . Assault 3: Sabinus driven to the walls
. . . . Sabinus killed, Titus' oath
. . . Temple destroyed
. . Jews sold 30 for a penny
. Pilate commits suicide
Second visitation of Christ prepared

---

architecture of history, in which events are continually built upon the past, is given concrete form in the hysteron proteron structure underlying *Siege of Jerusalem*: the first half of the poem lays the foundation that sets the stage for a culmination of action in the second half of the poem, just as the Passion of Christ lies at the "center" of Christian history. As Nicholson has stated the matter, "the poem destroys the Synagogue and in its place sets up a memorial, a lapidary tale that honors Christ's passion . . . [and] is saved by that which it does not say, by the future it does not describe, where the history of Christ's church is projected; the Temple is razed and the Church raised in its place."[120] Nicholson's term

---

[120] Nicholson, "Haunted Itineraries," p. 457. Though not mentioned by Nicholson, St. Ambrose's gloss on Luke 21:6 shows that the parallel razing and building of Synagogue and Church was precisely part of the thinking of the Church Fathers: "It was spoken then of the temple made with hands, that it should be overthrown. For there is nothing made with hands which age does not impair, or violence

"lapidary" is particularly apt: the poem is not only a monument to the Church, representing a microcosm of Christian history beginning with the death of Christ and — by showing the triumph of the New Law over the Old Law — providing a first judgment on the Jews that presupposes the final judgment on humanity, but it is also a monument in the sense that it stands only in remembrance of an act that has already been performed.[121] To continue to seek vengeance on Jerusalem for Christ's death — as Arthur does in *Alliterative Morte Arthure* — is at its best folly and at its worst damnable. Vengeance has already been achieved.

We might, as an analogy, view the hysteron proteron structure of the poem as a series of frames that act like shells, each pair of actions framing off another layer of the text. The kernel (or fruit) at the center of the structure, then, is of utmost importance toward understanding the goals of the entire work. In a very real sense, the center of the structure is its climax.[122] In the case of *Siege of Jerusalem*, what lies at the structural and literal center of the poem[123] is the mechanism of the siege itself: the surrounding of Jerusalem by palisades, the filling of an encircling ditch with the corpses of the battle-dead, and the stopping of the water course that brings vital sustenance to the city.

By that wrightes han wroght a wonder stronge pale	*By then; palisade*
Alle aboute the burwe, with bastiles manye,	*around the town, with towers*
That no freke myght unfonge withouten fele harmes,	*encircle; many*
Ne no segge undere sonne myght fram the cité passe.	*man under [the] sun*

---

throw down, or fire burn. Yet there is also another temple, that is, the synagogue, whose ancient building falls to pieces as the Church rises" (Aquinas, *Catena aurea*, 3.674).

[121] Jesus' enigmatic prophecy in John 2:18–21 might also be of note here: "The Jews, therefore, answered, and said to him: What sign dost thou shew unto us, seeing thou dost these things? Jesus answered and said to them: Destroy this temple; and in three days I will raise it up. The Jews then said: Six and forty years was this temple in building; and wilt thou raise it up in three days? But he spoke of the temple of his body." On one level, Christ is understood to be speaking of his death and resurrection; in this regard, St. Augustine makes much of the pronouns at work here, using the passage to illustrate Christ's divinity since Christ says that *He* will raise up His body (see Tractate 47.7, in Schaff, *Select Library*, 7.263). In addition, Christ can be understood to be speaking of the destruction of the Second Temple and its replacement by the body of Christ (i.e., the Christian Church) after the entombment (which lasted three days). Though the Second Temple was probably built in something closer to eighty-four years (20 BC to AD 64), the numeric values of the Greek letters in "Adam" add up to forty-six ($alpha[=1] + delta[=4] + alpha[=1] + mu[=40]$), further emphasizing that the Temple represents the old Adam and original sin. Jesus' role as a new Adam demarcates the old way (Judaism and the Old Testament) from the new (Christianity and the New Testament). This latter reading is also interesting for paralleling the destruction of the Temple with the Crucifixion, as if the one logically followed from the other. As we will see, this connection is made quite explicit in *Siege of Jerusalem*.

[122] In this respect, as the lines of the narrative turn retrograde and inward, the framing structure seems to act more along Boethian than Augustinian models, as linear tangents turn back to the center; see Boethius' *Consolation of Philosophy* 3.m.11.1–6: "Whoever with deep thought seeks out the truth / And wants not to go wrong down devious ways, / Must on himself turn back the light of his inward vision, / Bending and forcing his far-reaching movements / Into a circle."

[123] This center is structural in the sense that the turning point of any hysteron proteron structure is of central importance to the theme of the whole, and literal in the sense that the center of this particular hysteron proteron structure (lines 681–92) falls close to being the precise midpoint of the poem's 1340 total lines.

Suth dommyn the diches   with the ded corses,
Crammen hit myd karayn   the kirnels alle under,
That the stynk of the stewe   myght strike over the walles
To cothe the corsed folke   that hem kepe scholde.[124]

The cors of the condit   that comen to toun   *course of the canal*
Stoppen, evereche a streem,   ther any strande yede,   *current went*
With stockes and stones   and stynkande bestes,   *sticks; stinking [dead] beasts*
That they no water myght wynne   that weren enclosed. (*Siege*, lines 681–92)

This central moment in the poem, the kernel at the center of its structure, fulfills, in quite literal effect, Christ's pronouncement as he approached Jerusalem on Palm Sunday:

> And when he drew near, seeing the city, he wept over it, saying: "If thou also hadst known, and that in this day, the things that are to thy peace: but now they are hidden from thy eyes. For the days shall come upon thee: and thy enemies shall cast a trench about thee and compass thee round and straiten thee on every side, and beat thee flat to the ground, and thy children that are in thee. And they shall not leave in thee a stone upon a stone: because thou hast not known the time of thy visitation." (Luke 19:41–44)

The Romans have come seeking vengeance on the Jews for the death of Christ, and they have, indeed, "cast a trench" around the city and encompassed it with walls. They press upon the city on every side, and the loss of life within the city is grievous. In the ensuing second half of the poem, the pain of the children within the besieged city will be highlighted with the story of Marie and her child, oaths will be taken not to leave a stone standing upon another in the city, and plows will level the city "flat to the ground."

That this judgment must focus particularly on the fate of the Temple is shown as Luke goes on to record that Christ's first action on arriving in Jerusalem is to visit the Temple Mount and to "cleanse" the site of the money-changers (Luke 19:45–46). This revolutionary action produces an immediate response in the Jewish authorities: "And the chief priests and the scribes and the rulers of the people sought to destroy him" (Luke 19:47). Not long after coming to the Temple, Christ once more foretells its destruction and, presumably, that of the city, as well:

> And to some saying of the temple that it was adorned with goodly stones and gifts, he said: "These things which you see, the days will come in which there shall not be left a stone upon a stone that shall not be thrown down." (Luke 21:5–6; compare Matthew 24:1–2 and Mark 13:1–2)

The writer of the Gospel of Luke makes a direct tie between Christ's prophecy for the destruction of Jerusalem, the final condemnation of the Temple (and the Jewish cultus that it represented), and the actions of the high priests (led by Caiaphas) who were viewed as the direct killers of Christ.[125]

---

[124] Lines 685–88: *Then [they] choke the ditches with the dead bodies, / Cram it with carrion beneath all the battlements, / So that the stench from that stew (combination) might strike over the walls [of the city] / To infect the cursed folk (i.e., the living Jews) that should defend them (i.e., their fallen dead)*

[125] These connections were firmly supported by the Church Fathers, who were almost unanimous in associating the Jews' rejection of Christ to their "murder" of Christ and thus to their condemnation

As a poem that represents the vengeance of Titus and Vespasian for the death of Christ — one manuscript even goes so far as to provide the Latin synopsis *Hic incepit Distruccio Jerarusalem quomodo Titus & Vespasianus obsederunt & distruxerunt Jerusalem et vi[n]dicarunt mortem Domini Jhesu Christi* ["Here begins the destruction of Jerusalem in which Titus and Vespasian besieged and unmade Jerusalem and avenged the death of the Lord Jesus Christ"] at the beginning of the poem[126] — *Siege of Jerusalem* depicts the culmination of Christ's prophecies in Luke: Jerusalem (and, by proxy, the Jews) did not recognize the visitation of Christ and, for that blindness, is condemned. In fulfilling this motive of revenge, vengeance upon the killers of Christ is certainly not to be forgotten, and it is no coincidence that the encircling of the city is, in turn, framed by the capture of Caiaphas and the high priests and their gruesome execution.

All that remains, after this central moment in the text, is to "cleanse" the Temple and the old Jewish cultus once and for all: that is, the Temple must be destroyed. This destruction, too, was viewed as a fulfillment of Christ's prophecy. As Christ had said that Jerusalem's enemies would "not leave in thee a stone upon a stone" (Luke 19:44; 21:6), so will Jerusalem's conquerors utterly destroy the Temple. In taking over command of the army from his father,[127] Titus swears an oath to do just this; Vespasian replies (lines 1015–20):

"My wele and my worschup ye weldeth to kepe,	*prosperity; honor; you control*
For the tresour of my treuth upon this toun hengyth:	*troth; town hangs*
"I nold this toun were untake, ne this toures heye,[128]	
For alle the glowande golde upon grounde riche,	*glowing*
Ne no ston in the stede stondande alofte,	*stone in the place*
Bot alle overtourned and tilt, Temple and other."	*tilled, Temple and all*

And it is this same detail of overturning the Temple so that no stone stands upon another, and thus fulfilling the twin prophecies of Christ in Luke, that is emphasized in the aftermath of the siege (lines 1285–96):

So they wroughten at the wal alle the woke tyme,	*made; that week's time*
Tille the cyté was serched and sought al aboute,	*Until*
Maden wast at a wappe ther the walle stode,	*Made waste with one blow where*
Bothe in Temple and in tour alle the toun over.	*tower*

as a people and the destruction of the Temple by Titus and Vespasian. In his exposition of Psalm 79, for instance, St. Augustine calls the first three verses a prophecy fulfilled in the destruction and a sign of the inheritance of God passing from Israel to the Church of Christ (in Schaff, *Select Library*, 8.380–81). On the Gospel prophecies, Aquinas' *Catena aurea* cites numerous supports for associating Christ's directive with the destruction: for example, Hrabanus Maurus on Matthew 24:2 (1.799) and Gregory the Great, Origen, and Eusebius on Luke 19:41–44 (3.644–46).

[126] London, British Library MS Additional 31042 (commonly denoted as manuscript A), fol. 50r. See pp. 8–13 for information about the textual history of *Siege of Jerusalem*.

[127] Though one would not want to push the argument too far, it is possible that Vespasian and Titus might function theologically within the poem as a reflection of the Father and Son. Thrice in the Bible vengeance is said to be the purvey of God: "Revenge is mine, I will repay, saith the Lord" (Romans 12:19; compare Deuteronomy 32:25 and Hebrews 10:30). The point would seem to be that Vespasian and Titus are, at the very least, God's appointed avengers.

[128] *I wouldn't [know that] this town were untaken, nor these towers high*

Nas no ston in the stede   stondande alofte,   *Was no stone; place standing*
Morter ne mude-walle   bot alle to mulle fallen: *mud-brick wall; earth*
Nother tymbre ne tre,   Temple ne other,   *Neither timber*
Bot doun betyn and brent   into blake erthe.   *That wasn't razed and burned*

And whan the Temple was overtilt,   Tytus commaundys   *overthrown*
In plowes to putte   and alle the place erye;   *plowed up*
Suth they sow hit with salt,   and seiden this wordes: *Then they sowed; these*
"Now is this stalwourthe stede   distroied forevere."   *strong place destroyed*

Here, at the end of the poem, Christ's prophecies are at last fulfilled. Jerusalem, the Temple, and the killers of Christ have been utterly destroyed. No stone is left standing on another. It is no coincidence that the corresponding action at the beginning of the poem — the other end of this particular frame of the text — is the Crucifixion of Christ. Even the details of the actions share common ground: the Romans harrowing the city of Jerusalem ("In plowes to putte and alle the place erye" — line 1294) is surely meant to hearken back to the Jews setting the scourging post into the ground ("A pyler pyght was doun upon the playn erthe" — line 9). The exiled Jews are defined by their torment of Christ ("Ne non that leved in here lawe scholde in that londe dwelle / That tormented trewe God" — lines 1323–24), a torment depicted in quite graphic detail at the beginning of the poem (lines 10–18). The entire poem is ultimately framed by Christ: it begins with the Passion of Christ, and ends with Christ's prophecies fulfilled, His death avenged, and the path made ready for the *Parousia*, a Second Coming that surely lies just beyond the end of the poem. It is possible, perhaps, that the story's final lines (1337–40)

When alle was demed and don   they drowen up tentis,   *said and done; folded*
Trossen here tresour   and trompen up the sege,   *Pack; trumpet; siege*
Wenten syngyng away   and han here wille forthred,   *have their will furthered*
And hom riden to Rome.   Now rede ous oure Lord!   *ride home; guide us may*

allude to this ultimate act in human history, depicting a return to a home of two sorts: the physical city of Rome and the new spiritual home that Rome represents.

Within this Christ frame lies yet another framing figure: Pontius Pilate. Christ's Passion is set within the context of Pilate's role in bringing about His death, and the final act of Titus in passing judgment on the city is the imprisonment of Pilate at Viterbo ("And Pilat to prisoun was put to pynen forevere, / At Vienne, ther venjaunce and vile deth he tholed" — lines 1327–28). It is interesting to note that Pilate's imprisonment is here given a doctrinal twist: he will continue in "pyne forevere," perhaps referring to Pilate having a special place reserved in Hell.

These framing layers of story work throughout the poem. In some cases they are simple parallels of detail, such as Titus' decision to sell the Jews thirty to a penny (lines 1319–20), corresponding to the selling of Christ for thirty pennies (line 154, recalling Matthew 26:15), or the shifting of scene from Titus and Vespasian in Judaea to Nero in Rome (lines 897 ff.), corresponding to the shifting of scene from Nero in Rome to Titus and Vespasian in Judaea (lines 297 ff.). But far more interesting are thematic parallels that hint at deeper levels of interpretation, like the structural correspondence between the story of Christ (as told by the messenger Nathan in lines 101 ff.) and the story of Marie (lines 1081 ff.): the parallel is surely meant to recall Matthew 27:25, where the Jewish crowd in Jerusalem chooses Barabbas over Christ, saying to Pilate: "His [Christ's] blood be upon us and upon our children," a statement that comes into hideous reality not only in the broad outlines of the siege, but also in the specific murder of Marie's child. And similar connections might be found in the structural relationships, for example, between the story of Veronica and the healing of Vespasian (lines 221 ff.) and the story of Josephus and the healing of Titus (lines 1029 ff.).

The complexities of this hysteron proteron structure have only begun to be broached here, but it is important to recall that the entire structure serves to emphasize the theme of the whole: vengeance for the death of Christ. Thus, the architecture of history and the architecture of the poem work in tandem to produce a poem that spoke profoundly to the end of the fourteenth century.

THE LAUD MANUSCRIPT AND ITS VOCABULARY

Because copy L of *Siege of Jerusalem* is the oldest of the generally complete manuscripts to contain the poem, it is the version of the poem that is most frequently edited.[129] Given the greater number of witnesses in the family of manuscript *beta*, however, it is difficult to ignore the remaining manuscript tradition. We are left with two fairly distinct versions of the poem, and to give greater authority to the minority tradition simply on the basis of date may (or may not, of course) fly in the face of the poem's provenance. Put another way, to lay aside the *beta* manuscript tradition may be laying aside a more accurate representation of the poem's original form or, at the very least, what appears to have been a more popular form of the poem.[130] Length has also been noted in favor of the *alpha* manuscript tradition, but this, too, might be misleading since the scattered twenty-five lines found only in copy L may very well reflect scribal additions. The penchant of scribes for adding material is, after all, far more rampant than the desire to excise occasional lines. On the other hand, much of the additional material — modifications to the portents of Jerusalem's destruction and a detailed description of Pilate's suicide, for example — is quite interesting and the earlier date does weigh heavy in such a decision. Most convincing, however, has been the work of Hoyt N. Duggan in studying the b-verse of Middle English alliterative poetry; after thoroughly examining the extant manuscripts of *Siege* for inaccurate alliterative patterns, he concludes: "L is by far the best of the extant manuscripts, and though one will find numerous other examples of the statistically rare patterns in the other seven manuscripts, there would in all such cases be a satisfactory reading in L which is also statistically more regular."[131] In constructing this new text of *Siege of Jerusalem*, therefore, I have decided to follow the editors of the only other available full texts of the poem and to present an edition representing L. While it is a founding principle of the Middle English Texts Series to hold closely to a best-text theory of editing (i.e., the utilization of a copy-text), I have been hard-pressed to rely on L as extensively as I might have preferred since, unfortunately, the scribe

---

[129] The textual history of the poem is provided on pp. 8–13.

[130] Early commentators believed that L also most closely resembled the poet's dialect, but the exhaustive work of more recent scholars indicates that P (and, to a slightly lesser degree, A) should hold that honor: *Siege of Jerusalem* is undoubtedly a Northern poem, and L is undoubtedly an Oxfordshire manuscript. Given the early date of P (it is probably a close contemporary of L in that regard), it would certainly be the preferred base-text for the poem if only it were complete; see *Siege of Jerusalem*, ed. Hanna and Lawton, pp. lxxxvi–xcvi.

[131] Duggan, "Final -*e* and the Rhythmic Structure of the B-Verse," p. 125.

(or exemplar) of L was often inaccurate in his transcription insofar as we are able to reconstruct the original appearance of the text. As a brief look at the Textual Notes will indicate, the text of this edition is, therefore, far more heavily emended than I would otherwise prefer.

In emending L, I chose two primary texts from each of the branches of the more widely represented *beta* family. To represent the *delta* tradition, the choice of base-text came down to copies U and D since the remaining manuscripts are largely fragmentary. Despite the fact that U is the more ornate of the manuscripts, I chose the text of D since, like Thorlac Turville-Petre, I find it to be, aesthetically, the "best representative" of the tradition.[132] For the *gamma* tradition, I chose the text of P since it most closely represents the poet's own dialect and is contemporary in date with L; where the fragmentary P is lacking, the alternative text utilized is A, which is penultimate in approximating the original dialect of the poem. The text presented here, then, is that of L, generally emended by P, A, and D, a principle similar to that taken by the most recent editors of the poem.[133]

In addition to minor adjustments of the text, there are two broad exceptions to my use of L as a base-text for this edition: the presentation of the text in quatrains and the division of the text into passus. That *Siege* was originally composed in quatrains was first theorized by Max Kaluza in 1892.[134] Quatrain division of *Siege* was accepted by Kölbing and Day in their early edition of the poem (though they did not print an accordingly divided text), and has since been accepted by other critics, such as Duggan, as well as the most recent editors of the poem, Hanna and Lawton (who do print an accordingly divided text).[135] Though the manuscript evidence for these quatrain divisions is slight — copies E and C show four-line divisions, and copy U shows eight-line divisions — Hanna and Lawton, for example, conclude that an "assessment of manuscript variation indicates that they are authorial, whether explicitly marked in the extant manuscripts or not."[136] Even further, they argue persuasively that

> The poet perceived his mode of composition in a way perhaps fundamentally different from other alliterative poets; in addition to his adherence to traditional forms of composition by the formulaic phrase, he quite persistently shaped his developing narrative within syntactic

---

[132] *Siege of Jerusalem*, ed. Turville-Petre, p. 159.

[133] I have minimized citations to other manuscripts in my Textual Notes in order to prevent undo overlap with the edition of Hanna and Lawton, who provide a full textual apparatus comparing all extant manuscripts; thus, I have only provided manuscript alternatives and editorial variations where I have adjusted L or where the primary editors of the poem have done so. The reader interested in viewing additional alternative manuscript readings is strongly encouraged to consult the excellent work presented by Hanna and Lawton in their critical edition.

[134] Kaluza, "Strophische Gliederung." Kaluza's further theory that alliterative poems such as *Siege* could be divided into strophes has been soundly rejected by all subsequent editors of the poem; see, for example, Kölbing and Day, p. ixn1, and Day's more extensive refutation in "Strophic Division." Duggan provides similar conclusions in "Strophic Patterns."

[135] Among other critical discussions of the matter, see especially the work of Duggan, "Strophic Patterns"; Duggan is quick to point out that the choice of the term "quatrain" to describe these divisions is somewhat unfortunate, as the "quatrains" of such poems generally "lack the formal determination" of a "prosodic unit" that we would normally associate with quatrains (pp. 226–27). Hanna and Lawton discuss the matter on pp. lxx–lxxi of their edition.

[136] *Siege of Jerusalem*, ed. Hanna and Lawton, p. lxx.

patterns conceived as joining at least distichs, "half-stanzas" or "hemistichs," if not the full
four-line unit. . . . The quatrains of *The Siege of Jerusalem* are therefore syntactic devices like
the rhyme royal stanza of *Troilus and Criseyde* and consist mainly of one or two self-contained
syntactic units.[137]

While nothing short of an autograph copy can prove conclusively the authorial nature of
such divisions, I find the evidence persuasive enough to abandon the presentation of the poem
in L and here present the poem as divided into quatrains. In five instances, then, "faulty"
quatrains (i.e., those short at least a line) have been corrected by the insertion of material
from the *beta* tradition (lines 681–84, 877–80, 1121–24, 1233–36, and 1309–12); at lines
425–28 a line from L has been removed to achieve the four-line structure. These adjustments
leave three quatrains that are faulty across the whole of the extant manuscript tradition: lines
25–28, 41–44, and 1333–36. Though I am rather loathe to do so, I have incorporated the
"missing" lines of these quatrains into the lineation of my text in order to facilitate the
reader wishing to cross-reference between this volume and that of Hanna and Lawton. My
hesitancy to "count" these missing lines is, I hope, understandable when the full weight of
manuscript evidence argues against their existence. This is not to say that lines are not
missing from our existing text, for the fact that we have some lacunae is without doubt. Indeed, there are four additional gaps in the text that are not numbered by Hanna and Lawton
(and there may, of course, be even more).[138] While Hanna and Lawton are quite confident
that reference to the poem's sources is enough to determine the number of missing lines,[139]
I cannot be completely assured about the number of missing lines in certain locations (as
a quatrain that appears short a line could well be missing one, five, or even more lines). Better,
I should think, simply to indicate the lacuna in all such instances, though my interest in the
practicalities of usage sways me from following this principle in the present work.

The second broad exception to the acceptance of L as base-text is my decision to divide
the poem into seven passus and a prologue despite the fact that copy L shows only three major
textual divisions. Here again, the manuscript record is spotty: copies P, A, V, U, and C all
show some markings of passus division, though not all are agreed on the number of passus
(P shows six; A, V, U, and C show seven), while copy E breaks the text into six major
divisions with large capitals (though one of these divisions is not in the same location as
those found in P).[140] That all extant copies show some degree of division, however, argues
in favor of some authorial basis — the question, then, is one of number. Though Kölbing
and Day accepted L's divisions as authorial, I am inclined to follow Hanna and Lawton's
division of the text into six passus and a prologue; the seventh possible division, reflected
in U, V, and C at line 738, breaks the text in the midst of a stanza. It is worth noting that
these divisions match quite neatly with my hypothesis of a hysteron proteron structure

---

[137] *Siege of Jerusalem*, ed. Hanna and Lawton, pp. lxxi and lxxvii. Their intervening and following
discussion of the poet's style is particularly useful in showing the intricacies of the poet's technique
in utilizing this construction.

[138] These lacunae appear after lines 216, 938, 940, and 942.

[139] In private correspondence, Lawton states that he and Hanna actually had no trouble writing
in the missing lines, though they did not, of course, publish them as part of their edition.

[140] A very useful table showing the correspondences between the divisions in the various manuscripts is provided by Hanna and Lawton on p. lxxii of their edition.

behind the whole of the poem (see Figure 2, above) — though one cannot discount the fact that such coincidental division may be more the result of an observant reader than of an authorial hand.

The vocabulary of alliterative poetry is often more difficult than that which is found in most other forms of Middle English verse since alliterative poetry typically relies on what we might think of as "archaisms" held over from an earlier English period along with the richness of colloquial idioms. The vocabulary of *Siege of Jerusalem*, however, with its interest in presenting a dramatic, now-you-are-there account of the siege itself, goes even beyond the norm of typical alliterative poems. In addition to archaic alliterative forms that at times seem closer to Aelfric than to Chaucer, the poet utilizes a wide range of what we might term "war" vocabulary: specialized vocabulary for armor, weapons, siege engines, fortifications, warriors, and military tactics all appear within the poem's lines.[141] A few of these terms are borrowed from Old Norse: *farcostes*, for example, a type of seacraft mentioned in line 289, is derived from ON *farkostr*; and *brynye*, a coat of mail mentioned at lines 281, 748, 959, 1123, and 1242, is derived from ON *brynja*.[142] But the vast majority of the war vocabulary is French in origin, imported either directly from the continent or through the medium of Anglo-Norman. Hence words like *arblastes* in lines 671 and 840, meaning crossbows (from OF *arbaleste*); *avental* in line 760, a term for the faceplate of a helmet (from OF *esventail*);[143] *bastiles* in line 682, meaning tall, fortified besieging towers (from F *bastille*); *belfray* in lines 390, 392, 413, 591, and 1192, a type of siege tower (from OF *berfrei*); *brytaged* in lines 338 and 413, referring to wooden galleries (from OF *bretesche*); *fanward* in lines 433 and 553, meaning the vanguard of a military force (from OF *avangarde*); *garrite* in line 651, a watch-tower used in siege operations (from OF *garite*); *hurdighs* in line 580, a wooden fortification carried by animals (from OF *hourdeis*); *kernels* in lines 625, 660, 679, 686, and 1195, meaning battlement embrasures (from OF *crenel*); *masers* in line 886, a soldier equipped with a mace (from OF *massier*); *nakerer* in lines 856 and 1183, a kettle-drum player (from OF *naquere*); *pesan* in line 515, an armored plate of sheet of mail protecting the neck and upper torso (from OF *pizane*); *quarels* in lines 626 and 657, a term for a square-headed crossbow bolt (from OF *quarel*); *quarters* in line 626, another term for a crossbow (from OF *quartot*); and *spryngoldes* in line 841, a specific type of siege catapult (from AN *springalde*). Because such vocabulary is foreign to modern readers, I have made every attempt to gloss these terms consistently. I have also provided an explanatory note for the first occurrence of these and other instances of war vocabulary.[144]

---

[141] *Siege of Jerusalem* is by no means alone in this fact; *Alliterative Morte Arthure*, for example, has many of the instances of war vocabulary cited here; see above for more on the relationship between these poems. I am grateful to Kölbing and Day's excellent editorial work for making this list far easier to compile than it might have been.

[142] It is interesting to note that whatever hand is responsible for the D text of the poem, a concerted effort seems to have been made to reduce the number of "foreign" words in the text since all occurrences of the word *brynye* have been replaced with various Middle English terms in the D text.

[143] See the explanatory note to this line, however, for a different glossing of the term based on *Alliterative Morte Arthure*.

[144] Further discussion of the lexis of the poem is provided in *Siege of Jerusalem*, ed. Hanna and Lawton, pp. lxxvii–lxxxi; they also discuss the general style of the poem in more detail on pp. lxxiv–lxxxvi.

The text presented here has been regularized in accordance with the standard editorial practices of the Middle English Texts Series, with the following addenda: thorn is translit-erated as *th*, and yogh is transliterated as *g* or *y* depending not only on Modern English orthography but also on alliterative patterns. Hyphens have been placed where words sepa-rated in the Middle English represent a Modern English compound word. Punctuation and capitalization is, of course, editorial, as is the division of the poem into quatrains and passus.[145]

MANUSCRIPTS

Indexed as item 1583 in Brown and Robbins, eds., *Index of Middle English Verse*, and Cutler and Robbins, eds., *Supplement to the Index of Middle English Verse*:[146]

- L: Bodleian Library, MS Laud Misc. 656, fols. 1v–19r. [Base-text for this edition.]
- A: British Library, MS Additional 31042, fols. 50r–66r.
- C: British Library, MS Cotton Caligula A.ii, part I, fols. 111r–125r.
- V: British Library, MS Cotton Vespasian E.xvi, fols. 70r–75v.
- U: Cambridge University Library, MS Mm.v.14, fols. 187r–206v.
- Ex: Exeter, Devon Record Office, MS 2507, binding fragment.
- D: London, Lambeth Palace Library, MS 491, part I, fols. 206r–227v.
- P: Princeton University Library, MS Taylor Medieval 11, fols. 104vb–110vb.
- E: San Marino, Huntington Library, MS HM 128, fols. 205r–216r.

---

[145] On the reconstruction of these textual divisions based on the surviving manuscript tradition, see Hanna and Lawton's excellent discussion: *Siege of Jerusalem*, ed. Hanna and Lawton, pp. lxix–lxxiv.

[146] For more details on the manuscripts, see pp. 8–9.

[PROLOGUE]

1   In Tyberyus tyme,   the trewe emperour,
     Sire Sesar hymsulf,   seysed in Rome,
     Whyle Pylat was provost   undere that prince riche
     And Jewen justice also   in Judeus londis.[1]

5   Herodes, undere his emperie,   as heritage wolde,
     Kyng of Galilé was y-called   whan that Crist deyed;
     They Sesar sakles were,   that oft synne hatide,
     Throw Pylat pyned He was   and put on the Rode.[2]

     A pyler pyght was doun   upon the playn erthe,[3]
10   His body bonden therto,   and beten with scourgis.   *bound; beaten*
     Whyppes of quyrboyle   by-wente His white sides   *pliable leather beset*
     Til He al on rede blode ran,   as rayn in the strete.[4]

     Suth stoked Hym on a stole   with styf mannes hondis,
     Blyndfelled Hym as a be   and boffetis Hym raghte:[5]
15   "Gif thou be prophete of pris,   prophecie!" they sayde,   *If; prophet of worth*
     "Whiche berne here aboute   bolled Thee laste?"   *man; struck You*

     A thrange thornen croune   was thraste on His hed,
     Umbecasten Hym with a cry   and on a Croys slowen.[6]

---

[1] Lines 1–4: *In the time of Tiberius, this legitimate emperor, / [Ruling as] Sir Caesar himself, held sway in Rome, / While [Pontius] Pilate was provost under that rich prince (i.e., Tiberius) / And also judge of the Jews in Judaea's lands*

[2] Lines 5–8: *[And] Herod, under his (i.e., Tiberius') imperial rule, by hereditary right, / Was called the king of Galilee when Christ died; / Though Caesar, who often hated sin, was innocent, / Through Pilate He (i.e., Christ) was pained (tortured) and put on the Cross*

[3] *A pillar was set upon the flat ground*

[4] *Until His whole body ran red with blood, as rain [does] upon the street*

[5] Lines 13–14: *Then [they] struck Him upon a stool with stiff men's hands, / Blindfolded Him as a bee and gave Him blows*

[6] Lines 17–18: *A crown of straight thorns was thrust upon His head, / [And they] surrounded Him with a cry and on a Cross slew [Him]*

	For al the harme that He hadde, hasted He noght	
20	On hem the vyleny to venge that His veynys brosten,[1]	

Bot ay taried on the tyme gif they tourne wolde,	
Gaf hem space that Hym spilide, they hit spedde lyte.[2]	
Fourty wynter, as Y fynde, and no fewere yyrys,	*I find; years*
Or princes presed in hem that Hym to pyne wroght,[3]	

25	Til hit tydde on a tyme that Tytus of Rome	*Until it befell; Titus*
	That alle Gascoyne gate and Gyan the noble	*Who; Gascony ruled; Guienne*
	[. . . .]	
	[. . . .]	

	Whyle noye noyet hym in Neroes tyme,	*trouble harassed; Nero's*
30	He hadde a malady unmeke inmyddis the face:[4]	
	The lyppe lyth on a lumpe, lyvered on the cheke;	*lip lay; clotted; cheek*
	So a canker unclene hit cloched togedres.[5]	

	Also his fadere of flesche is ferly bytide:	*father; is marvelously afflicted*
	A bikere of waspen bees bredde in his nose,	*hive of wasp-bees bred*
35	Hyved upon his hed; he hadde hem of youthe	*Hived; them since youth*
	And Waspasian was caled the waspene bees after.	*[he] was called Vespasian*

	Was never syknes sorere than this sire tholed,	*sickness; this man suffered*
	For in a liter he lay, laser at Rome;	*litter; diseased*
	Out of Galace was gon to glade hym a stounde,	
40	For in that cuthe he was kyng they he car tholede.[6]	

	Nas ther no leche upon lyve this lordes couth helpe,	
	Ne no grace growyng to gayne here grym sores.[7]	
	[. . . .]	
	[. . . .]	

---

[1] Lines 19–20: *Despite all the harm that He had [from them], He did not haste / To revenge the villainy on those who had burst His veins*

[2] Lines 21–22: *Instead [He] waited for the time when they might convert, / Gave those who slew Him time, though it availed little*

[3] *Before [He] set the princes upon those who [had] given Him pain*

[4] *He had a cruel malady amidst [his] face*

[5] *As a cancer unclean it clenched [his lips] together*

[6] Lines 39–40: *Out of Galatia [he] was taken to cheer him a short time, / For in that country he was king though he suffered ill*

[7] Lines 41–42: *There was no doctor alive [who] could help these lords, / Nor herbs growing that could benefit their grim sores*

45   Now was ther on Nathan,   Neymes sone, of Grece,
        That sought oft over the se   fram cyté to other,
        Knewe contreys fele,   kyngdomes manye,
        And was a marener myche   and a marchaunt bothe.[1]

        Sensteus out of Surye   sent hym to Rome   *Cestius; Syria*
50   To the athel Emperour   — an eraunde fram the Jewes —   *noble; errand*
        Caled Nero by name   that hym to noye wroght,   *came to trouble*
        Of his tribute to telle,   that they withtake wolde.   *they would hold back*

        Nathan toward Nero   nome on his way   *went*
        Over the Grekys grounde   myd the grym ythes,   *amid the fierce waves*
55   An heye setteth the sayl   over the salt water,   *On high set the sail*
        And with a dromound on the deep   dryveth on swythe.[2]

        The wolcon wanned anon   and the water skeweth,   *sky waned; grew dark*
        Cloudes clateren on loude   as they cleve wolde.[3]
        The racke myd a rede wynde   roos on the myddel   *storm; red wind rose*
60   And sone sette on the se   out of the south syde.   *soon set upon the sea*

        Hit blewe on the brode se,   bolned up harde;   *swelled*
        Nathannys nave anon   on the north dryveth,   *Nathan's ship soon*
        So the wedour and the wynd   on the water metyn
        That alle hurtled on an hepe   that the helm gemyd.[4]

65   Nathan flatte for ferde   and ful under hacchys,
        Lete the wedour and the wynde   worche as hem lyked;
        The schip scher upon schore,   schot froward Rome
        Toward uncouth costes,   kayrande on the ythes,[5]

        Rapis unradly   umbe ragged tourres.
70   The brode sail at o brayd   to-bresteth a-twynne:[6]
        That on ende of the sschip   was ay toward heven,   *one end; [the] heavens*
        That other doun in the deep,   as alle drenche wolde.   *as [if] all would drown*

---

[1] Lines 45–48: *Now was there one [man named] Nathan, Naym's son, of Greece, / Who often journeyed over the sea from [one] city to another, / [Who] knew many countries, many kingdoms, / And was both a great mariner and merchant*

[2] *And with a drumond (a large ship) on the deep drives on quickly*

[3] *The clouds thundered loudly as [if] they would break apart*

[4] Lines 63–64: *The weather and the wind so meet on the water / That [he] who governed the helm was hurtled into a heap*

[5] Lines 65–68: *Nathan dropped flat for fear and fell under the hatches, / Let the water and the wind do what they would; / The ship ran swiftly past shores, shot away from Rome / Toward unknown coasts, carried on the waves*

[6] Lines 69–70: *Moving rapidly among ragged towers [of water]. / The broad sail in one moment burst in two*

Over wilde wawes he wende,   as alle walte scholde,[1]

Stroke stremes throw   yn stormes and wyndes;   *Struck through streams*

75   With mychel langour atte laste,   as our Lord wolde,   *great wretchedness*

Alle was born at a byr   to Burdewes havene.[2]

By that were bernes atte banke;   barouns and knyghtes   *men at the shore*

And citezeins of the syght   selcouth hem thoght   *thought [it a] marvel*

That ever barge other bot   or berne upon lyve   *[a] barge or boat or man alive*

80   Unpersched passed hadde: the peryles were so many.   *Unperished; perils*

They token hym to Titus,   for he the tonge couthe;   *could speak the language*

And he fraynes how fer   the flode hadde hym y-ferked.   *asks; far; carried*

"Sire, out of Surré,"   he seide, "Y am come,   *Syria*

To Nero, sondisman sent,   the seignour of Rome,   *[as a] messenger; leader*

85   "Fram Sensteus, his serjant,   with certayn leteres,   *Cestius, his officer*

That is justise and juge   of the Jewen lawe.   *judge of the Jewish law*

Me were lever at that londe   — lord, lene that Y were —

Than alle the gold other good   that ever God made."[3]

The kyng into conseyl   calleth hym sone   *called him (i.e., Nathan)*

90   And saide: "Canste thou any cure   or craft upon erthe

To softe the grete sore   that sitteth on my cheke?

And Y schal thee redly rewarde   and to Rome sende."[4]

Nathan nyckes hym with nay,   sayde he non couthe:

"Bot were thou, kyng, in that kuthé   ther that Crist deyed,[5]

95   Ther is a worldlich wif,   a womman ful clene,   *worldly wife; very pure*

That hath softyng and salve   for eche sore out."   *healing and salve*

"Telle me tyt," quod Titus,   "and thee schal tyde better,   *quickly; you will do*

What medecyn is most   that that may useth,   *greatest*

Whether gommes other graces,   or any goode drenches,[6]

100   Other chauntementes or charmes?   Y charge thee to say."   *enchantments*

---

[1] *Over wild waves he went, [so wild it seemed] as [if] all would be overturned*

[2] *All was borne by a favorable wind to the haven of Bordeaux*

[3] Lines 87–88: *"It would be better to me [to be] at that land — lord, grant that I were — / Than [to have] all the gold or goods that God ever made"*

[4] Lines 90–92: *And said: "Do you know any cure or craft on earth / To ease the massive sore that sits on my cheek? / And[, if you do,] I shall quickly reward you and send [you] to Rome"*

[5] Lines 93–94: *Nathan answers him with a no, says he could do nothing: / "But if you, king, were in that country where Christ died . . ."*

[6] *Whether [they are] gums or grasses, or any special drinks*

"Nay, non of tho," quod Nathan,   "bot now wole Y telle: *those*
Ther was a lede in our londe,   while He lif hadde,   *man in our land; was alive*
Preved for a prophete   throw preysed dedes   *Proved [to be] a prophet*
And born in Bethleem one by,   of a burde schene,   *Bethlehem; fair maiden*

105   "And ho a mayde unmarred   that never man touched,   *she; (i.e., a virgin)*
As clene as clef   ther cristalle of sprynges.[1]
Without hosebondes helpe   save the Holy Goste,
A kyng and a knave child   ho conceyved at ere;   *a male child she; ear*

"A taknyng of the Trinyté   touched hire hadde,   *token; had touched her*
110   Thre persones in o place   preved togedres: *one; acknowledged together*
Eche grayn is o God   and o God bot alle,   *part is one God*
And alle thre ben bot one   as eldres us tellen.   *as [our] elders tell us*

"The first is the Fadere   that fourmed was never,
The secunde is the Sone   of His sede growyn,
115   The thridde in Heven myd Hem   is the Holy Goste,   *third; with Them*
Nether merked ne made   bot mene fram Hem passyth.   *appointed; conjointly*

"Alle ben they endeles,   and even of o myght   *endless (i.e., immortal); equally*
And weren inwardly endeles   or the erthe bygan.   *before*
As sone was the Sone   as the self Fadere,   *quickly*
120   The heye Holy Goste   with Hem hadde They ever.   *high*

"The secunde persone, the Sone,   sent was to erthe
To take careynes kynde   of a clene mayde;
And so unknowen He came   caytifes to helpe,
And wroght wondres ynowe ay   tille He wo driede.[2]

125   "Wyne He wroght of water   at o word ene,   *with one word alone*
Ten lasares at a logge   He leched at enys,   *lepers; lodge; leeched (healed) at once*
Pyned myd the palsy   He putte hem to hele,[3]
And ded men fro the deth   ever ilke day rered.   *dead; death; raised*

"Croked and cancred   He kevered hem alle,   *Crook-backed and cancered; cured*
130   Both the dombe and the deve,   myd His dere wordes,   *mute; deaf; with*
Dide myracles many mo   than Y in mynde have;   *more miracles; I know of*
Nis no clerk with countours   couthe aluendel rekene.[4]

---

[1] *As pure as [a] cliff where crystals spring out*

[2] Lines 121–24: *The second person [of the Trinity], the Son, was sent to earth / To take the carrion's nature (i.e., a fleshly body) from a pure woman; / And so He came in disguise to help wretches, / And [He] wrought many wonders until he suffered woe*

[3] *Those pained with paralysis He put to heel (i.e., made them walk)*

[4] *There is no accountant with counters who could count half of them all*

"Fyf thousand of folke, is ferly to here,   *Five; [it] is wondrous to hear*
With two fisches He fedde and fif berly loves,   *barley loaves*
135 That eche freke hadde his fulle, and yit ferre leved   *each man; yet lived long*
Of battes and of broken mete basketes twelve.   *pieces [of bread]; meat*

"Ther suwed Hym of a sorte seventy and twey   *sowed; one group seventy-two*
To do what He dempte, disciples were hoten.   *He deemed; were called*
Hem to citees He sende His sawes to preche,   *He sent them; teachings*
140 Ay by two and by two til hy were a-twynne.   *Always; until they were apart*

"Hym suwed of another sorte semeliche twelve,   *twelve goodly [men]*
Pore men and noght prute, aposteles were hoten,   *not proud; were called*
That of kaytefes He ches His Churche to encresche,   *caitiffs; chose; increase*
The outwale of this worlde, and this were her names: *outcasts; these; their*

145 "Peter, James, and Jon, and Jacob the ferthe,   *fourth*
And the fifthe of His felawys Phelip was hoten;   *fifth of His fellowship*
The sixte Symond was caled, and the seveth eke   *sixth; seventh*
Bertholomewe, that his bone never breke nolde;   *whose bones would never*

"The eyght man was Mathu, that is myche y-loved;   *eighth; much-loved*
150 Taddé and Tomas — here ben ten even —   *here are [an] even ten*
And Andreu the elleveth, that auntred hym myche   *eleventh; adventured*
Byfor princes to preche, was Petrus brother.   *Before; [and who] was*

"The laste man was unlele and luther of his dedis: *disloyal; wicked in his deeds*
Judas, that Jhesu Crist to the Jewes solde.
155 Suth hymsulf he slowe for sorow of that dede;   *slew; deed*
His body on a balwe-tree to-breste on the myddel.   *gallows-tree burst in*

"Whan Crist hadde heried Helle and was to Heven passed,   *harrowed*
For that mansed man Mathie they chossyn.   *To replace that accursed; chose*
Yit unbaptized were bothe Barnabé and Poule,
160 And noght knewen of Crist, bot comen sone after.[1]

"The princes and the prelates, agen the Paske tyme,   *at the time of Passover*
Alle thei hadde Hym in hate for His holy werkes.
Hit was a doylful dede whan they His deth caste;   *woeful deed; plotted*
Throw Pilat pyned He was, the provost of Rome.   *Through Pilate tortured*

165 "And that worliche wif that arst was y-nempned   *honorable; first was named*
Hath His visage in hire veil — Veronyk ho hatte —   *face on; she's called*
Peynted prively and playn that no poynt wanteth;   *Painted; missing no detail*
For love He left hit hire til hire lyves ende.   *it [to] her until her life's*

---

[1] Lines 159–60: *As yet both Barnabas and Paul were not baptized, / And did not know Christ, but [they] came [to the fold] soon afterward*

"Ther is no gome on this grounde   that is grym wounded,   *man on this earth*
170   Meselry ne meschef   ne man upon erthe,   *[By] illness or mischief or man's [work]*
That kneleth doun to that cloth   and on Crist leveth,   *Who kneels; believes*
Bot alle hapneth to helle   in an hand-whyle."[1]

"A, Rome renayed!" quod the kyng.   "The riche emperour,   *Ah; traitorous*
"Cesar, synful wrecche,   that sent hym fram Rome,   *him (i.e., Pilate)*
175   Why nadde thy lycam be leyd   low under erthe[2]
Whan Pilat provost was made   suche a prince to jugge?"   *judge*

And or this wordes were   wonne to the ende,[3]
The cankere that the kyng hadde   clenly was heled,   *cancer; was fully healed*
Without faute the face   of flesche and of hyde,   *Without scarring*
180   As newe as the nebbe   that never was wemmyd.   *face; blemished*

"A, corteys Crist!"   seide the kyng than.   *Ah, courteous*
"Was never worke that Y wroght   worthy Thee to telle,   *to tell You*
Ne dede that Y have don,   bot Thy deth mened;   *deed; death lamented*
Ne never sey Thee in sight,   Goddis Sone dere.   *see; God's dear Son*

185   "Bot now bayne me my bone,   blessed Lord,   *promote my petition*
To stire Nero with noye   and newen his sorowe,   *stir; trouble; renew*
And Y schal buske me boun   hem bale forto wyrche:[4]
To do the develes of dawe   and Thy deth venge!   *To slay these devils*

[PASSUS 1]

"Telle me tit," quod Titus,   "what tokne He lafte   *quick; token He left*
190   To hem that knew Hym for Crist   and His crafte leved?"   *believed*
"Nempne the Trinyté by name,"   quod Nathan, "at thries,   *Name; at once*
And thermyd baptemed be   in blessed water!"   *therewith be baptized*

Forth they fetten a font   and foulled hym ther,   *fetched a font-stone; baptized*
Made hym Cristen kyng   that for Crist werred.   *who fought for Christ*
195   Corrours into eche coste   than the cours nomen[5]
And alle his baronage broght   to Burdewes haven.   *Bordeaux's*

Suth with the sondes-man   he sought unto Rome,   *messenger (i.e., Nathan); went*
The ferly and the faire cure   his fadere to schewe;   *marvel; show*

---

[1] *And does not become fully healed in an instant*

[2] *Why had not your (Caesar's) body been laid low under the earth*

[3] *And before these words were finished to the end*

[4] *And I shall prepare myself to work ills [on] them*

[5] *Then couriers took the roads to each coast*

And he, gronnand glad,   grete God thanked   *(i.e., Vespasian), groaning gladly*
200 And, loude criande on Crist,   carped and saide: *crying; shouted*

"Worthy, wemlese God,   in whom Y byleve,   *unblemished*
As Thou in Bethleem was born   of a bryght mayde,   *pure woman*
Sende me hele of my hurt,   and heyly Y afowe   *wholly I avow*
To be ded for Thy deth,   bot hit be dere yolden."   *unless; requited (avenged)*

205 That tyme Peter was pope   and preched in Rome   *[At] that time*
The lawe and the lore   that our byleve asketh.   *our faith preaches*
Folowed fele of the folke   and to the fayth tourned,   *Many folk followed [him]*
And Crist wroght for that wye   wondres ynow.   *man wonders enough*

Therof Waspasian was ware,   that the waspys hadde,   *aware; wasps*
210 Sone sendeth hym to   and he the sothe tolde[1]
Of Crist and the kerchef   that kevered the sike,   *cloth that cured the sick*
As Nathan, Neymes sone, seide   that to Nero come.[2]

Than to consayl was called   the knyghtes of Rome   *Then to council were*
And assenteden sone   to sende messageres: *[they] quickly agreed*
215 Twenti knyghtes were cud   the kerchef to fecche   *appointed; fetch*
And asked trewes of the empererour   that erand to done.   *permission; do*

[. . . .]

Ac, without tribute or trewes,   by tenfulle wayes[3]
The knyghtes with the kerchef   comen ful blyve;   *returned very quickly*
The pope gaf pardoun to hem   and passed theragens[4]
220 With processioun and pres   of princes and dukes.   *and [a] crowd*

And whan the womman was ware   that the wede owede   *aware who; owned*
Of Seint Peter the pope,   ho platte to the grounde,   *she fell flat*
Umbefelde his fete   and to the freke saide: *Embraced his feet; man*
"Of this kerchef and my cors   the kepyng Y thee take."[5]

225 Than bygan the burne   biterly to wepe   *Then began the man*
For the doylful deth   of his dere mayster,   *doleful death; dear teacher*
And longe stode in the stede   or he stynte myght,   *place before he might stop*
Whan he unclosed the clothe   that Cristes body touched.   *unwrapped*

---

[1] *[And] Soon sends for him (i.e., Peter), and he (i.e., Peter) the truth told [to Vespasian]*

[2] *[Just] as Nathan, Naym's son, who [had] come to Nero, had said*

[3] *But, without [receiving] tribute or safe conduct, by troubled paths*

[4] *The pope (i.e., Peter) gave pardon to them and moved towards them*

[5] *I give the protection of this veil and my body to you*

	The wede fram the womman he warp atte laste,	*cloth; took at last*
230	Receyved hit myd reverence and rennande teris.	*running tears*
	To the palace myd pres they passed on swythe	*with [the] crowd; quickly*
	And ay held hit on hey that alle byhold myght.	*always; high*

	Than twelf barouns bolde the emperour bade wende,	*ordered to go*
	And the pope departe fram the pople faste;	*people*
235	Veronyk and the vail Waspasian they broght,	*[to] Vespasian*
	And Seint Peter the pope presented bothe.	

	Bot a ferly byfelle forthmyd hem alle;	*marvel happened before them all*
	In her temple bytidde tenful thynges:	*their temple difficult things occurred*
	The mahound and the mametes to-mortled to peces	
240	And al to-crased as the cloth throgh the kirke passed.[1]	

	Into the palice with the prente than the pope yede;	*palace; veil then; went*
	Knyghtes kepten the clothe and on knees fallen.	*worshiped*
	A flavour flambeth therfro; they felleden hit alle:	
	Was never odour ne eyr upon erthe swetter.[2]	

245	The kerchef clansed hitself and so clere wexed	*purified; grew so bright*
	Myght no lede on hit loke for light that hit schewed.	*man; showed*
	As hit aproched to the prince, he put up his hed;	*(i.e., Vespasian); head*
	For comfort of the cloth he cried wel loude:	

	"Lo, lordlynges, here: the lyknesse of Crist,	*lords, hear*
250	Of whom my botnyng Y bidde for His bitter woundis."	*healing I ask*
	Than was wepyng and wo and wryngyng of hondis	*hands*
	With loude dyn and dit for doil of Hym one.	*noise; clamor; grief*

	The pope availed the vaile, and his visage touched,[3]	
	The body suth al aboute, blessed hit thrye.	*then; thrice*
255	The waspys wenten away and alle the wo after:	
	That er was laser-liche, lyghtter was nevere.[4]	

| | Than was pypyng and play,   departyng of stryf; | *piping (music)* |
| | They yelden grace to God,   this two grete lordes. | *gave thanks; these* |

---

[1] Lines 239–40: *The idols of Mohammed crumbled to pieces / And broke all to bits as the cloth passed through the church*

[2] Lines 243–44: *A scent erupted from there; they all sensed it: / There was never a smell or an air on earth that was sweeter*

[3] *The pope used the veil, and his (i.e., Vaspasian's) face touched*

[4] *What before was leper-like had never been better*

| | The kerchef carieth fram alle   and in the eyr hangyth, | *hangs in the air* |
| 260 | That the symple pople myght hit se   into soper-tyme.[1] | |

	The Vernycle after Veronyk Waspasian hit called,	*Vernicle*
	Garde hit gayly agysen in gold and in selvere.	*Had it arrayed beautifully*
	Yit is the visage in the vail, as Veronyk hym broght;	*Still [today]; face; veil*
	The Romaynes hit holdeth at Rome, and for a relyk hit holden.	*relic*

	This whyle Nero hadde noye and non nyghtes reste,	*Meanwhile; trouble*
265	For his tribute was withholde, as Nathan told hadde.	*withheld*
	He commaundith knyghtes to come consail to holde,	*council*
	Erles and alle men the emperour aboute.	*Earls*

	Assembled the senatours sone, upon haste,	*quickly, in haste*
270	To jugge who jewes myght best upon the Jewys take;	*judge; [the] judgment*
	And alle demeden by dome tho dukes to wende	
	That were cured throw Crist, that they on Croys slowen.[2]	

	That on Waspasian was of the wyes twey	*one; two men*
	That the travail undertoke, and Titus another,	*Who the work*
275	A bold burne on a blonke and of his body comyn:	
	No ferther sib to hymself bot his sone dere:[3]	

	Crouned kynges bothe and mychel Crist loved,	*Crowned; much*
	That hadde hem geven of His grace and here grem stroyed.[4]	
	Moste thei hadde hit in hert here hestes to kepe	*their words to keep*
280	And here forwardis to fulfille that thei byfor made.	*their promises*

	Than was rotlyng in Rome, robbyng of brynnyis,	*rattling; rubbing of mailcoats*
	Schewyng of scharpe, scheldes y-dressed.	*Showing of swords, shields*
	Laughte leve at that lord, leften his sygne,	*[They] took leave of; lifting insignia*
	A grete dragoun of gold, and alle the gyng folwed.[5]	*gathering followed*

| 285 | By that schippis were schred,   yschot on the depe, | *By then; rigged, issued* |
| | Takled and atired   on talterande ythes:[6] | |

---

[1] *So that the common people might see it until supper-time*

[2] Lines 271–72: *And unanimously [they] deemed by decree to send those dukes / Who were cured by Christ, who they (i.e., the Jews) on [the] Cross slew*

[3] Lines 275–76: *A bold man on horseback (i.e., a knight) and come from his body (i.e., Vespasian's family): / No more distantly related to him than being his own dear son*

[4] *Who had given them (i.e., Titus and Vespasian) of His grace and their ills destroyed*

[5] Lines 281–84: *Then there was rattling in Rome, rubbing of mailcoats, / Showing of swords, shields prepared. / [They] took leave of that lord (i.e., Nero), lifting his insignia, / A great dragon of gold, and all the gathered men followed*

[6] *Tackled and readied on rolling waves*

Fresch water and wyn   wounden yn faste,   *wine hoisted in quickly*
And stof of alle maner store   that hem strengthe scholde.[1]

Ther were floynes aflot,   farcostes many,
290   Cogges and crayers,   y-casteled alle;[2]
Galees of grete streyngthe   with golden fanes,   *Galleys; pennants*
Brayd on the brod se   aboute foure myle.   *Scattered; broad sea; four miles*

They tyghten up tal-sail   whan the tide asked,   *the top sail*
Hadde byr at the bake   and the bonke lefte,   *wind at their backs; bank*
295   Soughte over the se   with soudeours manye,   *soldiers*
And joyned up at port Jaf   in Judeis londys.   *Jaffa in Judaea's lands*

Suree, Cesaris londe,   thou may seken ever;   *Syria, Caesar's land; seek*
Ful mychel wo moun be wroghte   in thy wlonk tounnes.[3]
Cytees under Syone,   now is your sorow uppe: *Mt. Zion; here*
300   The deth of the dereworth Crist   dere schal be yolden.   *dearly shall be avenged*

Now is, Bethleem, thy bost   y-broght to an ende;   *boast*
Jerusalem and Jerico,   for-juggyd wrecchys,   *condemned wretches*
Schal never kyng of your kynde   with croune be ynoyntid,   *lineage; anointed*
Ne Jewe, for Jhesu sake,   jouke in you more.   *Nor; rest; again*

[PASSUS 2]

305   They setten upon eche side   Surrie withyn,   *beset; [trapping] Syria*
Brente ay at the bak   and ful bare laften;   *Burned always; left everything bare*
Was noght bot roryng and rich   in alle the riche tounnes   *roaring and smoke*
And red laschyng lye   alle the londe overe;   *red rushing (i.e., fire) that spread*

Token toun and tour,   teldes ful fele,   *Took; very many houses*
310   Brosten gates of brass   and many borwe wonnen,   *Broke [down]; towns won*
Holy the hethen here   hewyn to grounde,   *Utterly; hewn*
Both in bent and in borwe,   that abide wolde.   *field; town, whoever would stay*

The Jewes to Jerusalem,   ther Josophus dwelde,   *where*
Flowen as the foule doth   that faucoun wolde strike.   *as do the fowl that the falcon*
315   A cité undere Syon   sett was ful noble   *city*
With many toret and toure   that toun to defende.   *turrets and towers*

---

[1] *And stuff of all manner of stores in order that they should have strength [for the war]*

[2] Lines 289–90: *There were floins (i.e., small ships) afloat, many farcosts (i.e., large ships), / Cogs (i.e., bigger ships) and crayers (i.e., small vessels), all well-fortified.*

[3] *Very much woe may be wrought on your proud towns*

Princes and prelates   and poreil of the londe,   *poor people*
Clerkes and comens   of contrees aboute   *commoners of countries*
Were schacked to that cité   sacrifice to make   *Had flocked*
320   At Paske-tyme, as preched hem   prestes of the lawe.[1]

Many swykel at the sweng   to the swerd yede;   *crafty; went*
For penyes passed non,   thogh he pay wolde,   *pennies (ransom)*
Bot diden alle to the dethe   and drowen hem after   *drew them*
With engynes to Jerusalem   there Jewes were thykke.   *[siege] engines; thick*

325   They sette sadly a sege   the cité alle aboute,   *resolutely set a siege*
Pighten pavelouns doun   of pallen webbes,   *Set pavilions; [made] of pall cloth*
With ropis of riche silk   raysen up swythe   *raised up quickly*
Grete tentis as a toun   of torkeys clothys.   *[made] of turkish cloth*

Choppyn over the cheventayns,   with charboklis foure,[2]
330   A gay egle of gold   on a gilde appul   *gilded apple*
With grete dragouns grym   alle in gold wroghte,
And lyk to lyouns also   lyande ther undere.   *lying underneath them*

Paled and paynted   the paveloun was umbe,   *Palisaded; about*
Stoked ful of storijs,   stayned myd armys[3]
335   Of quaynte coloures to know,   kerneld alofte,   *crenelated*
An hundred stondyng on stage   in that stede one.[4]

Toured with torettes   was the tente thanne,   *Towered with turrets*
Suth britaged aboute,   bright to byholde.   *Then barricaded*
Er alle the sege was sette   yit of the cité comyn   *Before; siege*
340   Messengeres, were made   fram maistres of the lawe.   *masters of law*

To the chef cheventayn   they chosen here wey,   *chief chieftain; made their way*
Deden mekly by mouthe   here message attonys,   *their message at once*
Sayen: "The cité hath us sent   to serchen your wille,   *Said*
To here the cause of your comyng,   and what ye coveyte wolde."   *hear*

345   Waspasian no word   to the wyes schewed   *men showed*
Bot sendeth sondismen agen,   twelve sikere knyghtes,[5]
Gaf hem charge to go   and the gomes telle   *Gave them; men*
That alle the cause of her come   was Crist forto venge: *their coming; avenge*

---

[1] *At Passover, as priests of their law preached to them*

[2] *Covering over the chieftain's [tent], with four carbuncles*

[3] *Filled (or covered) completely with histories, painted with arms (i.e., family armorial insignia)*

[4] *A hundred [could be] standing on stage in that place alone*

[5] *But sends messengers in return, twelve trusty knights*

350 "Sayth, Y bidde hem be boun,   bischopes and other,   *be ready*
Tomorow or mydday,   moder-naked alle,   *before; stark-naked*
Up here gates to yelde,   with yerdes an hande,[1]
Eche whight in a white scherte   and no wede ellys,   *man; no other clothes*

"Jewyse for Jhesu Crist   by juggement to take,   *Jews*
And brynge Cayphas, that Crist   throgh conseil bytrayede.   *betrayed*
355 Or Y to the walles schal wende   and walten alle overe;   *go and throw [them]*
Schal no ston upon ston   stonde by Y passe."   *stand by [the time] I leave*

This sondismen sadly   to the cité yede   *These messengers resolutely; went*
Ther the lordes of the londe   lent weren alle,   *Where; were all dwelling*
Tit tolden here tale   and wondere towe made   *Quickly; made a great row*
360 Of Crist and of Cayphas   and how they come scholde.   *Caiaphas; (the Jews)*

And when the knyghtes of Crist   carpyn bygonn,   *began shouting*
The Jewes token alle twelf   without tale more,   *took; more talk*
Here hondis bounden at here bak   with borden stavys   *Their hands; wooden*
And of flocken here fax,   and here faire berdis,   *tore off their hair; beards*

365 Made hem naked as a nedel   to the nether hove,   *lowest reaches*
Here visage blecken with bleche,   and al the body after,   *blacken with blacking*
Suth knyt with a corde   to eche knyghtes swere   *Then knit; knight's neck*
A chese, and charged hem   here chyventayn to bere: *A [piece of] cheese*

"Sayth, unbuxum we beth   his biddyng to yete,   *we are unwilling; to follow*
370 Ne noght dreden his dom: his deth have we atled.   *dread; judgment; planned*
He schal us fynde in the felde,   ne no ferre seke,   *field; farther seek*
Tomorowe pryme or hit passe,   and so your prince tellith."   *prime (dawn)*

The burnes busken out of burwe,   bounden alle twelf,   *men hastened; bound*
Agen message to make   fram the maister Jewes.   *Return; Jewish leaders*
375 Was never Waspasian so wrothe   as whan the wyes come   *angry; men came*
That were scorned and schende   upon schame wyse.[2]

This knyghtes byfor the kyng   upon knees fallen   *These*
And tolden the tale   as hit tid hadde: *had happened*
"Of thy manace ne thy myght   they maken bot lyte:
380 Thus ben we tourned of our tyre   in tokne of the sothe[3]

"And bounden for our bolde speche;   the batail they willeth   *battle*
Tomorowe prime or hit passe.   They put hit no ferre.   *farther*

---

[1] *Up their gates to yield, with rods (signs of authority) in hand*

[2] *Who were scorned and reproached in [this] shameful way.*

[3] *Thus are we turned out of our clothes (attire) in token of the truth*

Hit schal be satled on thyself   the same that thou atlest;   *settled; planned*
Thus han they certifiet thee   and sende thee this cheses."   *have; certified [to]*

385   Wode wedande wroth   Waspasian was thanne,   *Raging mad [with] anger*
      Layde wecche to the walle   and warned in haste   *Put watches; advised*
      That alle maner of men   in the morowe scholde   *morning*
      Be sone after the sonne   assembled in the felde.   *soon; sun*

      He streyght up a standard   in a stoure wyse,   *erected; headquarters; stern way*
390   Bild as a belfray   bretful of wepne;   *Built; full to the brim with weapons*
      Whan oght fauted in the folke   that to the feld longed,
      Atte the belfray to be   botnyng to fynde.[1]

      A dragoun was dressed,   drawyn alofte,   *A dragon [banner] was prepared*
      Wyde-gapande, of gold,   gomes to swelwe,   *Wide-gaping; [as if] men to swallow*
395   With arwes armed in the mouthe,   and also he hadde   *arrows*
      A fauchyn under his feet   with foure kene bladdys.   *falchion; keen blades*

      Therof the poyntes were pight   in partyis foure
      Of this wlonfulle worlde   ther thei werre fondyn;
      In forbesyn to the folke   this fauchoun thay hengede
400   That they hadde wonnen with swerd   al the world riche.[2]

      A bal of brennande gold   the beste was on sette,   *burnished; beast*
      His taille trayled theraboute   that tourne scholde he nevere   *tail*
      Whan he was lifte upon lofte   ther the lord werred,   *lifted; where; warred*
      Bot ay lokande on the londe   tille that al laughte were.   *ever looking; taken*

405   Therby the cité myght se   no setlyng wolde rise   *settlement*
      Ne no treté of no trewes   bot the toun yelde,   *treaty or no truce; yield*
      Or ride on the Romayns,   for they han her rede take   *Before; counsel taken*
      Ther britned to be   or the burwe wynne.   *to be slain or the town [to] win*

      His wynges brad were abrode   boun forto flee,   *extended; ready*
410   With belles bordored aboute   al of bright selvere,
      Redy, whan oughte runnen   to ryngen ful loude   *Ready, if anyone ran away*
      With eche a wap of the wynde   that to the wynges sprongyn.   *gust*

      I-brytaged bigly aboute   the belfray was thanne[3]
      With a tenful toure   that over the toun gawged.   *troubling tower; gauged*

---

[1] Lines 391–92: *When the men who were to go to the battlefield lacked anything, / At this structure they could find assistance*

[2] Lines 397–400: *The [four] points [of the falchion] were pointed in the four directions / Of this proud world where they had found war (i.e., made conquests); / They hung these falchions as a proof to the people / That they had won with the sword all the rich world*

[3] *Ringed strongly about [with wooden platforms] the siege-tower was then*

415	The batail by the brightnesse burnes myght knowe	*battlefield; men*
	Foure myle therfro, so the feldes schonen.	*fields shone*
	And on eche pomel were pyght penseles hyghe[1]	
	Of selke and sendel with selvere y-betyn:	*silk and cendal; beaten*
	Hit glitered as gled fure, ful of gold riche,	*glowing fire*
420	Over al the cité to se, as the sonne bemys.	*sun beams*
	Byfor the foure gates he formes to lenge	*Before; sets to remain*
	Sixti thousand by somme while the sege lasteth;	*sum; siege*
	Sette ward on the walles that noght awey scaped,	*watch; no one escaped*
	Sixe thousand in sercle the cité alle aboute.	*circle*
425	Was noght while the nyght laste bot nehyng of stedis,	*neighing of steeds*
	Strogelyng in stele wede, and stuffyng of helmes,	*Struggling into steel armor*
	Armyng of olyfauntes and other arwe bestes	*elephants; slow beasts*
	Agen the Cristen to come with castels on bake.	*Against; castles on [their] backs*
	Waspasian in stele wede and his wyes alle	*all his men*
430	Weren dight forth by day and drowen to the vale	*arrayed; came to the valley*
	Of Josophat, ther Jhesu Crist schal juggen alle thinges,	*where; judge*
	Bigly batayled hym ther to biden this other.	*Strongly battled*
	The fanward Titus toke, to telle upon ferste,	*vanguard*
	With sixtene thousand soudiours assyned for the nones;	
435	And as mony in the myd-ward were merked to lenge[2]	
	Ther Waspasian was with princes and dukes.	*Where*
	And sixtene thousand in the thridde with a thryvande knyght,	*valiant*
	Sire Sabyn of Surrie, a siker man of armes,	*trusty*
	That prince was of Provynce and michel peple ladde,	*Who; many people led*
440	Fourty hundred in helmes and harnays to schewe.	*harnesses*
	And ten thousand atte tail at the tentis lafte,	*in the rear; tents*
	Hors and harnays fram harmyng to kepe.	
	By that bemys on the burwe blowen ful loude,	*trumpets in the town*
	And baners beden hem forth. Now blesse us our Lorde!	*banners bade them*

[PASSUS 3]

445	The Jewes assembled were sone and of the cité come	*soon*
	An hundred thousand on hors with hamberkes atired,	*halberks attired*

---

[1] *And on each pommel (i.e., tower top) were placed high pennons*

[2] Lines 434–35: *With sixteen thousand soldiers expressly assigned; / And just as many were marked to remain in the midguard*

Without folke upon fot   at the foure gates   *not counting men on foot*
That preset to the place   with pauyes on hande.   *pressed; with shields*

450   Fyf and twenti olyfauntes,   defensable bestes,   *elephants; beasts*
       With brode castels on bak   out of burwe come;   *broad castles; town*
       And on eche olyfaunte   armed men manye,
       Ay an hundred an hey,   an hundred withyn.[1]

       Tho drowen dromedarius doun   develich thicke,   *dromedaries; devilishly*
       An hundred and y-heled   with harnays of mayle,   *covered; mailed harnesses*
455   Eche beste with a big tour   ther bold men were ynne,   *beast; tower, where; in*
       Twenty, told by tale,   in eche tour evene.

       Cameles closed in stele   comen out thanne   *Camels enclosed in steel came*
       Faste toward the feld;   a ferlich nonbre   *[in] an amazing number*
       Busked to batail,   and on bak hadde   *Armed for battle*
460   Ech on a toret of tre   with ten men of armes.   *Each one a wooden tower*

       Chares ful of chosen,   charged with wepne   *Chariots; weapons*
       A wondere nonbre ther was,   whoso wite lyste.   *number; desired [to] know*
       Many doughti that day,   that was adradde nevere,   *brave men; who were afraid*
       Were fond fey in the feld   er that fight endid.   *found dead; before*

465   An olyfaunt y-armed   came out at the laste,
       Kevered myd a castel,   was craftily y-wroght,   *Covered*
       A tabernacle in the tour   atyred was riche,   *was attired richly*
       Pight as a paveloun   on pileres of selvere.   *Set; pillars*

       A which of white selvere   was sett therynne   *A chest*
470   On foure goions of gold   that hit fram grounde bare;   *pivots*
       A chosen chayre therby   on charbokeles twelfe,   *chair; carbuncles*
       Betyn al with bright gold   with brennande sergis.   *Beaten; burning candles*

       The chekes of the chayre   were charbokles fyne,   *sides*
       Covered myd a riche clothe,   ther Cayphas was sette.   *where; sitting*
475   A plate of pulsched gold   was pight on his breste   *polished; set*
       With many preciose perle   and pured stones.   *pearls and noble*

       Lered men of the lawe   that loude couthe synge   *Learned; could sing*
       With sawters seten hym by   and the psalmys tolde   *psalters sat beside him*
       Of doughty David the kyng   and other dere storijs: *brave; dear stories*
480   Of Josue, the noble Jewe,   and Judas the knyght.   *Joshua; Judas Maccabeus*

---

[1] *At least one hundred on high, [and] a hundred within*

Cayphas of the kyst   kyppid a rolle   *chest took a roll*
And radde how the folke ran   throgh the rede water   *read; (i.e., Red Sea)*
Whan Pharao and his ferde   were in the floode drouned;   *army; drowned*
And myche of Moyses lawe   he mynned that tyme.   *he related [at] that time*

485   Whan this faithles folke   to the feld comen   *came*
And batayled after the bent   with many burne kene,   *field; keen men*
For baneres that blased   and bestes y-armed   *blazed*
Myght no man se throw the sonne   ne uneth the cité knowe.   *hardly*

Waspasian dyvyseth   the vale alle aboute,   *observes*
490   That was with baneres overbrad   to the borwe wallis,   *overspread; town walls*
To barouns and bold men   that hym aboute were
Seith: "Lordlynges a londe,   lestenyth my speche: *Lords of land, hear*

"Here nys king nother knyght   comen to this place,   *There is neither king nor*
Baroun ne bachelere   ne burne that me folweth,   *bachelor (petty knight); man*
495   That the cause of his come   nys Crist forto venge   *coming is not to avenge*
Upon the faithles folke   that Hym fayntly slowen.   *deceitfully*

"Byholdeth the hethyng   and the harde woundes,   *Look [to] the scorning*
The byndyng and the betyng,   that He on body hadde: *beating*
Lat never this lawles ledis   laugh at His harmys   *Let; these lawless men*
500   That bought us fram bale   with blod of His herte.   *evil; heart*

"Y quycke-clayme the querels   of alle quyk burnes   *I renounce; living men*
And clayme of evereche kyng   — save of Crist one —   *except; alone*
That this peple to pyne,   no pité ne hadde:
That preveth His Passioun,   whoso the Paas redeth.[1]

505   "Hit nedith noght at this note   of Nero to mynde,
Ne to trete of no trewe   for tribute that he asketh:
That querel Y quik-cleyme   whether he wilneth
Of this rebel to Rome   bot resoun to have.[2]

"Bot more thing in our mynde   myneth us today: *[one] more; we remember*
510   That by resoun to Rome   the realté fallyth,   *supreme rule falls*
Bothe the myght and the mayn,   maistre or ellys,   *strength, master or not*
And lordschip of eche londe   that lithe under Heven.   *lord; lies*

---

[1] Lines 503–04: *Because these people (i.e., the Jews) [put Christ] to torture, and had no pity: / That is proved by His Passion, [for] whomever reads the Pasch*

[2] Lines 505–08: *It is not necessary in these circumstances to remember Nero, / Nor to consider any truce for the tribute that he desires: / That quarrel I renounce even if he desires / With this rebel to Rome to have only negotiations*

"Lat never this faithles folke   with fight of us wynne
Hors ne harnays,   bot they hit hard byen,
515   Plate, ne pesan,   ne pendauntes ende,[1]
While any lyme may laste,   or we the lif have.   *limb*

"For thei ben feynt at the fight,   fals of byleve,   *faint; belief*
And wel wenen at a wap   alle they wold quelle.[2]
Nother grounded on God   ne on no grace tristen,   *Neither; trusting*
520   Bot alle in storijs of stoure   and in strength one.   *stories of battle*

"And we ben dight today   Drighten to serve: *are called; [the] Lord*
Hey Heven kyng   hede to His owne!"   *High Heaven's; [takes] heed*
The ledes louten hym alle   and aloude sayde: *men bow*
"Today, that flethe any fote,   the Fende have his soule!"[3]

525   Bemes blowen anon,   blonkes to neye,   *Trumpets; horses [begin] to neigh*
Stedis stampen in the felde   undere stele wedes.   *Steeds; field; steel clothes*
Stithe men in stiropys   striden alofte;   *Strong; striding up on high*
Knyghtes croysen hemself,   cacchen here helmys,[4]

With loude clarioun cry   and alle kyn pypys,   *clarion; all kinds [of] pipes*
530   Tymbris and tabourris   tonelande loude,   *Timbrels and drums intoning*
Geven a schillande schout.   Schrynken the Jewes,   *Gave a resounding*
As womman wepith and waylith   whan hire the water neyeth.[5]

Lacchen launces anon,   lepyn togedris,   *Took lances; leapt*
As fure out of flynt-ston   ferde hem bytwene.   *fire; [it] fared between them*
535   Doust drof upon lofte,   dymedyn alle aboute   *dust drove; dimmed*
As thonder and thicke rayn   throbolande in skyes.   *jostling in the skies*

Beren burnes throw,   brosten here launces;[6]
Knyghtes crosschen doun   to the cold erthe;   *crash*
Fought faste in the felde,   and ay the fals undere[7]
540   Doun swowande to swelt   without swar more.   *swooning to die; word*

Tytus tourneth hym to,   tolles of the beste,   *toils with the best*
For-justes the jolieste   with joynyng of werre.   *Fights the strongest*

---

[1] Lines 513–15: *Never let this faithless people win from us in fighting / [Either] horse or harness, unless they buy it through difficulty, / [Nor] armor, nor pizane, nor [even the] end of a pendant*

[2] *And [might] well think at a [single] blow [that] they all would [be] slain*

[3] *"Today, whoever flees a single foot, [may] the Fiend (i.e., Satan) have his soul!"*

[4] *Knights cross themselves, take up their helms*

[5] *As [a] woman weeps and wails when she gives birth*

[6] *[They] bear through men, bursting their lances*

[7] *[They] Fought strongly in the field, and always the false (i.e., the Jews) [fell] beneath [them]*

Suth with a bright bronde   he betith on harde   *Then; sword; beats*
Tille the brayn and the blod   on the bent ornen.   *brain; field runs*

545 Sought throgh another side   with a sore wepne,   *flank [of the army]*
Bet on the broun stele   while the bladde laste,   *Beat; blade lasts*
An hey breydeth the brond   and as a bore loketh,[1]
How hetterly doun,   hente whoso wolde!   *Hews fiercely; receive [it]*

Alle brightned the bent   as bemys of sonne   *field; beams*
550 Of the gilden gere   and the goode stones;   *Off the golden gear*
For schyveryng of scheldes   and schynyng of helmes   *shivering of shields*
Hit ferde, as alle the firmament   upon fure were.   *went, as [if]; sky was on fire*

Waspasian in the vale   the fanward byholdeth,   *vanguard sees*
How the hethyn here   heldith to grounde;   *there were holding ground*
555 Cam with a fair ferde   the fals forto mete.   *[He] came; strong force*
As greved griffouns   girden in samen.   *angered; [they] strike together*

Spakly here speres   on sprotes they yeden,
Scheldes as schidwod   on scholdres to-cleven,
Schoken out of schethes   that scharpe was y-grounde,
560 And mallen metel   throgh unmylt hertes.[2]

Hewen on the hethen,   hurtlen togedre,
For-schorne gild schroud,   schedered burnee.
Baches woxen ablode   aboute in the vale,
And goutes fram gold wede   as goteres they runne.[3]

565 Sire Sabyn setteth hym up   whan hit so yede,   *went*
Rideth myd the rereward   and alle the route folweth,   *Rides; rout*
Kenely the castels   came to assayle
That the bestes on here bake   out of burwe ladden.   *their backs; town led*

Atles on the olyfauntes   that orible were,   *[He] takes aim; horrible*
570 Girdith out the guttes   with grounden speres: *Tears out the guts*
Rappis rispen forth   that rydders an hundred
Scholde be busy to burie   that on a bent lafte.[4]

---

[1] *On high brandishes the sword and looks like a boar*

[2] Lines 557–60: *Quickly they drive their spears into splinters, / Split the shields on their shoulders into firewood, / Shake out of sheaths what was sharply ground (their swords), / And thrust the metal [blades] through un-mild hearts*

[3] Lines 561–64: *[They] hew upon the heathen, hurtle together, / Gilt shrouds (i.e., clothing) are torn to pieces, mailcoats are shattered: / The streams in the valley grew bloody, / And gushes from golden armor ran like gutters*

[4] Lines 571–72: *[Such] entrails break forth that a hundred ridders (i.e., field-strippers) / Would be hard-pressed to bury what was left upon the field*

Castels clateren doun,   cameles brosten,   *clatter; camels burst [open]*
Dromedaries to the deth   drowen ful swythe;   *are driven quickly*
575   The blode fomed hem fro   in flasches aboute   *foamed from them; pools*
That kne-depe in the dale   dascheden stedes.   *dashed steeds*

The burnes in the bretages   that above were   *men; wooden towers*
For the doust and the dyn   — as alle doun yede   *dust; went*
Al for-stoppette in stele —   starke-blynde wexen   *Completely locked; grew*
580   Whan hurdighs and hard erthe   hurtled togedre,   *hurdighs*

And under dromedaries   dyed in that stounde.   *died in that place*
Was non left upon lyve   that alofte standeth —   *alive, who stands upright*
Save an anlepy olyfaunt   at the grete gate   *Except one single elephant*
Ther as Cayphas the clerke   in a castel rideth.

585   He say the wrake on hem wende   and away tourneth   *sees the destruction*
With twelf maystres made   of Moyses lawe.   *masters*
An hundred helmed men   hien hem after,   *go after them*
Er they of castel myght come,   caughten hem alle,   *Before*

Bounden the bischup   on a bycchyd wyse   *Bound; in [such a] bitter way*
590   That the blode out barst   ilka band undere,   *burst out under each bond*
And broghten to the berfray,   and alle the bew-clerkes   *fine clerks (scholars)*
Ther the standard stode,   and stadded hem ther.   *Where; placed them there*

The beste and the britage   and alle the bright gere —   *wooden tower*
Chaire and chaundelers   and charbokel stones,
595   The rolles that they redde on,   and alle the riche bokes —   *read from*
They broghte myd the bischup,   thou hym bale thoughte.[1]

Anon the feythles folke   fayleden herte,   *failed [in their] hearts*
Tourned toward the toun   and Tytus hem after: *Titus [came] after them*
Fele of the fals ferde   in the felde lefte,   *Many; army; field [were] left*
600   An hundred in here helmes   myd his honde one.   *helms with his hand alone*

The fals Jewes in the felde   fallen so thicke   *fall*
As hail froward Heven,   hepe over other;   *from; heaping over each other*
So was the bent over-brad,   blody by-runne,   *field covered over*
With ded bodies aboute   alle the brod vale.   *broad valley*

605   Myght no stede doun stap   bot on stele wede,   *steed; step; steel clothing*
Or on burne, other on beste,   or on bright scheldes;   *man, or on beast*
So myche was the multitude   that on the molde lafte   *high; number; earth*
Ther so many were mart;   merevail were ellis.   *dead*

---

[1] *They brought with the bishop (i.e., Caiaphas), though [they] thought him evil*

	Yit were the Romayns as rest as they fram Rome come,	*well-rested*
610	Unriven eche a renk and noght a ryng brosten;	*Unharmed; man; broken*
	Was no poynt perschid of alle here pris armure:	*pierced; prize armor*
	So Crist His knyghtes gan kepe tille complyn tyme.	*until compline time*

	An hundred thousand helmes of the hethen syde	*helms (i.e., soldiers)*
	Were fey fallen in the felde or the fight ended,	*dead; before*
615	Save seven thousand of the somme, that to the cité flowen,	
	And wynnen with mychel wo the walles withynne.[1]	

	Ledes lepen to anon, louken the gates,	*Men leap; lock*
	Barren hem bigly with boltes of yren,	*Bar them strongly; iron*
	Brayden up brigges with brouden chaynes	*Raise up the drawbridges*
620	And portecolis with pile picchen to grounde.	*[the] portcullis with pins drops*

	Thei wynnen up whyghtly the walles to kepe,	*bravely; to defend*
	Frasche, unfounded folke, and grete defence made;	*[These] fresh, untried*
	Tyeth into tourres tonnes ful manye[2]	
	With grete stones of gret and of gray marble.	*grit*

625	Kepten kenly with caste the kernels alofte,[3]	
	Quarten out querels with quarters attonys.	*Hurling bolts; crossbows at once*
	That other folke at the fote freschly assayled[4]	
	Tille eche dale with dewe was donked aboute.	*Until; made wet*

	Withdrowen hem fro the diche, dukes and other —	*They withdrew; ditch*
630	The caste was so kene that come fram the walles —	*[For] the casting*
	Comen forthe with the kyng clene as they yede,	*Came; [as] unharmed; went*
	Wanted noght o wye, ne non that wem hadde.	*Lacking; one man; injury*

	Princes to here pavelouns passen on swythe,	*their; quickly*
	Unarmen hem as tyt and alle the nyght resten[5]	
635	With wacche umbe the walles to many wyes sorowe;	*watch around; men's*
	They wolle noght the hethen here thus harmeles be lafte.	*heathen; be left*

[PASSUS 4]

| | As rathe as the rede day   ros yn the schye, | *Soon; rose in the sky* |
| | Bemes blowen on brode   burnes to ryse. | *Trumpets blow aloud to wake the men* |

---

[1] Lines 615–16: *Except seven thousand of their total number, who fled to the city / And won with much sadness [a return to] within the walls*

[2] *[They] took into towers a great number [of] barrels*

[3] *[They] defended boldly with [the] casting [of stones from] the battlements on high*

[4] *That the other folk (i.e., the Romans) at the foot [of the wall] freshly assailed [them]*

[5] *Unarmed themselves as quickly [as possible] and all that night rested*

	The kyng comaundeth a-cry that comsed was sone,[1]	
640	The ded bodies on the bonke bare forto make:	*field to make bare*
	To spoyle the spilt folke, spare scholde none,	*loot; dead (spilled)*
	Geten girdeles and gere, gold and goode stones,	*Gathering belts*
	Byes, broches bryght, besauntes riche,	*Bracelets; byzants*
	Helmes hewen of gold, hamberkes manye.	*hauberks*
645	Kesten ded upon ded, was deil to byholde,	*[They] cast dead; grievous*
	Made wayes full wide and to the walles comen;	*pathways*
	Assembleden at the cité saut to bygynne,	*to begin [the] assault*
	Folke ferlich thycke at the foure gates.	*marvelously thick*
	They broghten toures of tre that they taken hadde[2]	
650	Agen evereche gate, garken hem hey;	*Against every; placed them high*
	Bygonnen at the grettist a garrite to rere,	*Began; watchtower to raise*
	Groded up fro the grounde on twelf grete postes.	*Built*
	Hit was wonderlich wide, wroght upon hyghte,	
	Fyve hundred in frounte to fighten at the walles.	
655	Hardy men upon hyghte hyen at the grecys	*hew at the stairs*
	And bygonnen with bir the borow to assayle.	*with [a] rush; city*
	Quarels, flambande of fure, flowen out harde,	*Bolts, flaming with fire*
	And arwes unarwely, with attyr envenymyd,	*arrows swiftly; poisoned*
	Taysen at the toures, tachen on the Jewes;	*Aiming; attacking*
660	Throgh kernels cacchen here deth many kene burnes.[3]	
	Brenten and beten doun beldes full thycke,	*[They] burnt; buildings*
	Brosten the britages and the brode toures.	*Burst the galleries; broad*
	By that was many bold burne the burwe to assayle.[4]	
	The hole batail boun, aboute the brode walles	*whole battle raging*
665	That were byg and brode and bycchet to wynne,	*difficult*
	Wondere heye to byholde with holwe diches undere,	*hollow trenches beneath*
	Heye-bonked above upon bothe halves,	*High-banked*
	Right wicked to wynne, bot yif wyles helpe.	*without strategies*
	Bowmen atte bonke benden here gere,	*at the bank bend their gear*
670	Schoten up scharply to the schene walles	*Shoot; fair walls*

---

[1] *The king commanded with a cry what was soon begun*

[2] *They brought [siege] towers [made] of wood that they had taken*

[3] *Through the crenelations many good men catch their deaths*

[4] *By that [means] were many bold men [prepared] to assail the town*

With arwes and arblastes   and alle that harme myght,   *arrows and crossbows*
To affray the folke   that defence made.   *terrify*

The Jewes werien the walles   with wyles ynowe,   *defend; wiles enough*
Hote playande picche   amonge the peple yeten: *Hot boiling pitch; cast*
675 Brennande leed and brynston,   many barels fulle,   *Burning lead and brimstone*
Schoten schynande doun   right as schyre water.   *Shoot shining; bright*

Waspasian wendeth fram the walles   wariande hem alle;   *cursing them all*
Other busked were boun,   benden engynes,[1]
Kesten at the kernels   and clustred toures,   *Cast; crenelations and clustered*
680 And monye der daies worke   dongen to grounde.   *many dear days' work falls*

By that wrightes han wroght   a wonder stronge pale   *By then; palisade*
Alle aboute the burwe,   with bastiles manye,   *around the town, with towers*
That no freke myght unfonge   withouten fele harmes,   *encircle; many*
Ne no segge undere sonne   myght fram the cité passe.   *man under [the] sun*

685 Suth dommyn the diches   with the ded corses,
Crammen hit myd karayn   the kirnels alle under,
That the stynk of the stewe   myght strike over the walles
To cothe the corsed folke   that hem kepe scholde.[2]

The cors of the condit   that comen to toun   *course of the canal*
690 Stoppen, evereche a streem,   ther any strande yede,   *current went*
With stockes and stones   and stynkande bestes,   *sticks; stinking [dead] beasts*
That they no water myght wynne   that weren enclosed.

Waspasian tourneth to his tente   with Titus and other,   *retires*
Commaundeth consail anon   on Cayphas to sitte,   *council; sit [in judgment]*
695 What deth by dome   that he dey scholde   *death by judgment; die*
With the lettered ledes   that they laughte hadde.   *the scribes; had captured*

Domesmen upon deyes   demeden swythe
That ech freke were quyk-fleyn,   the felles of clene:
Firste to be on a bent   with blonkes to-drawe,
700 And suth honget on an hep   upon heye galwes,[3]

The feet to the firmament,   alle folke to byholden,   *to the sky (i.e., by the feet)*
With hony upon ech half   the hydeles anoynted;   *honey; hideless*

---

[1] *Other [men] were prepared quickly, set engines*

[2] Lines 685–88: *Then [they] choke the ditches with the dead bodies, / Cram it with carrion beneath all the battlements, / So that the stench from that stew (combination) might strike over the walls [of the city] / To infect the cursed folk (i.e., the living Jews) that should defend them (i.e., their fallen dead)*

[3] Lines 697–700: *The judges upon the dais decide quickly / That each man would be flayed alive, cleaned of flesh: / [But] First to be drawn upon a field by horses, / And then hanged all together upon a high gallows*

| | Corres and cattes   with claures ful scharpe | *Dogs and cats; claws* |
| | Foure kagged and knyt   to Cayphases theyes; | *caught and latched; thighs* |

705	Twey apys at his armes to angren hym more,	*Two apiece; to torment*
	That renten the rawe flesche upon rede peces.	*rent; into red pieces*
	So was he pyned fram prime with persched sides	*pained from prime; pierced*
	Tille the sonne doun sett in the someretyme.	*Until the sun set*

	The lered men of the lawe a litel bynythe	*learned; beneath*
710	Weren tourmented on a tre, topsailes walten,	*tormented; turned upside-down*
	Knyt to everech clerke kene corres twey,	*Tied; two keen dogs*
	That alle the cité myght se the sorow that they dryven.	*suffered*

	The Jewes walten over the walles for wo at that tyme,	*hurl [themselves]*
	Seven hundred slow hemself for sorow of here clerkes,	*slew themselves*
715	Somme hent here heere and fram the hed pulled,	*grabbed their hair*
	And somme doun for deil daschen to grounde.	*sorrow dashed*

	The kyng lete drawen hem adoun whan they dede were,	
	Bade: "A bole-fure betyn to brennen the corses,	*Build a bale-fire; burn*
	Kesten Cayphas theryn and his clerkes alle,	*Cast*
720	And brennen evereche bon into browne askes.	*Burn every bone; ashes*

	Suth wende to the walle on the wynde syde,	*Then go*
	And alle abrod on the burwe blowen the powdere:	*across; town blow; soot*
	'Ther is doust for your drynke!' adoun to hem crieth,	*powder*
	And bidde hem bible of that broth for the bischop soule."	*imbibe*

725	Thus ended coursed Cayphas and his clerkes twelf,	*cursed*
	Al to-brused myd bestes, brent at the laste,	*mangled by beasts, burned*
	In tokne of tresoun and trey that they wroght,	*return for; trouble*
	Whan Crist throw here conseil was cacched to deth.	*put to death*

	By that was the day don: dymmed the skyes,	
730	Merked montayns and mores aboute,	*Darkened; moors*
	Foules fallen to fote and here fethres rysten,	
	The nyght-wacche to the walle and waytes to blowe.[1]	

	Bryght fures aboute betyn abrode in the oste;	*fires; army (host)*
	The kyng and his consail carpen togedre,	*speak together*
735	Chosen chyventayns out and chiden no more,	*Choose chieftains; quarrel*
	Bot charged the chek-wecche and to chambre wenten,	*check-watch*

---

[1] Lines 731–32: *Birds fall to their feet and their feathers shake out. / The night-watch [goes] to the wall and waits to sound [the alarm]*

Kynges and knyghtes,   to cacchen hem reste.   *to get their rest*
Waspasian lyth in his logge,   litel he slepith,   *lies in his lodging, he sleeps little*
Bot walwyth and wyndith   and waltreth aboute,   *wallows and turns and tosses*
740   Ofte tourneth for tene   and on the toun thynketh.   *turns for sadness*

Whan schadewes and schire day   scheden attwynne,
Leverockes upon lofte   lyfteth here stevenes;
Burnes busken hem out of bedde   with bemes full loude
Bothe blowyng on bent   and on the burwe walles.[1]

745   Waspasian bounys of bedde,   busked hym fayre   *rises; hastened*
Fram the face to the fourche   in fyne gold clothes.   *fork (crotch)*
Suth putteth the prince   over his pallen wedes   *clothes made of pall*
A brynye, browded thicke,   with a brestplate: *coat of mail, braided thick*

The grate of gray steel   and of gold riche.   *The lance-seat*
750   Therover he casteth a cote,   colour of his armys;   *puts on a coat, [the] color*
A grete girdel of gold   without gere othere   *wide belt; gear*
Layth umbe his lendis   with lacchetes ynow.   *about his loins; lashes enough*

A bryght burnesched swerd   he belteth alofte,   *he belts above*
Of pure polisched gold   the pomel and the hulte.   *pure refined; hilt*
755   A brod schynande scheld   on scholdire he hongith,   *broad shining shield*
Bocklyd myd bright gold,   above at the necke.   *Buckled*

The glowes of gray steel,   that were with gold hemmyd,
Hanleth harnays   and his hors asketh.[2]
The gold-hewen helme   haspeth he blyve,   *helm he buckles quickly*
760   With viser and avental   devysed for the nones.   *visor; aventail*

A croune of clene gold   was closed upon lofte,
Rybaunde umbe the rounde helm,   ful of riche stones,   *Ribboned about*
Pyght prudely with perles   into the pure corners,   *Set proudly*
And so with saphyres sett   the sydes aboute.

765   He strideth on a stif stede   and striketh over the bente   *strong steed; field*
Light as a lyoun   were loused out of cheyne.   *loosed out of confinement*
His segges sewen hym alle,   and echon sayth to other: *men all saw him*
"This is a comlich kyng   knyghtes to lede!"   *goodly*

He boweth to the barres,   or he bide wolde,   *barriers, before he would stop*
770   And bet on with the brond   that all the bras rynges: *beat; sword so that*

_____

[1] Lines 741–44: *When shadows and bright day divide in two, / Larks aloft lift up their voices; / Men hasten out of bed [to the sound of] loud trumpets / Blowing on the field and on the town walls*

[2] Lines 757–58: *The gauntlets of grey steel, which were hemmed with gold, / Handle the harness after he asks for his horse*

"Cometh, caytifes, forth,   ye that Crist slowen,   *wretches; slew*
Knoweth Hym for your kyng,   or ye cacche more.   *before you get more [guilt]*

"Wayteth doun fro the walle,   what wo his on hande:
May ye fecche you no fode   thogh ye fey worthe!
775   And thogh ye waterles wede,   wynne ye hit never,
O droppe thogh ye dey scholde   daies in your lyve![1]

"The pale that I pight have,   passe hit who myght,   *palisade; set*
That is so byg on the bonke   and hath the burowe closed,   *bank; town*
Fourty to defenden   agens fyve hundred —   *against*
780   Thogh ye were etnes ech on   in scholde ye tourne!   *giants; you go [again]*

"And more manschyp were hit   mercy to byseche
Than metles marre   there no myght helpys."
Was non that warpith a word,   bot waytes here poyntes
Gif any stertis on stray   with stones hem to kylle.[2]

785   Than, wroth as a wode bore,   he wendeth his bridul:
"Gif ye as dogges wol dey,   the devel have that recche!
And or I wende fro this walle,   ye schul wordes schewe;
And efte spakloker speke   or Y your speche owene!"[3]

By that a Jewe, Josophus,   the gentyl clerke,   *By that time; Josephus*
790   Hadde wroght a wondere wyle   whan hem water fayled: *marvelous stratagem*
Made wedes of wolle   in wete forto plunge,[4]
Water-waschen as they were,   and on the walle hengen.   *Water-soaked*

The wedes dropeden doun,   and dryen yerne.   *dripped; quickly*
Rich rises hem fro;   the Romayns byholden,   *Stink*
795   Wenden wel here wedes   hadde wasschyng so ryve   *Know; their clothes; plentiful*
That no wye in the wone   water schold fayle.   *man; place can lack water*

Bot Waspasian the wile   wel ynow knewe,   *trick*
Loude lawghthe therat   and lordlynges byddis: *laughs*

---

[1] Lines 773–76: *Look down from the walls, [see] what woe is at hand: / You cannot fetch [more] food, even if you are dying [from starvation]! / And as you go waterless [now], [so] will you never get it again: / [Not] one drop even if you should die [by thus passing the remaining] days in your life*

[2] Lines 781–84: *"Thus it would be more wise (man-like) to seek mercy now / Than to perish without food where no might can help you." / There was no one [among the Jews] who said a word [in reply to Vespasian], but [they] awaited their chance / To kill with stones any [Roman] who wanders astray*

[3] Lines 785–88: *Then, angry as a mad boar, he (Vespasian) turns his bridle: / "If you would die like dogs, the devil take whoever cares! / But before I turn from this wall, you will [indeed] say something; / And [you must] speak more wisely in reply before I [will] acknowledge your speech!*

[4] *[He] made [the besieged Jews] plunge wool clothes into water*

"No burne abasched be,   thogh they this bost make;   *man be weak; boast*
800   Hit beth bot wyles of werre,   for water hem fayleth."   *It is only*

Than was nothyng bot note   newe to bygynne,   *troubles*
Assaylen on eche a side   the cité by halves,   *[They] assail*
Merken myd manglouns   ful unmete dyntes.
And myche of masouns note   they marden that tyme.[1]

805   Therof was Josophus ware,   that myche of werre couthe,   *aware; war knew*
And sette on the walle side   sakkes myd chaf,   *sacks of chaff*
Agens the streyngthe of the stroke   ther the stones hytte,   *strike where; hit*
That alle dered noght a dyghs   bot grete dyt made.   *harmed not a bit; noise*

The Romayns runne to anon   and on roddes knytte   *on poles attached*
810   Sithes for the sackes,   that selly were kene,   *Scythes; were very sharp*
Raghten to the ropis,   rent hem in sondere,   *Cut at*
That alle dasschande doun   into the diche flatten.   *dashing; ditch flattened*

Bot Josophus the gynful   here engynes alle   *crafty*
Brente with brennande oyle   and myche bale wroght.   *Burned; burning; woe*
815   Waspasian wounded was ther   wonderlich sore   *very badly*
Throw the hard of the hele   with an hande-darte   *heel*

That boot throw the bote   and the bone nayled   *That bit; boot*
Of the frytted fote   in the folis syde.[2]
Sone assembled hym to   many sadde hundred
820   That wolden wrecken the wounde,   other wo habiden.   *avenge; or woe endure*

They braydyn to the barres,   bekered yerne,   *rushed; barriers, engaged quickly*
Fought right felly,   foyned with speres,   *fiercely, thrust*
Jokken Jewes throgh.   Engynes by thanne   *Battered; Siege engines by then*
Were manye bent at the bonke   and to the burwe threwen.   *bank; town*

825   Ther were selcouthes sen,   as segges mowe here:
A burne with a balwe ston   was the brayn clove,
The gretter pese of the panne   the pyble forth striketh,
That hit flow into the feld,   a forlong or more;[3]

A womman, bounden with a barn,   was on the bely hytte   *pregnant; child*
830   With a ston of a stayre,   as the storyj telleth,   *stone from a siege-ladder*

---

[1] Lines 803–04: *Make with mangonels (machines for hurling large stones) many unanswered blows. / And they marred a great deal of masons' work at that time*

[2] *Of the leather-wrapped foot into the horse's side*

[3] Lines 825–28: *There were marvels seen [then], as men might hear: / A man with an evil stone was cloven to the brain, / The largest piece of which was so struck out by that rock / That it flew out into the field, a furlong or more*

That the barn out brayde   fram the body clene   *child [was] flung out*
And was born up as a bal   over the burwe walles;   *borne; town walls*

Burnes were brayned   and brosed to deth;   *Men; brained and bruised*
Wymmen wide open   walte undere stones;   *thrown*
835 Frosletes fro the ferst   to the flor thrylled;   *Fortifications; ground fell*
And many toret doun tilte   the Temple aboute.

The cité had ben seised   myd saut at that tyme
Nad the folke be so fers   that the Fende served,[1]
That kilden on the Cristen,   and kepten the walles   *Who killed; kept*
840 With arwes and arblastes   and archelers manye,   *arrows; crossbows; catapults*

With speres and spryngoldes   sponnen out hard,   *missiles thrown*
Dryven dartes adoun,   geven depe woundes,   *Drive; cause deep wounds*
That manye renke out of Rome   by restyng of sonne   *a man; setting of the sun*
Was mychel levere a leche   than layke myd his toles.[2]

845 Waspasian stynteth of the stoure,   steweth his burnes   *battle, stows; men*
That were forbeten and bled   undere bryght yren;   *wounded; iron*
Tyen to here tentis   myd tene that they hadde,   *Retire; their tents with sadness*
Al wery of that werk   and wounded ful sore.   *weary; very badly*

Helmes and hamberkes   hadden of sone,   *took off soon*
850 Leches by torchelight   loken here hurtes,   *Physicians; looked [to] their hurts*
Waschen woundes with wyn   and with wolle stoppen,   *wool bandaged [them]*
With oyle and orisoun,   ordeyned in charme.   *prescribed charms*

Suth evereche a segge   to the soper yede;   *Then every man; supper went*
Thogh they wounded were   was no wo nempned   *woe named*
855 Bot daunsyng and no deil   with dynnyng of pipis   *dancing; grief; dinning*
And the nakerer noyse   alle the nyght-tyme.   *drummers' noise*

Whan the derk was doun   and the day sprongen,   *day dawned*
Sone after the sonne   sembled the grete,   *sun assembled the great [men]*
Comen forth with the kyng   conseil to here,   *hear*
860 Alle the knyghthod clene   that for Crist werred.   *pure; warred*

Waspasian waiteth a-wide,   his wyes byholdeth   *looks all-around; men*
That were freschere to fight   than at the furst tyme,   *more ready*
Prayeth princes on ernest   and alle the peple after
That eche wye of that werre   schold his wille specke: *man; war*

---

[1] Lines 837–38: *The city [would] have been seized with assault at that time / [If] the folk hadn't been so fierce who served the Fiend (i.e., the "pagan" Jews)*

[2] *Would much prefer a doctor than [to] fight with his weapons*

865	"For or this toun be tak, and this toures heye,	
	Michel torfere and tene us tides on hande."[1]	
	They tourned alle to Titus and hym the tale graunten	*opportunity grant*
	Of the cité and the sege to seyn for hem alle.	*siege; speak*

Than Titus tourneth hem to   and talkyng bygynneth: — *turns to them*
870 "Thus to layke with this lese folke   us lympis the worse,[2]
For they ben fele of defence,   ferce men and noble, — *are hard; fierce*
And this toured toun   is tenful to wynne. — *towered; difficult*

"The worst wrecche in the wone   may on walle lygge, — *place; wait on the wall*
Strike doun with a ston   and stuny many knyghtes, — *[And]; stun*
875 Whan we schul hone and byholde   and litel harme wirche,
And ay the lothe of the layk   light on usselve.[3]

"Now mowe they ferke no ferre   here fode forto wynne;
Wolde we stynt of our strif,   whyle they here store marden?[4]
We scholde with hunger hem honte,   to hoke out of toun, — *hunt, to proceed*
880 Without weme or wounde   or any wo elles. — *injury or wound*

"For ther as fayleth the fode   ther is feynt strengthe, — *where food is short*
And ther as hunger is hote,   hertes ben feble." — *strong; feeble*
Alle assenteden to the sawe   that to the sege longed, — *saying; siege*
Apaied as the prince   and the peple wolde. — *Contented*

885 To the kyng were called   constables thanne,
Marchals and masers,   men that he tristith; — *mace-bearers; trusted*
He chargeth hem chefly   for chaunce that may falle, — *charged them chiefly*
With wacche of waled men   the walles to kepe: — *a watch of chosen*

"For we wol hunten at the hart   this hethes aboute,
890 And hure racches renne   amonge this rowe bonkes,[5]
Ride to the rever   and rere up the foules, — *river and raise; birds*
Se faucouns fle,   fele of the beste." — *See falcons fly; fall*

---

[1] Lines 865–66: *For before this town is taken, and these high towers, / Much trouble and sadness awaits us close at hand*

[2] *Thus to engage with these lesser people turns out worse for us*

[3] Lines 875–76: *When [this is the case] we must hesitate and watch and work little harm, / Since ever the evil of the fight comes down on us*

[4] Lines 877–78: *Now may they go no farther from here to get their food; / Would we cease of our fight, while they used up their stores?*

[5] Lines 889–90: *For we will hunt for the deer [in] these heaths about, / And hear hunting dogs run along these rough shores*

Ech segge to the solas   that hymself lyked,   *man [goes] to the solace*
Princes out of pavelouns   presen on stedes,   *press on horses*
895   Torneien, trifflyn   and on the toun wayten.   *Joust, loiter*
This lyf they ledde longe: oure Lord gyve us grace!   *life; [for a] long [time]*

[PASSUS 5]

In Rome Nero hath now   mychel noye wroght: *evil*
To deth pyned the pope   and mychel peple quelled,[1]
Petre, apostlen prince,   and Seint Poule bothe,   *prince of the Apostles*
900   Senek and the senatours;   and alle the cité fured;   *Seneca; burned*

His modire and his mylde wif   murdred to dethe;   *mother; mild; murdered*
Combred Cristen fele,   that on Crist leved.   *Harassed many; believed*
The Romayns resen anon,   whan they this rewthe seyen,   *rose; evil saw*
To quelle the emperour quyk   that hem unquemed hadde.[2]

905   They pressed to his paleys,   porayle and other,   *palace, poor people*
To brytten the bold kyng   in his burwe riche;   *slay; rich burrow*
The cité and the senatours,   assented hem bothe,   *both [of] them assented*
Non other dede was to doun: they han his dome yolden.   *have; doom given*

Than flowe that freke,   frendles, alone,   *flew; man (i.e., Nero), friendless*
910   Out at a pr004e posterne,   and alle the peple folwed.   *poor toilet*
With a tronchoun of tre,   toke he no more   *staff of wood*
Of alle the glowande gold   that he on grounde hadde.   *glowing*

On that tronchoun with his teth   he toggeth and byteth,   *teeth he tugged; bit*
Tille hit was piked at the poynt   as a prikkes ende.   *Until; sharpened*
915   Than abideth that burne   and biterlych speketh   *man; bitterly*
To alle the wyes that ther were   wordes aloude: *people*

"Tourneth, traytours, agen!   Schal never the tale rise   *Turn; arise*
Of no karl by the coppe,   how he his kyng quelde."   *churl; cup; killed*
Hymself he stryketh myd that staf,   streght to the hert,   *strikes; straight*
920   That the colke to-clef,   and the kyng deyed.   *core was cleft; died*

Six monthe after, and no more,   this myschef bytydde,   *happened*
That Waspasian was went   to werry on the Jewes;   *war upon*
Foure mettyn myle out of Rome   to mynden forevere,   *measured miles*
That erst was emperour of alle   thus ended in sorow.   *before*

---

[1] *Tortured the pope to death and many people killed*

[2] *To quench the life of the emperor who had troubled them*

925   The grete togedres gan,   geten hem another,   *great [men] (i.e., aristocracy); go*
        On Gabba, a gome   that mychel grem hadde   *Galba, a man; trouble*
        Throgh Othis Lucyus, a lord   that hym longe hated.   *Otho*
        And at the last that lord   out of lyf hym broght: *lord (i.e., Otho)*

        Amydde the market of Rome   they metten togedres;   *Amid; came together*
930   Othis fallith hym fey,   gaf hym fale woundes   *felled him mortally; deadly*
        That foure monthes and more   hadde mayntened the croune;   *Who [for]*
        And tho deyed the duke   and diademe lefte.   *then died; crown left*

        And whan that Gabba was gon   and to grounde broght,   *brought (i.e., buried)*
        Othis entrith on ernest   and emperour was made;   *entered [Rome]*
935   That man in his majesté   was monthes bot thre,
        Than he yeldeth Sathanas the soule   and hymself quelled.[1]

        The Romayns raisen a renk   Rome forto kepe,   *raised a man*
        A knyght that Vitel was calde,   and hym the croune raughte . . .[2]

        [. . . .]

        Bot for Sire Sabyn's sake,   a segge that was noble,   *Sabinus' sake, a man who*
940   Waspasian brother of blode,   that he brytned hadde . . .   *had killed*

        [. . . .]

        Waspasian upon Vitel   to vengen his brother   *avenge*
        Sent out of Surrie   segges to Rome . . .   *Syria; men*

        [. . . .]

        That as naked as an nedul   the newe emperour,   *needle*
        For Sire Sabyns sake,   alle the cité drowe;   *drew him (i.e., Vitellius)*

945   Suth gored the gome   that his guttes alle   *Then gored the man*
        As a boweled beste   into his breche felle.   *breeches*
        Doun yermande he yede   and yeldeth the soule,   *screaming he went; yields*
        And they kayght the cors   and kast into Tybre.   *corpse; Tiber River*

        Seven monthes this segge   hadde septre on hande,   *man; scepter*
950   And thus loste he the lyf   for his luther dedes.   *terrible deeds*
        Another segge was to seke   that septre schold have,   *to [be] sought*
        For alle this grete ben gon   and never agayn tournen.   *great [men] were gone*

---

[1] *Then he yielded [to] Satan his soul and killed himself*

[2] *A knight who was called Vitellius, and he attained the crown*

	Now of the cité and of the sege wolle Y sey more,	*city (i.e., Jerusalem); siege*
	How this comelich kyng, that for Crist werreth,	*warred*
955	Hath holden yn the hethen men this other half wynter,	*Has held in*
	That never burne of the burwe so bold was to passe.	*man of the town*

	As he to dyner on a day with dukes was sette,	*dinner*
	Comen renkes fram Rome, rapande swythe,[1]	
	In bruneys and in bryght wede and with bodeworde newe,	*garb; message*
960	Louten alle to the lord, and lettres hym raughten;	*Bowed; gave him letters*

	Sayn: "Comelich kyng! The knyghthod of Rome,	*Saying*
	Throgh the senatours assent and alle the cité ellis,	*also*
	Han chosen thee for chyventayn, here chef lord to worthe,[2]	
	And riche emperour of Rome. Thus redeth this lettres."	*So read these letters*

965	The lord unlappeth the lef, this lettres byholdeth,	*leaf; beheld*
	Overloketh ech a lyne to the last ende.	*Carefully read each line*
	Bordes born were doun, and the burne riseth,	*Tables; man*
	Calleth consail anon and kytheth this speche:	*made this speech*

	"Ye ben burnes of my blod, that Y best wolde,	*are men of my blood*
970	My sone is next to myself, and other sib manye:	*nearest; many other relations*
	Sire Sabyn of Surrie, a segge that Y triste,	*man; trust*
	And other frendes fele that me fayth owen.	*many, who owe me loyalty*

	"Now is me bodeword broght of blys froward Rome,	*message; bliss from*
	To be lord over that lond as this lettres speketh.	*these*
975	Sire Sabyn of Surrie, sey thee byhovyth	*you must say*
	How Y myght savy myself and I so wroght;	*save; if I did this*

	"For Y have heylych heyght here forto lenge	*solemnly vowed; remain*
	Tille I this toured toun have taken at my wille	*towered*
	And me the gates ben get and golden the keyes,	*been given and yielded*
980	And suth houshed on hem that this hold kepyn,	*then*

	"Brosten and betyn doun this britages heye	*Burst; beaten; high fortifications*
	That never ston in that stede stond upon othere.	*place stand*
	Kythe thy consail, sire knyght," this kyng to hym sayde,	*Pronounce*
	"For Y wol worche by thy witt gif worschip may folowe!"	*work; wit, if honor*

985	Than seith Sire Sabyn anon: "Semelich lord,	*Honored*
	We ben wyes thee with, thy worschup to further,	*honor*
	Of longe tyme bylafte, and ledes thyn owen;	*For a long time; your own men*
	That we doun is thy dede, may no man demen elles.	*What we do; claim else*

[1] *Men came from Rome, traveling quickly*

[2] *Have chosen you as chieftain, their chief lord to be*

990
"The dom demed was ther: who doth by another   *judgment made; does*
Schal be soferayn hymself,   sein in the werke.[1]
For as fers is the freke   atte ferre ende,   *fierce; man at the far end*
That of fleis the fel   as he that foot holdeth.   *flays off the skin*

"Bytake Tytus, thy sone,   this toun forto kepe,   *Commit*
And to the doughti duke   Domyssian, his brother.   *brave; Domitian*
995
Here I holde up myn honde   myd hem forto lenge   *with them to remain*
With alle the here that I have   while my herte lasteth. *all the forces*

"And thou schalt ride to Rome   and receyve the croune,
In honour emperour to be   as thyn eure schapith.   *your fortune (destiny)*
So may the covenaunt be kept   that thou to Crist made: *promise*
1000
Thyself dest, that thy soudiours   by thyn assent worchen."[2]

Than with a liouns lote   he lifte up his eyen,
To Titus tourneth anon,   and hym the tale schewed.
And as Sire Sabyn hadde seid,   he hym sone granteth,
With his brother and the burnes,   as he hym blesse wolde:[3]

1005
"I wol tarie at this toun   til I hit taken have,   *remain*
Made weys throw the walles   for wenes and cartes,   *paths; wagons*
Oure bothere heste to holde,   gif me hap tydith,[4]
Or here be to-hewen,   or I hennes passe."   *hewn, before I hence*

A boke on a brode scheld   was broght on to swere: *book; shield; swear*
1010
Alle burnes boden to the honde   and barouns hit kyssen,   *men stretched toward*
To be leel to that lord   that hem lede scholde,   *loyal; them should lead*
Sire Titus, the trewe kyng,   tille they the toun hadde.   *until*

Fayn as the foul of day   was the freke thanne,   *Glad; day-bird; man (Vespasian)*
Kysseth knyghtes anon   with carful wordes:
1015
"My wele and my worschup   ye weldeth to kepe,   *prosperity; honor; you control*
For the tresour of my treuth   upon this toun hengyth: *troth; town hangs*

"I nold this toun were untake,   ne this toures heye,[5]
For alle the glowande golde   upon grounde riche,   *glowing*
Ne no ston in the stede   stondande alofte,   *stone in the place*
1020
Bot alle overtourned and tilt,   Temple and other."   *tilled, Temple and all*

---

[1] *Shall be [as if done by the] sovereign himself, seen in the work*

[2] *You do yourself, what your soldiers work by your order*

[3] Lines 1001–04: *Then with a lion's look [upon his face] he (i.e., Vespasian) lifted up his eyes, / To Titus turns at once, and told him the tale. / And just as Sir Sabinus had said, [so] he (i.e., Titus) soon grants to him, / With his brother and the men, as if he (i.e., Titus) wanted to bless him (i.e., Vespasian)*

[4] *The promise of both of us to maintain, if my health remains good*

[5] *I wouldn't [know that] this town were untaken, nor these towers high*

Thus laccheth he leeve   at his ledes alle,   *he takes leave from his men*
Wende wepande away   and on the walles loketh,   *Goes weeping; looked*
Praieth God, as he gooth,   hem grace forto sende
To hold that they byhot han   and never here hertis chaunge.[1]

1025   Now is Waspasian went   over the wale stremys   *wild sea*
Even entred into Rome   and emperour maked.   *And so entered*
And Titus for the tydyng   hath take so mychel joye   *news; taken so much joy*
That in his synwys soudeynly   a syknesse is fallen.   *sinews; sickness*

The freke for the fayndom   of the fadere blysse,   *man; joyousness*
1030   With a cramp and a colde   caught was so hard
That the fyngres and feet,   fustes and joyntes   *fists*
Was lythy as a leke   and lost han here strengthe.   *Were weak as a leaf*

He croked agens kynde   and as a crepel woxen,[2]
And whan they sey hym so,   many segge wepyth;   *saw him so [beset]; men wept*
1035   They sente to the cité   and soughten a leche   *physician*
That couthe kevere the kyng,   and condit delyveryn.   *could cure; safe conduct*

Whan they the cyté hadde sought   with seggys aboute,   *men*
Fynde couthe they no freke   that on the feet couthe,   *could; who could walk*
Save the self Josophus   that surgyan was noble,   *Except; surgeon*
1040   And he graunteth to go   with a goode wylle.   *accepted*

Whan he was comen to the kyng   and the cause wyste   *case knew*
How the segge so sodeynly   in syknesse is fallen,   *man*
Tille he have complet his cure   condit he asketh   *Until; safe-conduct*
For what burne of the burwe   that he brynge wolde.   *whichever man; town*

1045   The kyng was glad alle to graunte   that the gome wylned,   *man desired*
And he ferkith hym forth,   fettes ful blyve   *goes forth, fetches very quickly*
A man to the mody kyng   that he moste hated,   *moody; he (i.e., Titus)*
And yn bryngeth the burne   to his beddes syde.   *man to his bedside*

Whan Tytus saw that segge   sodeynly with eyen,   *with [his] eyes*
1050   His herte in an hote yre   so hetterly riseth   *hot anger so quickly rose*
That the blode bygan with the hete   to brede in the vaynes,
And the synwes resorte   in here self kynde.[3]

---

[1] Lines 1023–24: *Prays God, as he goes, to send them grace / To keep what they have promised and to never change their hearts*

[2] *He became crooked against nature and as a cripple grew*

[3] Lines 1051–52: *That the blood began to spread in his veins as a result of the heat, / And his sinews [began to] return to their proper nature*

Feet and alle the fetoures as they byfore were,   *features*
Comyn in here owen kynd, and the kyng ryseth,   *proper nature*
1055 Thonketh God of His grace and the goode leche   *Thanked; physician*
Of alle save that his enemy was yn on hym broght.

Than sayth Josophus: "This segge hath thee holpyn, *has helped you*
And here hath be thy bote, thogh thou hym bale wolde; *deliverer; harm*
Therfor graunte hym thy grace agen his goode dede, *for his good deed*
1060 And be frende with thy foman that frendschup hath served!" *your enemy*

The kyng saghtles with the segge that hym saved hadde, *reconciles*
And ther graunted hym grace to go where he wolde. *wherever he wanted*
With Josophus he made joye and jewels hym raughte: *gave*
Besauntes, byes of gold, broches and ryngys.   *Bezants, bracelets*

1065 Bot alle forsaketh the segge and to the cité yede   *went*
With condit as he come; he kepith no more.   *he keeps nothing more*
And Tytus segyth the toun ther tene is on hande *besieges; where woe*
For hard hunger and hote that hem is bylompyn.   *befallen*

Now of the tene in the toun were tore forto telle *hardship; difficult*
1070 What moryne and meschef for mete is byfalle; *mortality; for [lack of] food*
For fourty dayes byfor they no fode hadde:
Nother fisch ne flesch freke on to byte,   *man; bite*

Bred, browet ne brothe, ne beste upon lyve,   *Bread, soup; beast alive*
Wyn ne water to drynke bot wope of hemself. *but what they wept*
1075 Olde scheldes and schone scharply they eten; *shields and shoes soon they ate*
That liflode for ladies was luther to chewe.   *food; hard*

Fellen doun for defaute flatte to the grounde, *Fell down from starvation*
Ded as a dore-nayl, eche day many hundred.   *door-nail*
Wo wakned thycke: as wolves they ferde; *Woe stirred up thickly; became*
1080 The wyght waried on the woke alle his wombe-fille.[1]

On Marie, a myld wyf, for meschef of foode,   *One*
Hire owen barn that ho bare ho brad on the gledis,[2]
Rostyth rigge and rib with rewful wordes,   *Roasted side*
Sayth, "Sone, upon eche side our sorow is alofte:

1085 "Batail aboute the borwe our bodies to quelle, *around the town; kill*
Withyn hunger so hote that negh our herte brestyth. *almost our hearts burst*

---

[1] *The strong warred upon the weak to completely fill his belly*

[2] *Her own child that she bore she cooked on the coals*

Therfor yeld that I thee gaf,   and agen tourne   *give back what I gave you*
And entre ther thou cam out,"   and etyth a schouldere.   *enter where; eats*

The smel roos of the rost   right into the strete,   *rose; roast*
1090 That fele fastyng folke   felden the savere;   *many starving folk smelled the savor*
Doun thei daschen the dore: dey scholde the berde[1]
That mete yn this meschef   hadde from men layned.   *meat; hidden*

Than saith that worthi wif,   in a wode hunger,   *crazed hunger*
"Myn owen barn have I brad   and the bones gnawen;   *child; roasted*
1095 Yit have I saved you som,"   and forth a side feccheth   *[she] fetches*
Of the barn that ho bare —   and alle hire blode chaungeth.   *she bore; their*

Away they went for wo,   wepyng ech one   *woe, weeping*
And sayn: "Alas! In this lif   how longe schul we dwelle?   *endure*
Yit beter were at o brayde   in batail to deye   *one blow in battle to die*
1100 Than thus in langur to lyve   and lengthen our fyne."   *languish to live; end*

Than they demeden a dom   that deil was to hure:
To voiden alle by vile deth   that vitelys destruyed —
Wymmen and weyke folke   that weren of olde age,
That myght noght stonde in stede   bot her stor mardyn —[2]

1105 After to touche of trewe,   to trete with the lord.
Bot Titus graunteth noght for gile   that the gomes thenke,
For he is wise that is war   or hym wo hape,
And with falsede afere   is fairest to dele.[3]

To worchyn undere the wal   wayes they casten,   *mine; plot*
1110 Whan Tytus nold no trewe   to the toun graunte;   *would not a truce*
With mynours and masouns   myne they bygonne,   *miners; mine they began*
Grobben faste on the grounde,   and God gyve us joye!   *Digging*

[PASSUS 6]

As Tytus after a tyme   umbe the toun redeth   *around; rides*
Wyth sixty speres of the sege,   segges a fewe,   *siege, and a few men*

---

[1] *Down they smashed the door: die should the man*

[2] Lines 1101–04: *Then they passed a judgment that was terrible to hear: / To execute by cruel death all those who used vital [supplies] — / Women and weak people who were of old age, / Who might not [be able to] stand in place but their stores depleted —*

[3] Lines 1105–08: *After [which] to touch [on the subject] of truce, to treat with the lord. / But Titus grants [them] nothing because of the guile that the men (i.e., the Jews) intend, / For he is wise who is aware before woe happens [to him] / And it is best to deal with falsehood at a distance*

| 1115 | Alle outwith the ost,   out of a kave | *away from the army; cave* |
| | Up a buschment brake,   alle of bright hedis, | *an ambush broke; helms* |

	Fyf hundred fightyng men, and fellen hem aboute	*fell about them*
	In jepouns and jambers. Jewes they were,	*tunics and greaves*
	Hadde wroght hem a wey and the wal myned.	*themselves; undermined*
1120	And Titus tourneth hem to without tale more.	*turns toward them*

	Schaftes schedred were sone and scheldes y-threlled,	*broken; pierced*
	And many schalke throw-schot with the scharpe ende,	*men shot through*
	Brunyes and bright wede blody by-runne;	*Armor; gear run with blood*
	And many segge at that saute soughte to the grounde,	*men at that assault*

1125	Hacchen upon hard steel with an hetter wylle,	*[They] hack; [such] a savage*
	That the fure out flewe as of flynt-stonys:	*sparks fly about*
	Of the helm and the hed hewen at-tonys,	*Off; head [are] hewn at once*
	The stompe undere stede feet in the steel leveth.	*stump; horse hooves; remains*

	The yong duk Domycian of the dyn herde	*noise heard*
1130	And issed out of the ost with eghte hundred speres,	*issued*
	Fel on the fals folke, umbe-feldes hem sone,	*Fell upon; surrounds them*
	As bestes bretnes hem alle and hath his brother holpen.	*beasts slaughters*

	Than Titus toward his tentis tourneth hym sone,	*turns quickly*
	Maketh mynours and men the myne forto stoppe;	*Orders*
1135	After profreth pes for pyté that he hadde	*Afterwards [he] offers peace*
	Whan he wist of here wo that were withyn stoken.	*knew of their woe; trapped*

	Bot Jon the jenfulle, that the Jewes ladde,	*crafty, who; led*
	An other Symond, of his assent, forsoken the profre,	*Simon; forsook the offer*
	Sayn lever in that lif lengen hem were,	
1140	Than any renke out of Rome rejoyced here sorowe.[1]	

	Sale in the cité was cesed by thanne;	*Selling; ceased*
	Was noght for besauntes to bye that men bite myght:	*nothing; bezants to buy*
	For a ferthyng-worth of fode floryns an hundred	*farthing's worth; florins*
	Princes profren in the toun to pay in the fuste.	*offer; pay in hand (fist)*

1145	Bot alle was boteles bale, for whoso bred hadde	
	Nold a gobet have gyven for goode upon erthe.[2]	
	Wymmen falwed faste and here face chaungen,	*blanched; their faces*
	Feynte and fallen doun that so faire were,	*Faint*

---

[1] Lines 1139–40: *Saying [that they] preferred in that position to remain, / Than [to have] any man from Rome rejoice [in] their sorrow*

[2] Lines 1145–46: *But all was incurable evil, for whoever had bread / Would not have given a morsel [to someone else] for [all of the] goods upon the earth*

Swounen, swallen as swyn,   and som swart wexen,
1150   Som lene on to loke   as lanterne-hornes.[1]   *mortality; thick*
The morayne was so myche   that no man couthe telle   *bury; town*
Where to burie in the burwe   the bodies that were ded,

Bot wenten with hem to the walle   and walten hem overe;   *went; threw them*
Into the depe of the diche   the ded doun fallen.
1155   Whan Titus told was the tale,   to trewe God he vouched   *vowed*
That he propfred hem pes   and grete pité hadde.   *offered them peace*

Tho praied he Josophus to preche,   the peple to enforme   *begged*
Forto save hemself   and the cité yelde.   *themselves; yield*
Bot Jon forsoke the sawe   so forto wyrche,   *forsook the message*
1160   With Symond, that other segge   that the cyté ladde.   *man who led the city*

Myche peple for the prechyng   at the posterne gatis   *Many; secret gates*
Tyen out of the toun   and Tytus bysecheth   *Came*
To forgyve hem the gult   that they to God wroght;   *guilt*
And he graunteth hem grace   and gaylers bytaught.   *[to] jailers sent*

1165   Bot whan they metten with mete,   unmyghty they were   *met; food, powerless*
Any fode to defye,   so faynt was here strengthe.   *digest*
Ful the gottes of gold   ilka gome hadde: *guts; each person had*
Lest fomen fongen hem schold,   here floreyns they eten.[2]

Whan hit was broght up abrode   and the bourd aspyed,   *it was discovered; trick*
1170   Withouten leve of that lord,   ledes hem slowen,   *men slay them*
Goren evereche a gome   and the gold taken,   *Butcher each person*
Fayner of the floreyns   than of the frekes alle.   *Happier*

Ay were the gates unget   tille two yeres ende,   *Always; un-gotten until*
So longe they sought hit by sege   or they the cité hadde;   *siege, before*
1175   Eleven hundred thousand Jewes   in the menewhyle
Swalten while the sweng last   by swerd and by hunger.   *Died; fighting*

Now Titus conseil hath take   the toun to assayle,
To wynne hit on eche wyse   of warwolves handes,
Never pyté ne pees   profre hem more,   *nor peace [to] offer them again*
1180   Ne gome that he gete may   to no grace taken;   *Nor*

Armen hem as-tyt   alle for the werre,   *quickly; battle*
Tyen even to the toun   with trompis and pypys,   *trumpets and pipes*

---

[1] Lines 1149–50: *Swoon, swell like pigs, and some grow black, / Some [grow as] thin to look upon as lantern-horns (i.e., so thin as to be transparent)*

[2] *Lest enemies should take them, they had eaten their florins*

With nakerers and grete noyce   neghen the walles   *drummers; noise come near*
Ther many styf man and stoure   stondith alofte.   *Where many strong*

1185   Sire Sabyn of Surrye   on a syde yede;   *went*
        The yong duke Domycian   drow to another.
        Fiftene thousand fyghtyng men   ilka freke hadde,   *each man had*
        With many maner of engyne   and mynours ynowe.   *miners enough*

        Tytus at the toun gate,   with ten thousand helmes,
1190   Merketh mynours at the wal   where they myne scholde,   *Orders*
        On ech side for the assaute   setteth engynes   *assault he sets siege engines*
        And bold brenyed men   in belfrayes heye.   *armored; high fortifications*

        Was noght bot dyn and dyt   as alle deye scholde,   *noise and blows*
        So eche lyvande lyf   layeth on other;   *living life lays*
1195   At eche kernel was cry   and quasschyng of wepne,   *corner; crashing of weapons*
        And many burne atte brayd   brayned to deth.   *men in a moment [are] brained*

        Sire Sabyn of Surrye,   whyle the saute laste,   *while the assault lasts*
        Leyth a ladder to the wal   and alofte clymyth,   *Lays; climbs*
        Wendeth wyghtly theron   — thogh hym wo happned —
1200   And up stondith for ston   or for steel-ware.[1]

        Syx he slow on the wal,   Sire Sabyn alone;   *Six he slew*
        The seventh hitteth on hym   an unhende dynte   *seventh hits; a hideous blow*
        That the brayn out brast   at both nosethrylles.   *brain burst out; nostrils*
        And Sabyn, ded of the dynt,   into the diche falleth.   *dead from the blow*

1205   Than Tytus wepyth for wo   and warieth the tyme,   *weeps; curses the moment*
        Syth he the lede hath lost   that he love scholde: *Since; man has lost*
        "For now is a duke ded   the doughtiest Y trowe   *bravest I believe*
        That ever stede bystrode   or any steel wered."   *rode a horse; armor wore*

        Than Tytus on the same side   setteth an engyne,   *sets*
1210   A sowe wroght for the werre,   and to the wal dryveth   *siege engine; war; drives*
        That alle overwalte ther hit went,   and wyes an hundred
        Were ded of that dynt   and in the diche lyghten.[2]

        Than Tytus heveth up the honde   and Heven Kyng thonketh,[3]
        That they the dukes deth   han so dere boughte;   *have so dearly*

---

[1] Lines 1199–1200: *Makes his way onto the wall with strength — though woe would happen to him — / And stands up in spite of the stones or arrows [launched at him by the Jews]*

[2] Lines 1211–12: *[So hard] that all were overthrown wherever it turned, and hundreds of men / Were killed by its blows and fell into the ditch*

[3] *Then Titus throws up his hand and thanks the King of Heaven (i.e., Christ)*

1215   The Jewes preien the pees   — this was the Paske-evene —
         And to the comelich kyng   the keyes out raughten.[1]

         "Nay, traytours," quod Tytus,   "now take hem yourselfen,
         For schal no ward on the wal   us the way lette: *guard from your wall*
         We han geten us a gate   agenes your wille;   *have seized for ourselves a gate*
1220   That schal ben satled soure   on youre sory kynde!"   *settled sorely*

         Or the gates were yete   — al the yeres tyme —[2]
         Over the cyté were seyn   selcouthe thynges.   *marvelous*
         A bryght brennyng swerd   over the burwe henged   *burning; hung*
         Without hond other helpe   save of Heven one.   *hand or help; alone*

1225   Armed men in the ayere   upon ost-wyse,   *air like an army*
         Over the cyté were seyn   sundrede tymes.   *several*
         A calf agen kynde   calved in the Temple   *against its nature*
         And eued an ewe-lombe   at the offryng-tyme.   *gave birth [to] a baby lamb*

         A wye on the wal   cried wondere heye: *man; cried loudly*
1230   "Voys fram est, voys fram west,   voys fram the foure wyndis,"   *A voice from east*
         And sayd: "Wo, wo, wo   worth on you bothe,   *fall on you both*
         Jerusalem, the Jewen toun,   and the joly Temple!"

         The same tyme the toun   was taken and wonnen
         Yit sayth the wye on the walle   another word more: *Yet says the man*
1235   "Wo to this worldly wone   and wo to myselve!"   *place*
         And deyd, whan he don hadde,   throw dynt of a slynge.   *died; blow from*

         And than the vilayns devysed hem   and vengaunce hit helde,
         And wyten her wo   the wronge that they wroghte
         Whan they brutned in the burwe   the byschup, Seint Jame;
1240   Noght wolde acounte hit for Crist,   the care that they hadde.[3]

         Bot up yeden here gates,   and yelden hem alle   *go; [they] yield themselves*
         Without brunee and bright wede,   in here bare chertes;   *in their bare shirts*
         Fram none tille the merke nyght   never ne cesed,   *morning to dark; ceased*
         Bot evere man after man   mercy bysought.   *sought mercy*

1245   Tytus into the toun   taketh his wey: *makes his way*
         Myght no man stande on the stret   for stynke of ded corses.   *corpses*

---

[1] Lines 1215–16: *The Jews plead [for] peace — this was Passover — / And to the noble king bring forth the gate keys*

[2] *Before the gates were given over — all that year's time —*

[3] Lines 1237: 40: *And then the people thought about them (these omens) and considered it all [God's] vengeance, / And knew their woe was due to the wrong that they did / When they killed in the town the bishop, Saint James; / [Yet] no one would equate it with Christ['s suffering], the misfortunes that they had*

The peple in the pavyment   was pité to byholde   *street*
That were enfamyned and defeted   whan hem fode wanted.   *famished*

1250   Was noght on ladies lafte   bot the lene bones   *nothing; lean*
       That were fleschy byfore   and fayre on to loke;   *fair to look upon*
       Burges with balies   as barels or that tyme
       No gretter than a grehounde   to grype on the medil.[1]

       Tytus tarieth noght for that,   bot to the Temple wendith   *tarries; goes*
       That was rayled the roof   with rebies grete;   *shingled*
1255   With perles and peritotes   alle the place ferde   *chrysolites; looked*
       As glowande gled-fure   that on gold flikreth.   *glowing burning coals; flickers*

       The dores ful of dyemauntes   dryven were thicke   *diamonds*
       And made merveylous lye   with margeri-perles;   *marvelously light; pearls*
       Derst no candel be kende   whan clerkes scholde rise —   *Needed no; kindled*
1260   So were they lemaunde lyght   and as a lampe schonen.   *brilliantly alight; shone*

       The Romayns wayten on the werke,   warien the tyme   *search; dread*
       That ever so precious a place   scholde perische for synne.   *perish for [its] sin*
       Out the tresour to take   Tytus commaundyth: *treasure*
       "Doun bete the bilde,   brenne hit into grounde."   *Raze the building, burn*

1265   Ther was plenté in the place   of precious stonys:
       Grete gaddes of gold   whoso grype lyste,   *bars; for whoever wanted to grab them*
       Platis, pecis of peys,   pulisched vessel,   *pieces of weight, polished vessels*
       Bassynes of brend gold   and other bryght gere;   *Basins of burnished*

       Pelours, masly made   of metalles fele,   *Pillars, sturdily*
1270   In copper craftly cast   and in clene selvere;   *copper; silver*
       Peynted with pure gold   alle the place over.
       The Romayns renten hem doun   and to Rome ledyn.   *tore them down; took*

       Whan they the cyté han sought   upon the same wyse,   *searched*
       Telle couthe no tonge   the tresours that they founden: *No tongue could tell*
1275   Jewels for joly men   and jemewes riche;   *rich double rings*
       Floreyns of fyne gold   ther no freke wanted;   *no man lacked*

       Riche peloure and pane   princes to were;   *fur and fabric; wear*
       Besantes, bies of gold,   broches, and rynges,   *Bezants, bracelets*
       Clene clothes of selke   many carte-fulle —   *silk*
1280   Wele wanteth no wye,   bot wale what hym lyketh.   *Wealth; man; chooses*

---

[1] Lines 1251–52: *Burgesses with bellies like barrels before that time / [Were now] no bigger than a greyhound to grip around the middle*

Now masouns and mynours   han the molde soughte,   *have searched the earth*
With pykeyse and ponsone   persched the walles: *picks and punches pierced*
Hewen throw hard ston,   hurled hem to grounde   *Hacked*
That alle derkned the diche   for doust of the poudere.   *darkened; dust*

1285   So they wroughten at the wal   alle the woke tyme,   *made; that week's time*
Tille the cyté was serched   and sought al aboute,   *Until*
Maden wast at a wappe   ther the walle stode,   *Made waste with one blow where*
Bothe in Temple and in tour   alle the toun over.   *tower*

Nas no ston in the stede   stondande alofte,   *Was no stone; place standing*
1290   Morter ne mude-walle   bot alle to mulle fallen: *mud-brick wall; earth*
Nother tymbre ne tre,   Temple ne other,   *Neither timber*
Bot doun betyn and brent   into blake erthe.   *That wasn't razed and burned*

And whan the Temple was overtilt,   Tytus commaundys   *overthrown*
In plowes to putte   and alle the place erye;   *plowed up*
1295   Suth they sow hit with salt,   and seiden this wordes: *Then they sowed; these*
"Now is this stalwourthe stede   distroied forevere."   *strong place destroyed*

Tytus suth sett hym   on a sete riche,   *then set himself; seat*
Alle the Jewes to jugge   as justise hymself.
Criours callen hem forth   as hy that Crist slowen,   *Criers; they who Christ slew*
1300   And beden Pilat apere,   that provost was thanne.   *order Pilate [to] appear*

Pilat proffrith hym forth,   apered at the barre,   *proffers; appeared at court*
And he frayneth the freke   alle with faire wordis,   *he (i.e., Titus) asks the man*
Whan Crist of dawe was don   and to the deth yede,   *day was done; went*
Of the hethyng that He hadde   and the hard woundis.   *Of the scorn*

1305   Than melys the man   and the matere tolde,   *remembers*
How alle the ded was don   whan He deth tholed;   *deed; suffered*
For thritty penyes in a poke   His postel Hym solde: *pennies; bag His apostle*
So was He bargayned and bought,   and as a beste quelled.   *beast killed*

"Now corsed be he," quod the kyng,   "that the acate made;   *bargain made*
1310   He wexe marchaunte amys,   that the money fenged   *merchant amiss; took*
To sille so precyous a prince   for penyes so fewe   *sell*
They eche a ferthyng had fourmed   floryns an hundred.   *[Even if]; farthing*

"Bot I schal marchaundise make   in mynde of that other,   *memory*
That schal be hethyng to hem   or I hennes passe:
1315   Alle that here bodyes wol by   or bargaynes make,[1]
By lowere pris forto passe,   than they the Prophete solde."   *price*

---

[1] Lines 1314–15: *That shall be hateful to them, before I go hence: / Anyone who their (i.e., the Jews') bodies will buy or bargains make [of them]*

He made in the myddis of the ost   a market to crye,   *midst; host (army)*
Alle that cheffare wolde chepe   chepis to have;[1]
Ay for a peny of pris,   whoso pay wolde,   *Ever*
1320 Thrytty Jewes in a throm   throngen in ropis.   *in a crowd bound*

So were they bargayned and bought   and broght out of londe,   *[that] land*
Never suth on that syde   cam segge of hem after;   *man of them*
Ne non that leved in here lawe   scholde in that londe dwelle,   *lived under*
That tormented trewe God.   Thus Titus commaundyth.   *Who*

1325 Josophus, the gentile clerke,   ajorned was to Rome: *ordered*
Ther of this mater and mo   he made fayre bokes.   *matter; books*
And Pilat to prisoun was put   to pynen forevere,   *was put to [be in] pain*
At Vienne, ther venjaunce   and vile deth he tholed.   *where; suffered*

The wye that hym warded   wente on a tyme   *man; guarded*
1330 Hymself fedyng with frut   and feffyt hym with a pere.   *provided; pear*
And forto paren his pere,   he praieth hym yerne   *peel; eagerly*
Of a knyf, and the kempe   kest hym a trenchour.   *man cast [to] him*

And with the same he schef   hymself to the herte,   *stabs*
And so the kaytif, as his kynde,   corsedlich deied.[2]
1335 [. . . .]
[. . . .]

Whan alle was demed and don   they drowen up tentis,   *said and done; folded*
Trossen here tresour   and trompen up the sege,   *Pack; trumpet; siege*
Wenten syngyng away   and han here wille forthred,   *have their will furthered*
1340 And hom riden to Rome.   Now rede ous oure Lord!   *ride home; guide us may*

Hic terminatur bellum Judaicum apud Jerusalem.[3]

---

[1] *Anyone who would buy merchandise would have bargains*

[2] *And so the caitiff, as was his nature, cursedly died*

[3] *Here ends the war against the Jews in Jerusalem*

EXPLANATORY NOTES

ABBREVIATIONS: **D**₈₆

ABBREVIATIONS: D_{86}: Duggan (1986); D_{88}: Duggan (1988); **H**: Hanna and Lawton (2003), editing L; **K**: Eugen Kölbing and Mabel Day (1932), editing L; ***MED***: *Middle English Dictionary*; ***OCD***: *Oxford Classical Dictionary*; ***OED***: *Oxford English Dictionary*; **T**: Turville-Petre (1989), editing D. **Whiting**: Whiting, *Proverbs, Sentences, and Proverbial Phrases*. For manuscript abbreviations, see p. 40.

1–12   *In Tyberyus tyme . . . as rayn in the strete.* As K notes (p. 91), these lines form "one sentence, translating the opening sentence of *Vindicta Salvatoris.*"

1   *Tyberyus.* Tiberius Julius Caesar Augustus (r. 14–37), the successor to Augustus Caesar. That Tiberius is a *trewe* emperor is surely meant to differentiate him from the criminal Nero and the number of would-be emperors wrought of the civil war which followed Nero's death and prompted Vespasian's eventual claim on the crown. These events are shown later in the poem, at lines 897–964.

3   *Pylat was provost.* Pontius Pilate, prefect of Judaea from 26–36.

5   *Herodes.* Herod Antipas, appointed tetrarch of Galilee and Peraea by Augustus Caesar following the death of Antipas' father, Herod the Great (d. 4 BC). He was eventually exiled in AD 39. According to Luke 23:6–12, Pontius Pilate tried to transfer the responsibility of Jesus' trial to Herod.

7   *oft synne hatide.* As H (p. 91) observes, this characterization might derive "upon the account of Tiberius's youth in Poly 4.4. (2:310–12)."

9   *upon the playn erthe.* Though it might appear to read as "on the barren earth" or, in a tautological construction, as "on the plain, the earth," this odd turn of phrase actually translates as "flat upon the ground." See *MED: plain(e),* adj. 1(a).

12   *Til He al on rede blode ran, as rayn in the strete.* While I have glossed this phrase as indicating that Christ's blood fell like rain onto the street (a proverbial usage; see Whiting R17), it is also possible to read the line as portraying Christ's blood running in rivulets like rain upon the street. Either possibility has iconographic support, as Christ's blood is often shown running on His body in rivulets and also springing out of Him (and curing Longinus in the process). The former usage, however, is perhaps supported by its appearance in *Alliterative Morte Arthure*, line 795, where the bear and the dragon fight and their blood "Runnand on red blood as rain of the heven."

14   *Blyndfelled Hym as a be.* The bee is a figure of blindness in the Middle Ages. K (p. 91) notes Maidstone's Penitential Psalm 253: "I stomble as doth þe blynde be," in *Richard Maidstone's Penitential Psalms.* The usage here is proverbial: Whiting B63.

15   *Gif thou be prophete of pris.* The *Siege*-poet seems particularly indebted to the Gospel of Matthew for many of the details concerning the Passion. For this scene, compare Matthew 26:68: "Prophesy unto us, O Christ. Who is he that struck thee?" It is interesting to note that this passage in Matthew directly follows the trial of Jesus before Caiaphas, the high priest of the Jews. The poet probably expects the reader to have Caiaphas' dominant role in bringing about Christ's death in the forefront of his mind.

20   *On hem the vyleny to venge.* As noted in the Introduction (pp. 30–36), it is the vengeance upon the Jews for the death of Christ that is to be the focus and the underlying structure of the entire poem.

25   *Tytus.* Titus Flavius Vespasianus (r. 79–81). The eldest son and namesake of Vespasian.

26   *Gascoyne gate and Gyan.* Neilson ("*Huchown,*" p. 329) notes an echo of *Parlement of the Thre Ages*, line 491: "Gascoyne and Gyane gatt."

36   *Waspasian was caled the waspene bees after.* Titus Flavius Vespasianus (r. 69–79). The derivation of his name from wasps given here is a false etymology, but one that enjoyed great popularity during the Middle Ages and is amusing to contemplate.

45   *Nathan.* Jacobus de Voragine's *Legenda aurea* names the messenger Alban, though the poet here follows *Vindicta Salvatoris.* In other traditions, the messenger is named Volusian. The name itself may carry specific significance here, as Nathan was a prophet associated with the courts of David and Solomon, and it was Nathan who rejected David's request to build a temple for God in Jerusalem, saying that, after David's death, God would raise one up from his seed and through him establish His kingdom. This son to come, Nathan prophesied, would be the one to build a temple to God in Jerusalem and a great dynasty under God (see 2 Kings [2 Samuel] 7:1–17). Though David's son Solomon, anointed by Nathan, built the First Temple in Jerusalem, Nathan's prophecy "became the focus of messianic hope for the postexilic community" since it promised an "everlasting dynasty for David" (*Mercer Dictionary of the Bible*, p. 604). Christian exegetes, not surprisingly, have seen in Nathan's words a prophecy about the coming of Christ, who was, after all, in the line of David and whose body could be regarded as the Temple to be resurrected (see p. 32n121, above). In *Siege*, Nathan's journey to Rome will ultimately set in motion the actions of Titus and Vespasian that culminate in the destruction of the Second Temple and the victory of a new temple to God (i. e., Christ); from this perspective, the name *Nathan* for the messenger is most fitting.

          of Grece. Nathan does not appear to be from Greece proper, as he clearly states that Christ was "in our lande" in line 95. Hellenistic communities were widespread throughout the lands surrounding the Mediterranean, and the Christian movement made many early converts among them. It is possible to hear a faint echo here of Acts 6:1–7, where the Seven (Stephen, Philip, Prochorus, Nicanor, Timon, Parmenas, and Nicolaus) are chosen to serve in order to help resolve a growing rift between the Hellenists and Hebrews. Identifying what the author of Acts meant by Hellenists is difficult to determine (he could have meant Greeks, Greek-speaking peoples, a heterodox movement, diaspora Jews, or even a group who accommodated Greek culture). Acts 11:20 also discusses evangelizing work by the early Christians among the Hellenists. Whether Nathan is meant to be associated with these early missionary movements is difficult to determine. For more on these passages in Acts and the possible historical matters behind them, see Livingston, "The Seven."

49   *Sensteus out of Surye.* This is probably Gaius Cestius Gallus, legate of Syria from 63 (or 65)–67. Cestius Gallus had to deal with a number of uprisings in Palestine during his rule, ultimately marching on the territory in 66 to restore peace (*OCD*); it was his failure to take Jerusalem, however, that led to the appointment of Vespasian to deal with the problems once and for all. K notes (p. xxiii) that the poet has adopted his role from Higden's *Polychronicon*, book 4, but H (p. xlv) makes a stronger case for reliance on Josephus at this point.

52   *his tribute to telle, that they withtake wolde.* The treatment of tribute is a recurrent theme in poems of the alliterative movement, seen in *Alliterative Morte Arthure*, *Wars of Alexander*, and *Destruction of Troy*. H posits (pp. xlv–vi and 94) that its appearance in the present poem is indebted to Josephus.

56   *on the deep dryveth on swythe.* Presumably a stock formula, since it can be found once in *Wars of Alexander* (line 64), twice in *Alliterative Morte Arthure* (lines 761 and 816), and once in *Cleanness* (line 416).

58   *Cloudes clateren on loude as they cleve wolde.* As Neilson notes ("*Huchown*," p. 283), there is a possible echo here of *Destruction of Troy*, line 5787: "Cloudis with the clamour claterit above." Similar lines also appear in *Wars of Alexander*, line 555 ("Cloudis clenly to-cleve clatird unfaire"), and *Sir Gawain and the Green Knight*, line 2201 ("hit clatered in þe clyff as hit cleue schulde").

59   *The racke myd a rede wynde roos on the myddel.* A "red wind" is literally a strong wind that carries sand from the deserts of North Africa northward across the Mediterranean Sea. Alternatively, the adjective could indicate a "harsh wind," from ME *roide*. The former is supported by Neilson ("*Huchown*," p. 283) and K's (p. 92) observations of similarity to *Destruction of Troy*, line 1984, "A rak and a royde wynde rose in hor saile." The latter is supported by the possibility that the *Siege*-poet adds the detail of the "red wind" from a gloss on Boethius' *Consolation of Philosophy* 2.m.6.12–13, which describes Nero's crimes against Rome and the Senate: "Quos Notus sicco violentus aestu / Torret ardentes recoquens harenas" ["those burnt by the harsh south wind / That bakes the hot dry sands"].

63   *So the wedour and the wynd on the water metyn.* H (p. 95) notes an echo of *Cleanness*, line 371 ("For when þe water of þe welkyn with þe worlde mette") and *Patience*, line 141 ("Þe wyndes on þe wonne water so wrastel togeder").

64   *That alle hurtled on an hepe that the helm gemyd.* H (p. 95) observes parallel lines in *Patience*, line 149 ("Þen hurled on a hepe þe helme and þe sterne"), and *Cleanness*, line 1211 ("By þat watz alle on a hepe hurlande swyþee").

89   *The kyng into conseyl.* Titus pulls Nathan aside so that they may speak more privately.

93   *nyckes hym with nay.* Proverbial: see Whiting N34, who cites numerous instances in *Cursor Mundi.*

102   *in our londe.* Probably a Hellenistic community in Judaea, not Greece. See the explanatory note to line 45.

105   *And ho a mayde unmarred that never man touched.* Oakden (*Alliterative Poetry in Middle English*, p. 100) notes a possible echo of *Cleanness*, line 867: "Þat ar maydenez vnmard for alle men ȝette."

106   *ther cristalle of sprynges.* Proverbial; see Whiting C588. H rightly notes (p. 97) that the comparison is probably meant to call to mind "conventional depictions of the Annunciation as a light shining through glass."

108   *ho conceyved at ere.* The poet here refers to the Annunciation — in which her pregnancy is announced to Mary by the angel Gabriel (Luke 1:26–38) — as the conception itself, a convention not far from many visual depictions of the event that show the Holy Spirit in the form of a dove entering at Mary's ear.

109   *touched.* It is interesting to note that the L reading here conveys a more personal moment at the Incarnation than does the reading of D (*trouthe*), which is far more doctrinal.

116   *mene fram Hem passyth.* The *Siege*-poet here supports Augustine's Double Procession of the Holy Spirit (i.e., that the Holy Spirit proceeds from the Father *and* the Son rather than from the Father *through* the son). Double Procession had long been the predominant view in the Catholic Church and a persistent point of conflict between East and West since the phrase *filioque* ("and the son") was added to the Nicene-Constantinopolitan Creed (451) at the Third Council of Toledo in 589. The addition of *filioque* to the Creed is considered the primary motivator in the Great Schism of 1054. On the Procession of the Holy Spirit, see Bell, *Many Mansions*, pp. 193–207.

117   *Alle ben they endeles, and even of o myght.* H (p. 98) finds the term *even* "perhaps theologically objectionable," but the doctrine that the Trinity is consubstantial (*homoousios*), co-eternal, co-eternally distinct, and ever in unison leads back to Athanasius (d. 373) but was resolved into orthodoxy by the Cappadocian Fathers: Basil the Great (d. 379), Gregory of Nyssa (d. c.395), and Gregory of Nazianzus (d. 389). Since the consubstantiality of the Trinity had been accepted at the Council of Nicaea in 325 (a council that condemned the Arian position of subordination within the Trinity), the positions of Athanasius and the Cappadocian Fathers, which became the standard in the Catholic Church, are often collectively called the Nicene Faith. See Bell, *Cloud of Witnesses*, pp. 65–74.

125   *Wyne He wroght of water at o word ene.* At a wedding in Cana, Christ turned six jars of water into wine, an act that John names as the first sign of Christ's power. See John 2:1–11. No doubt the linking of this story — along with the feeding of the five thousand at lines 133–36 and perhaps even the healings in between — with the story of Marie and the plight of the starving, dehydrated Jews (lines 1081–1104) is meant to show the powerlessness of the Jews to acquire those things most necessary for survival, things that Christ could have provided them.

126   *Ten lasares at a logge He leched at enys.* For the cleansing of the ten lepers, see Luke 17:11–19. A parallel story is that of the healing of the single leper, found in Luke 5:12–13 (compare Matthew 8:2–4 and Mark 1:40–42).

127   *Pyned myd the palsy He putte hem to hele.* Christ's healing of the paralyzed man is recorded in Luke 5:18–25 (compare Matthew 9:2–8 and Mark 2:3–12).

128   *And ded men fro the deth ever ilke day rered.* The Gospels record at least three "raisings": Jairus' daughter (Luke 8:41–56; compare Matthew 9:18–25 and Mark 5:22–42), the widow's son at Nain (Luke 7:11–15), and Lazarus (John 11:1–44). The last of these is said by John to be the seventh sign of Christ's power.

129   *Croked and cancred He kevered hem alle.* Probably an oblique reference to the healing of both the crippled woman (Luke 13:11–13) and the man with dropsy (Luke 14:1–4).

130   *the dombe and the deve.* The healing of the deaf man is recorded in Mark 7:31–37. The healing of the dumb could refer to either the healing of the mute, demon-possessed man recorded in Mark 9:32–33 or the blind, mute, demon-possessed man of Luke 11:14 (compare Mark 12:22). Given the poet's attention to details from Luke, I am inclined to think that it is the latter story that the poet has in mind: "And he was casting out a devil: and the same was dumb. And when he had cast out the devil, the dumb spoke: and the multitudes, were in admiration at it."

132   *Nis no clerk with countours couthe aluendel rekene.* Perhaps this is meant to echo John 20:30 ("Many other signs also did Jesus in the sight of his disciples, which are not written in this book") or the last verse of John's Gospel, 21:25: "But there are also many other things which Jesus did which, if they were written every one, the world itself, I think, would not be able to contain the books that should be written."

133–36   *Fyf thousand of folke . . . bascketes twelve.* The feeding of the five thousand appears in all four Gospels: Matthew 14:15–21, Mark 6:35–44, Luke 9:12– 17, and John 6:5–13. John provides the detail that the bread was made from barley.

135   *yit ferre leved.* Nathan is surely not referring to any sort of physical immortality being granted to the five thousand. He is probably arguing that those who partook in the feeding followed Christ, and thus through Christ's sacrifice and resurrection attained life everlasting.

137–40   *Ther suwed Hym of a sorte seventy and twey . . . Ay by two and by two til hy were atwynne.* The story of the Seventy-two (or, according to some traditions, the Seventy) is found in Luke 10. In particular, the poet seems to be recalling the opening of the story, Luke 10:1: "And after these things, the Lord appointed also other seventy-two. And he sent them two and two before his face into every city and place whither he himself was to come." Four different lists that claim to record the names of these disciples were produced in the early years of the church: *Epiphanii textus*, the list of Pseudo-Hippolyti, the list of Pseudo-Dorothei, and *Textus Syriaci*. All four lists are reproduced in Schermann, *Prophetarum Vitae Fabulosae*. It is interesting to note, however, that Eusebius of Caeserea claims that "no list of the Seventy is anywhere extant" (*Ecclesiastical History* 1.12.1). At the very least, this reference further reinforces the poet's reliance on the Gospel of Luke.

141–56   *Hym suwed of another sorte . . . to-breste on the myddel.* The choosing of the Twelve
          Apostles, and the subsequent catalog of them, is found in Luke 6:12–16 (com-
          pare Matthew 10:1–4 and Mark 3:13–19).

143   *His Churche to encresche.* This may be a reference to the sending forth of the
          Apostles (Luke 9:1–6) or to the Great Commission that ends Matthew (28:19–20):
          "Going therefore, teach ye all nations: baptizing them in the name of the Father
          and of the Son and of the Holy Ghost. Teaching them to observe all things what-
          soever I have commanded you. And behold I am with you all days, even to the
          consummation of the world."

154   *Judas, that Jhesu Crist to the Jewes solde.* Judas Iscariot's selling of Christ to the
          authorities for the sum of thirty pennies is a detail that will be revisited at the
          end of the poem when the Jews are sold thirty to the penny in retribution (lines
          1319–20). The circumstances of Judas' betrayal are given little time in the Gos-
          pels, the fullest account coming at Luke 22:1–6. That the sum paid was thirty
          pennies derives from a Christological reading of Zacharias 11:12.

155   *Suth hymsulf he slowe for sorow of that dede.* For the story of Judas' suicide, see
          Matthew 27:3–10.

156   *to-breste on the myddel.* The detail that Judas' body burst when he hanged himself
          is not recorded in the Gospels but in Acts 1:16–19. Judas' death is also reported
          in Matthew 27:3–8, though there is some difficulty corroborating the two accounts
          since Acts claims that Judas died after the crucifixion of Christ, and Matthew's
          account places the suicide before the Crucifixion. The poet is surely using Acts
          as his source here, though the suicide of Judas is a staple feature of the mystery
          cycles, and is given a separate play in York, Towneley, and N-Town; it is not
          included in Chester, however.

157   *Crist hadde heried Helle.* The harrowing of Hell, in which Christ literally "turned
          over" Hell, has no clear Biblical source but was one of the most popular med-
          ieval images of Christ's victory over sin, death, and the devil, appearing in *Piers
          Plowman* B.18 (C.20), the mystery plays, *Cursor Mundi,* and even within poems
          devoted entirely to the subject such as *Harrowing of Hell*; these various accounts
          derive, ultimately, from the apocryphal *Gospel of Nicodemus* (or *Acta Pilati*), of
          which a number of Middle English translations survive. Though the *Siege*-poet
          surely knew the story from many different sources, his direct source here is *Vin-
          dicta Salvatoris,* which uses *Gospel of Nicodemus* not only for the harrowing of Hell
          but also for the story of Veronica and her veil.

158   *For that mansed man Mathie they chossyn.* According to Acts 1:21–26, Matthias was
          chosen to maintain a full complement of twelve apostles after the betrayal and
          subsequent suicide of Judas Iscariot.

159   *Barnabé and Poule.* The conversion of Barnabas is given at Acts 4:36–27, that of
          Saul at 9:1–19 and 1 Corinthians 15:8. The two men are frequently linked with
          one another in Acts as the primary missionaries among the Gentiles (see their
          joint commissioning at 13:1–3, and their work together on Paul's first missionary
          journey at 13:13–15:36). It is appropriate for Nathan to bring them up here

since the conversion of Titus and Vespasian is, in essence, an extension of the Gentile mission.

165   *that worliche wif.* Apocryphal traditions, including the poet's source, *Vindicta salvatoris*, and one of the *Vindicta*'s primary sources, *The Gospel of Nicodemus*, equate Veronica with the woman healed of a twelve-year bleeding by touching the hem of Jesus' garment (Matthew 9:20–22). The identification is surely the result of the two stories' focus on the healing power of clothes associated with Jesus.

166   *Hath His visage in hire veil — Veronyk ho hatte.* The Vernicle, the veil of Saint Veronica that had an image of the face of Christ, was one of the most famous relics in the Middle Ages and a focus of many pilgrimages. Receiving a medal struck with an image of the veil was a well-known mark of evidence for having been on a pilgrimage to Rome, where the relic was kept. Chaucer describes the Pardoner, for example, as having such a medal "sowed upon his cappe" (*CT* I[A]685). See the explanatory note to line 261.

194   *Cristen kyng that for Crist werred.* While the idea of a Christian king making war for Christ might seem paradoxical, going to war for Christ was a common conceit in medieval concepts of knighthood. Bernard of Clairvaux, for example, exhorts the creation of a new chivalric ideal in his *Liber ad milites Templi* ("Letter to the Knights Templar"), a work subtitled as *De laude novae militae* ("In Praise of the New Knighthood") and written in support of the establishment of the Knights Templar: "This is, I say, a new kind of knighthood and one unknown to the ages gone by. It ceaselessly wages a twofold war both against flesh and blood and against a spiritual army of evil in the heavens." See Bernard, *Works of Bernard of Clairvaux*, ch. 1.

203   *heyly Y afowe.* As K (p. 94) notes, this half-line might be associated with *Parlement of Thre Ages*, line 178: "And heghely I a-vowe."

205   *Peter was pope.* Traditional accounts place Peter's martyrdom around the year 65, under the direction of Nero. According to some stories, he was accompanied in his death by Paul, a stance that the *Siege*-poet seems to take in line 899. Jesus' election of Peter as first pope is a prominent position of Catholic orthodoxy, ultimately derived from Matthew 16:17–19 and 18:18.

215–17 *Twenti knyghtes were cud . . . tenfulle wayes.* The logic of these lines is very confusing. Nero has certainly sent the knights to Judaea to demand the resumption of tribute, but it might also imply that he has sent them to acquire Veronica and the Vernicle, too. The knights were apparently given some sort of safe conduct for their mission, but the Jews revoked this truce in addition to refusing the tribute. The knights, however, do succeed in retrieving both Veronica and her veil despite the difficulties involved.

239   *The mahound and the mametes to-mortled to peces.* As a result of the widely held misconception that Muslims worshiped Mohammed as a god, the prophet's name (here *mawmetis*, from the OF *Mahumet*) came to be used to indicate a pagan idol of any sort. Thus when Saint Benedict first arrives at Monte Cassino in *South English Legendary*'s Life of Saint Benedict (*Seyn Benet*), he smashes the "maumets"

that he finds there (lines 50–51). As Neilson notes ("*Huchown*," p. 283), this line of *Siege* may be borrowed from *Destruction of Troy*, line 4312: "Bothe Mawhownus & maumettes myrtild in peces."

251–52   *Than was wepyng and wo and wryngyng of hondis / With loude dyn and dit for doil of Hym one*. As Neilson points out ("*Huchown*," p. 283), these two lines appear in various guises in *Destruction of Troy*: "Of wepyng, & wayle, & wryngyng of hondes" (line 8719, compare also line 9611); "Miche water þai weppit, wringyng of hond: / The dit & the dyn was dole to be-hold!" (lines 8679–80); "Of the dite & þe dyn was dole to be-holde" (line 1347).

260   *into soper-tyme*. Literally, "until supper-time." Though one cannot deny a literal reference to eating, it is more likely that a theological sense is meant: the veil is a reminder of Christ's presence until the people are witness to the actual presence of Christ in the Eucharist, the re-enactment of the Last Supper (Luke 22:7–23). One might additionally read in this passage a reference to Christ's return at the end of time, an event referred to as a feast in Apocalypse 3:20.

261   *Vernycle after Veronyk*. Remarkably, this etymology is accurate: the *OED* lists "vernicle" as a loan word from OF *veron(n)icle*, itself a variant of OF *veronique*, from the Latin *veronica*. According to Sumption, the Vernicle eventually "replaced the horse of Constantine as the emblem of Rome" and became an extremely popular goal of pilgrimages, especially in the fifteenth century: "Langland's palmer pinned it to his hat, as did Chaucer's pardoner. Public displays of the [Vernicle] were occasions for mass exhibitions of fierce repentance which astonished more than one visitor to Rome." See *Pilgrimage*, pp. 249–50.

270   *To jugge who jewes myght best upon the Jewys take*. The internal punning in this line is marvelous: *jewes* means "judgment," while *Jewys* means "Jews." The *Siege*-poet seems to be using the pun to push a theological point; as H (p. 107) puts it, "Jews deserve only justice, and a justice administered by those committed to their victim Jesus." Even further, it is possible that the poet understood the parallel between the terms to have etymological significance, even if this is not actually the case.

275   *A bold burne on a blonke and of his body comyn*. Neilson ("*Huchown*," p. 324) notes an echo of *Parlement of the Thre Ages*, line 110: "A bolde beryn one a blonke bownne for to ryde."

279–80   *most thei hadde hit in hert . . . here forwardis to fulfille*. The point the poet is at pains to make is that the two men are going to war not for Nero or for the reestablishment of tribute to Rome. They are going to uphold their own vows to avenge Christ (Titus' promise is given at lines 185–88; Vespasian's is given at lines 201–04). Vespasian will again drive home this fact in a speech to his men just before the first battle in Jerusalem, lines 493–522. It goes hardly without saying that the poet's ultimate source, Josephus' *Wars of the Jews* 3.1.1, mentions no motive for Vespasian other than following Nero's orders to reestablish Roman superiority over the region.

281–88   *Than was rotlyng in Rome . . . that hem strengthe scholde*. This portrayal of a quartermaster mustering — the moving of armies to the shore, the pageantry of the leadership, and the subsequent (and very practical) stocking of the Roman armada — has a close parallel in *Alliterative Morte Arthure*, lines 729–35.

281   *brynnyis*. Coats of mail, from ON *brynja*.

283–84   *leften his sygne, / A grete dragoun of gold*. See the explanatory note to lines 393–420, below.

288   *By that schippis were schred, yschot on the depe*. H observes (p. 108) that a nearly identical line appears in *Destruction of Troy*, line 5385.

289–90   *floynes aflot . . . y-casteled alle*. This small catalog lists the various sorts of ships that make up the Roman fleet: *floins, farecostes, coggis*, and *crayers*. Cogs are the largest vessels, followed in size by farcosts and crayers. As K notes (p. 95), all four ship types make appearances within only a few lines of *Alliterative Morte Arthure* as ships in Arthur's fleet: "Cogges and crayers then crosses their mastes" (line 738) and "floynes and fercostes and Flemish shippes" (line 743).

293–94   *They tyghten up tal-sail whan the tide asked, / Hadde byr at the bake and the bonke lefte*. Compare *Destruction of Troy*, lines 12489–90: "Thai past on the pale se, puld vp hor sailes, / Hadyn bir at þere backe, and the bonke leut." Neilson also notes ("*Huchown*," p. 283) an echo at line 1902: "Hade bir at his bake, and þe bankes leuyt."

296   *port Jaf*. Jaffa, the port most closely associated with Jerusalem in the Middle Ages (now a district of Tel Aviv).

307   *noght bot roryng and rich in alle the riche tounnes*. I do not think it would be a stretch to mark a pun in this line on *rich-riche*. The former means "smoke," the latter "rich." For the *Siege*-poet, the Jewish riches are fittingly going up in flames.

313   *Josophus*. Historically, Flavius Josephus was the primary leader of the Jews in Jotapata during its siege by the Romans. After the fall of that city, Josephus was captured by the Romans. He eventually became a mediating voice between the Romans and Jerusalem, though his many attempts to persuade the Jewish leaders of Jerusalem to surrender failed. After the destruction of the Temple, Josephus held the imperial favor of both Vespasian and Titus. He was given Roman citizenship, and he authored a number of histories in Greek, the most famous of which are *Antiquities of the Jews* and *Wars of the Jews* (see *OCD*). The latter of these is especially important as it records the fall of Judaea from an eyewitness perspective (see especially Books 3–6). His historical role is somewhat garbled in *Siege of Jerusalem*, which presents him as one of the leaders of the Jews in Jerusalem throughout much of the siege, though the poem does focus on Simon and John as the primary leaders of the Jews in Jerusalem and allows Josephus his place as the voice of reason among the Jews.

314   *flowen as the foule*. Proverbial; see Whiting F578.

316   *With many toret and toure that toun to defende*. Neilson notes ("*Huchown*," p. 283) an echo of *Destruction of Troy*, line 1551: "Mony toures vp tild þe toune to defende." This is also an echo of *Wars of Alexander*, line 1151.

320   *At Paske-tyme.* For the establishment of Passover, see Exodus 12 and Numbers 28: 16–25. Josephus began the tradition that the siege began at Passover, and there is no strong reason to disbelieve his account since the Romans would likely have seen the holiday as a strategically good time to strike. Josephus' claim that the siege lasted just over 140 days, making the destruction of the Temple fall on the ninth of Av, is more subject to debate. For the *Siege*-poet, the beginning of Passover would be doubly fitting for the start of the siege, since it often marks the beginning of Passion week.

326   *pallen webbes.* Cloth woven from pall, a very expensive material.

329   *charboklis.* Carbuncles are magnificent stones said to glow in the dark. As a result of their unique properties, these stones are often mentioned as evidence of material (often exotic) wealth in texts of the late Middle Ages (*MED*).

330   *A gay egle of gold on a gilde appul.* This golden eagle is the famed symbol of the Roman legions.

342   *Deden mekly by mouthe.* The meekness of the Jews stands in sharp contrast to the condescension of Vespasian, who refuses to even meet with the messengers. Though the Jews ultimately refuse Vespasian's unreasonable demands, the poet avoids condemning them for it; it is possible that Vespasian's actions are here meant to undermine such authoritative behavior on the part of leaders.

350   *moder-naked alle.* Proverbial; see Whiting M721. It is worth noting that two Roman senators approach Arthur's force similarly unattired as a mark of submission in *Alliterative Morte Arthure*, lines 2306–13.

351   *yerdes.* Traditionally, rods (Hebrew *mate[h]*) were used as markers of authority for the Jewish tribal leaders. See, for example, Genesis 38:18, where Juda produces his staff as a pledge to a disguised Thamar. The rod of Aaron figures prominently in the history of Israel, both in the cursing of Egypt (Exodus 7:9–20) and in the confirmation of his priesthood (Numbers 17). The latter is echoed in the N-town Cycle, where the sons of David are ordered by Episcopus to "brynge here du offryng / With whyte yardys in þer honde" ("The Marriage of Mary and Joseph" 10.127–28), and to place them on the altar whereby the one that blooms will identify Mary's husband (see also Isaias 11:1, which speaks of the rod that will come from the root of Jesse). Also possibly of note here is Psalm 22:4 of the Vulgate, wherein David is confronted by the Lord's rod and staff.

360   *Cayphas.* Caiaphas, the high priest who took part in the trial of Jesus according to the Gospels: "Then were gathered together the chief priests and ancients of the people, into the court of the high priest, who was called Caiphas and they consulted together that by subtlety they might apprehend Jesus and put him to death" (Matthew 26:3–4). See also Matthew 26:27–66; Mark 14:60–64 (though Caiaphas is not named); John 11:47–53, 18:19–28.

360   *And of flocken here fax, and here faire berdis.* As K notes (p. 95–96), the shaming of the Roman messengers has a biblical parallel in 2 Kings (2 Samuel) 10:4: "Wherefore Hanon took the servants of David, and shaved off the one half of their beards, and cut away half of their garments even to the buttocks, and sent them away."

Arthur takes similar action against Roman messengers in *Alliterative Morte Arthure*, lines 2330–70.

365   *naked as a nedel*. As naked as a needle. Proverbial: Whiting N64.

368   *chese*. The *MED* cites this usage of *cheese* as a "cake or lump of cheese," but this does little to construe the meaning behind the detail. The pieces of cheese apparently act either as marks of shame (here H supposes [p. 113] that "one should also understand the cheeses as smelly globes, and thus mockery of the imperial orbs prevalent in Roman decoration") or as symbols of the authority of the Jewish leaders' return message (in much the same way that a wax seal authenticates a royal letter). The detail is not in Josephus' account, so where the author of the *Bible en François* (the *Siege*-poet's immediate source for this passage) found it remains tantalizingly unclear. According to *Orach Chaim* 670, it is Jewish custom to eat cheese on Chanukah in commemoration of an act whereby Judith, the daughter of Yochanon, fed an Assyrian governor cheese to make him sleepy; when he fell asleep she cut off his head (see the parallel tradition of Judith and the general Holofernes in the apocryphal Book of Judith, where she gives him wine to put him to sleep). Judith's success saved future brides from the exploitation of "first night's rights," which the Assyrian had claimed (see the account in the *Mishna Berura*). It is possible that this importance of cheese was misinterpreted at some point in time and made its way into the textual tradition of our story as a mark of authority, though the line remains painfully elusive.

389   *standard*. According to the *MED*, "a tower used in a siege," though this is the only attribution. No doubt the meaning arises from the standards (i.e., flags or banners) that were fixed atop siege towers.

390   *belfray*. Probably a type of siege tower (from OF *berfrei*), though it is possible that *Bild as a belfray* is meant to act as a simile: the Roman tower is built as solidly as a bell-tower.

393–420 *A dragoun was dressed . . . as the sonne bemys*. Golden dragons are a common insignia in the Middle Ages, but Hamel points out that the source of this passage is quite likely to be the description of Emperor Otho's standard in the French poem *Florence de Rome*, lines 1264–69. The dragon banner obviously calls to mind Arthur's association with dragon standards (his own Welsh standard, for example), but in *Alliterative Morte Arthure* (line 2026) it is the Roman emperor Lucius Iberius, not Arthur, whose standard is a "dragon of gold." As Hamel notes, the chronicle sources (such as Geoffrey of Monmouth) agree that the golden dragon standard should be Arthur's, and the swapping of the standard to represent Roman imperial power is best explained by the indebtedness of *Alliterative Morte Arthure* to *Siege*; see *Morte Arthure*, ed. Hamel, pp. 46–52. It should also be noted that the dragon here described bears some affinity for the dragon that appears to Arthur in a dream in *Alliterative Morte Arthure* (lines 760–97). For other similar echoes between the two poems' dragons, see the explanatory notes to lines 283–84 and to line 396.

396   *A fauchyn under his feet*. I have glossed this as describing a falchion held by the dragon, but it is interesting to note that a "faucon" makes an appearance in the

description of the dragon in *Alliterative Morte Arthure* (line 788) and is usually glossed there as "falcon." Hamel posits that the detail of the falchion in *Siege* may also be from the French poem that probably acts as a source for this passage, *Florence de Rome*, which describes a lance atop its golden standard; see explanatory note to lines 393–420, above.

413   *I-brytaged.* "Provided with a parapet or barricade, fortified" (*MED*). In addition to a "defensive structure on a wall or tower, such as a parapet or bastille," *bretage* (from OF *bretesche*) can denote "a defensive structure on the back of an elephant." (*MED*).

419   *glitered as gled fure.* Proverbial; see Whiting G148–52.

421   *the foure gates.* Not, as H points out (p. 115), an accurate understanding of Jerusalem's layout. It would, however, be a layout familiar to the poet's readers.

431   *Josophat.* Though it is only one of several possible locations for the Last Judgment (another primary option being the Mount of Olives), the valley of Josaphat (or Jehoshaphat) was widely accepted during the Middle Ages as the most likely location for Christ's triumphant return, an opinion with the weight of scripture behind it:

> For behold in those days, and in that time when I shall bring back the captivity of Juda and Jerusalem: I will gather together all nations, and will bring them down into the valley of Josaphat. . . . Let them arise, and let the nations come up into the valley of Josaphat: for there I will sit to judge all nations round about. (Joel 3:1–2)

For more information about the traditions surrounding the location of the Last Judgment, see Hall, "Medieval Traditions about the Site of Judgment." The poet's immediate source here is *Legenda aurea*, but a parallel reference to Josaphat can be found in *Cursor Mundi*, line 22969. Placing this battle in the valley of Christ's final judgment upon humanity would be fitting for the poet since the course of the poem is preparing for the passing of final judgment upon the Jews. From a structural standpoint, this battle marks the beginning of the end of the poem, as the events of Caiaphas' capture represent the final piece in establishing the stage for the remainder of the poem's progress (for more on the structure of the poem, see Introduction, pp. 30–36). It is quite likely, as Hamel has noted, that the oddly out-of-place mention of "jousting . . . In the vale of Josephate" in *Alliterative Morte Arthure* (lines 2875–76) is another clue to the influence of *Siege* on that text (*Morte Arthure*, ed. Hamel, p. 50).

434–41   *sixtene thousand soudiours . . . And ten thousand atte tail.* The poet lists 16,000 men in the vanguard (i.e., at the front of the force) under the command of Titus, with another 16,000 in the main force of the army under Vespasian's command. Sabinus of Syria commands the rearguard, consisting of 16,000 more men, 4,000 of which are his own Syrians, with a final 10,000 men maintaining watch over the train and camp. The resulting Roman force of 58,000 men would have impressed upon any medieval reader the remarkable amount of manpower that the Romans bring to bear on the city. It is also meant to pale in comparison with the number of Jews — the Romans will win despite being greatly outnumbered.

445–88   *The Jewes assembled were sone . . . ne uneth the cité knowe.* Despite the huge numbers in the Roman force, they are clearly outnumbered in the battle: the Jews have 100,000 men on horseback, 25 elephants that each carry 200 men (5,000 men), another 100,000 dromedaries each holding 20 men (2,000,000 men), plus an undetermined number of camels each carrying 10 men. Not counting men on foot (though see the explanatory note to lines 613–15, below) and conservatively estimating 10 camels, the Jewish force is said to number 2,105,100; this gross exaggeration — Davis (*Besieged*, pp. 8–13) estimates the Jewish fighting force as 23,400 men — is certainly meant only to show the vastly superior numbers of Jews. For a brief discussion of how the Jewish army's exotic nature associates them with Saracens, see Chism, "*The Siege of Jerusalem*: Liquidating Assets," pp. 320–21. For more extended arguments on the association, see Hamel, "*The Siege of Jerusalem* as a Crusading Poem," and Nicholson, "Haunted Itineraries." Most of these arguments seem to ignore the poet's biblical sources for such material, however; see the explanatory note to line 449, below.

449   *Fyf and twenti olyfauntes.* That armed elephants have a role in the battle does not appear in the poet's sources, and was likely suggested to the poet from either 1 Maccabees 6 or Josephus' retelling of it in *Antiquities of the Jews* 12.9, where Antiochus V Eupator (who was probably nine years old, having just become king after the death of his father, Antiochus IV Epiphanes) uses fortified elephants in a battle against the Jews in Beth-zechariah, ten miles southwest of Jerusalem. This story details not only the elephants with wooden structures (see the explanatory note to line 460), but also the killing of one particularly large beast from beneath (1 Maccabees 6:43–46) — a feat that is probably echoed in Sir Sabinus' assault in lines 565–72. Whether the poet is utilizing 1 Maccabees or Josephus is not clear. As K notes (p. 96), fortified elephants also figure prominently in Alexander's fight against Darius in *King Alisaunder*, lines 2025–30 and 2521–38. It might be that, for the poet and his audience, elephants simply have the ring of Alexander and of the distant East, and that their presence at such a battle is therefore expected.

460   *toret of tre.* Other manuscripts read various forms of *hurdigh*, meaning some sort of wooden structure, often made of wicker, that acted as a palisade (from OF *hourdeis*). "A hurdle used for defense in battles and sieges; also, a palisade, bulwark, or other structure made of hurdles" (*MED*). In this case, what is meant are the fortified wooden structures atop the backs of the beasts.

469–72   *A which of white selvere . . . with brennande sergis.* H notes (pp. 117–18) that although this chest may owe something to the Ark of the Covenant (see Exodus 25), the description is mainly derived from 1 Maccabees 6:43.

477–78   *Lered men of the lawe . . . and the psalmys tolde.* Aside from being plainly anachronistic, this portrayal of the Jewish priests as Breviary-reading Christian clerics also borders on the heavily ironic. The *Siege*-poet would seem to be questioning the legitimacy of such learning, the very qualities he himself possesses.

479   *Of doughty David the kyng.* Alliterative *Morte Arthure* names David as the sixth of the nine worthies, and uses the same adjective to describe him: "The sixt was David

the dere, deemed with kinges / One of the doughtiest that dubbed was ever" (lines 3416–17). Both poems probably borrow the description from *Parlement of the Thre Ages*, which speaks of "David the doughty" (line 442).

480   *Josue, the noble Jewe.* Joshua, son of Nun, successor to Moses, and fifth of the nine worthies in *Alliterative Morte Arthure* (lines 3414–15).

Judas the knyght. Judas Maccabeus, whose name means "the hammerer," the primary leader of the Maccabean Revolt (167–164 BC) against the Seleucids. The chief sources for information on Judas are 1 and 2 Maccabees and Josephus' retelling of the same in *Antiquities of the Jews*. Caiaphas is presumably reading the story of how Judas turned back the Seleucid armies in the battle at Beth-zechariah. Judas Maccabeus is listed as the fourth of the nine worthies in *Alliterative Morte Arthure* (lines 3412–13). For more on Judas' role in history and in our poem, see Introduction, p. 3, and the explanatory note to line 449.

481   *rolle.* This detail, not in the poet's known sources, is startling in that it suggests that the *Siege*-poet has a fair idea of what a Jewish Torah looks like. One wonders how this is possible.

489–522   *Waspasian dyvyseth . . . hede to His owne.* On how Vespasian's speech reveals the foundational differences between the Jewish and Christian mythologies, see Van Court, "*The Siege of Jerusalem* and Augustinian Historians," pp. 230–31.

493–94   *Here nys king nother knyght comen to this place, / Baroun ne bachelere ne burne that me folweth.* As K notes (p. 96), the source for these lines is undoubtedly *Wynnere and Wastoure*, lines 327–28: "Ne es nothir kaysser, ne kynge, ne knyghte that the folowes, / Barone, ne bachelere, ne beryn that thou loueste."

495   *Crist forto venge.* King Arthur similarly decides to avenge the death of Christ by invading the Holy Land in *Alliterative Morte Arthure* (lines 3216–17), but his plan is condemned by the poem as vain and misguided and is closely followed by the news that his kingdom has been usurped by Mordred.

504   *That preveth His Passioun, whoso the Paas redeth.* It is unclear whether a particular passage of the scriptures is being referred to here for the reading of the Pasch, or if the whole of the Easter liturgy itself is meant. Christ's Passion — His sufferings in the period from the Last Supper to His death on the Cross — are intimately connected with the Paschal Feast (Easter), when His resurrection is celebrated. The word *Pasch* derives from the Jewish feast of Passover (Heb. *Pesach*), which was traditionally celebrated by the eating of a paschal lamb (Exodus 12: 1–28). Christian exegetes interpreted the serving of the paschal lamb as a prefiguration of the Passion of Christ, the Lamb of God (John 1:29). H supposes (p. 119) that the term is meant to convey Latin passus, the division of an alliterative poem, though this seems an unnecessarily complex reading.

505   *Hit nedith noght at this note of Nero to mynde.* Vespasian drops the political reasons for the expedition on the basis that all things temporal, including the temporal rule of the emperor, Nero, must ultimately submit to the rule of Christ, the King of Kings (Apocalypse 19:16). The need to avenge Christ, then, supersedes all political aims: even if the Jews gave up their rebellion against Rome and agreed

to pay tribute to the emperor once more, the siege would go on. Vespasian admits that his action is against the orders of the emperor.

510   *to Rome the realté fallyth*. It is possible that Vespasian's argument that mastery of all lands under Heaven belongs to Rome is meant to carry double meaning to readers: in the historical context of the poem's action, Vespasian is speaking of the Roman Empire; in the historical context of the poem's readership, Vespasian is speaking of the papacy in Rome.

511   *Bothe the myght and the mayn*. Neilson notes ("*Huchown*," p. 283) this as an echo of *Destruction of Troy*, line 5825: "all the might & the mayn."

515   *pesan*. Pizane (from OF *pizane*). "A piece of metal or mail attached to the helmet and extending over the neck and upper breast" (*MED*).

520   *Bot alle in storijs of stoure and in strength one*. As K notes (p. 97), there is possibly a distant echo of *Destruction of Troy* (line 9015) here: "stowrnes of strenght." The Jewish reliance on stories of battle rather than on battles themselves is immediately reflected in Caiaphas' reading of the past glory of Moses, David, Joshua, and Judas Maccabeus in lines 477–84.

529   *With loude clarioun cry and alle kyn pypys*. In some manuscripts, the pipes are more specifically designated to be cornmuse pipes. Carter defines these instruments as trumpets (*Dictionary of Middle English Musical Terms*, p. 80) and bagpipes with drones (p. 97), respectively. The line is probably echoed by lines 1809–10 of *Alliterative Morte Arthure*: "With cornus and clariouns these new-made knightes / Lithes unto the cry."

530   *Tymbris*. Carter defines a *timbre* (timbrel) as a "small percussion instrument consisting of a wooden cylinder, covered on one end with skin or parchment, and usually equipped with metal disks and a catgut snare; it was played by beating with the hands or by shaking to produce a jingling effect; a rudimentary tambourine" (*Dictionary of Middle English Musical Terms*, p. 500).

      tabourris. According to Carter, the main definition of *tabour* is a "small drum, an instrument of minstrelsy" (*Dictionary of Middle English Musical Terms*, p. 486), though it is the secondary meaning, "a larger drum used for military purposes (perhaps one with two skins and a cylinder of sufficient depth to provide the volume necessary for military signals, such as the German grosse Hersumper of the 14th century)" (p. 488), that is surely meant here.

536   *As thonder and thicke rayn throbolande in skyes*. Neilson ("*Huchown*," p. 283) hears an echo of *Destruction of Troy*, line 7619 (and compare line 12496, as well): "A thondir with a thicke Rayn thrublit in þe skewes."

547   *as a bore loketh*. For various proverbial comparisons with boars, see Whiting B387–92.

549   *Alle brightned the bent as bemys of sonne*. It is somewhat ambiguous whether the battlefield is brightened by the actual illumination of sunbeams or by the metaphorical illumination of falling blood.

553   *fanward*. The vanguard of a military force (from OF *avangarde*).

557   *Spakly here speres on sprotes they yeden*. Neilson ("*Huchown*," p. 284) notes a number of possible lines in *Destruction of Troy* as a source here: "Speires vnto sprottes sprongen" (line 1195; compare also lines 5783, 6406, 7248, 9666, and 11022). A similar construction also shows up in *Wars of Alexander*, line 790: "Al to spryngis in sprotis speres."

558   *Scheldes as schidwod on scholdres to-cleven*. Neilson ("*Huchown*," p. 284) notes an echo in *Wars of Alexander*, line 789 ("Sone into sheverand shidez shaftez to-bristen") as well as one in *Awntyrs of Arthur*, line 501 ("Schaftis of schene wode thay scheverende in schides").

564   *And goutes fram gold wede as goteres they runne*. K (p. 97) notes a possible echo of *Wars of Alexander*, line 4796: "As gotis out of guttars in golnand wedres." The usage is proverbial; see Whiting G495.

577–81   *The burnes in the bretages . . . dyed in that stounde*. The detailed exactness of this passage is remarkable: the dust and confusing noise of the battle effectively blinds even those who are atop the wooden towers on the field. The great beasts, similarly blinded, fall amid the chaos of blood, bodies, and weapons, and they take the towers down with them, scattering the men upon the ground. The men, locked in steel and unable to move quickly, are then trampled by the beasts.

570   *Girdith out the guttes with grounden speres*. Neilson ("*Huchown*," p. 284) sees this as an echo of *Destruction of Troy*, line 9406: "He gird hym thurgh the guttes with a grym speire."

580   *hurdighs*. See explanatory note to line 460.

582   *Was non left upon lyve that alofte standeth*. As K notes (p. 98), the line is very much like that found in *Destruction of Troy*, line 4764: "Was no lede opon lyfe þat a lofte stode."

594   *Chaire and chaundelers and charbokel stones*. As both Neilson ("*Huchown*," p. 284) and K (p. 98) note, this line may be derived from *Destruction of Troy*, line 3170: "Chaundelers full chefe and charbokill stones."

603   *So was the bent over-brad, blody by-runne*. Neilson ("*Huchown*," p. 284) notes the similarity to *Destruction of Troy*, line 11141: "All the bent of þat birr blody beronnen." *Alliterative Morte Arthure*, line 1863, appears to echo either *Troy* or *Siege* here, too: "The bente and the brode feld all on blood runnes!" The b-verse is formulaic.

608   *merevail were ellis*. This construction is a rather formulaic half-line of a similar type to that which occurs in *Alliterative Morte Arthure*, line 3595.

612   *complyn tyme*. Compline is the last of the seven daily offices formalized by the Rule of St. Benedict, to be completed just before the monastic house retired for the night. The service consists of psalms appropriate for the time of day, an evening hymn, and a canticle based on Luke 2:9 (*Nunc dimittis* [Now, Lord, let your servant depart in peace]). K notes (p. xxiii) the appropriateness of a reference to compline within this context, as the battle "stages the beginning of this divine

judgment on the Jews in the scene of the last judgment of all," the valley of Josaphat (see the explanatory note to line 431). One might also note that, in the structure of the poem, this reference to compline falls just as the poem moves into the central event of the work: the execution of Caiaphas and the setting of a siege upon Jerusalem.

613–15   *An hundred thousand helmes . . . Save seven thousand of the somme, that to the cité flowen.* This 100,000 may refer to the men on horseback (see the explanatory note to lines 445–88), or it may be the number of footmen involved in the battle. Regardless, the small number of survivors is just as exaggerated as the total numbers involved in the battle (the poet's source reads 53,000): 93,000 dead out of 100,000 would rate this not only as one of the bloodiest days of battle in history, but also one of the most lopsided. By contrast, some estimates of the death toll at the Battle of Towton on 29 March 1461 in Yorkshire, in which Edward IV won his crown over Lancastrian forces, hover around 28,000; the first day British losses at the Battle of the Somme have gone down to history as 57,470 out of roughly 100,000 men engaged, of which 19,420 were dead; and even the fall of Singapore on 15 February 1942 saw "only" 60,000 soldiers of the British army taken captive. Given such numbers, it might be more proper to term the engagement described in the poem as a massacre.

617–19   *Ledes lepen to anon . . . with brouden chaynes.* As K notes (p. 98), these lines are reminiscent of *Destruction of Troy*, lines 10462–64: "Þai wan in wightly, warpit to þe yates, / Barrit hom full bigly with boltes of yerne; / Braid vp the brigges in a breme hast."

620   *portecolis with pile.* A portcullis with pins that set into holes in the ground, helping to stabilize the gate against battering rams.

624–25   *With grete stones of gret and of gray marble. / Kepten kenly with caste the kernels alofte.* Neilson ("*Huchown*," p. 284) notes an echo of *Wars of Alexander*, line 1395: "Kenely thai kepe with castyng of stanes."

625   *kernels.* Battlements, especially crenelations (from OF *crenel*).

626   *querels.* A square-headed crossbow bolt (from OF *quarel*).

        quarters. A crossbow (from OF *quartot*).

643   *besauntes.* A bezant is literally a "gold coin of Byzantium," but the use of the word is extended in Middle English to include "several similar coins minted in Western Europe" as well as "various Biblical coins" (*MED*). The *MED* also cites usage of the word to denote "a bezant used as an ornament, an ornament resembling a bezant."

649   *toures of tre that they taken hadde.* That is, the wooden towers taken from the fallen elephants, now pressed into service by the besieging Romans.

651   *garrite.* A watchtower used in siege operations (from OF *garite*).

658   *And arwes unarwely with attyr envenymyd.* Neilson ("*Huchown*," p. 284) notes an echo of *Wars of Alexander*, line 1390: "Archers with arowes of atter envenmonyd."

670   *Schoten up scharply to the schene walles.* Neilson ("*Huchown*," p. 284) notes an echo
           of *Destruction of Troy*, line 4739: "Shottyn vp sharply at the shene wallis." See the
           explanatory note to line 820, as well. A similar line also shows up in *Wars of
           Alexander*, line 1391: "Schotis vp scharply at shalkis on þe wallis."

671   *arblastes.* A crossbow (from OF *arbaleste*).

674–77   *Hote playande picche . . . right as schyre water.* Though familiar to modern audiences
           from countless presentations in the movies, using burning oil to defend against
           a siege is first recorded in Josephus' defense of Jotapata, which ultimately lies
           behind this passage of Josephus' wiles (see note to line 789–96, below).

681–92   *By that wrightes han wroght a wonder strange pale . . . That they no water myght wynne
           that weren enclosed.* Aside from acting as a fulfillment to the prophecy of Jesus in
           Luke 19:41–44, this central climax of the hysteron proteron structure of the
           poem (see Introduction, pp. 30–36) might also echo back to Jeremias 4:16–17:
           "Say ye to the nations: Behold it is heard in Jerusalem, that guards are coming
           from a far country, and give out their voice against the cities of Juda. They are
           set round about her, as keepers of fields: because she hath provoked me to
           wrath, saith the Lord."

682   *bastiles.* Tall towers (from F *bastille*).

710   *tourmented on a tre, topsail walten.* It is possible that the description here is of an
           inverted crucifixion, though an upside-down hanging is also possible. As ven-
           geance for the death of Christ, an inverted crucifixion would seem appropriate,
           though it would also carry vestiges of the death of St. Peter, who is said to have
           demanded that he be crucified upside-down so as not to seem the equal of Christ.

724   *for the bischop soule.* That is, for the soul of Saint James the Less (James the Just,
           brother of the Lord), who was the supposed first bishop of Jerusalem (a fact prob-
           ably inferred from Acts 12:17 and 21:18). James was said to have been martyred
           in AD 57 at the Temple by a mob of Jews angry that Paul had escaped local pun-
           ishment by appealing to Rome and Caesar. James was thrown from the top of
           the pinnacle of the Temple, and then stoned to death while he prayed for Christ
           to forgive those who were persecuting him. Jacobus de Voragine's *Legenda aurea*
           recounts the story, noting that "Josephus states that it was in punishment of the
           murder of Saint James that the destruction of Jerusalem was permitted" (trans.
           Ryan and Ripperger, p. 264). Jacobus then proceeds to tell his account of the
           destruction. The passage of Josephus referred to is in *Antiquities of the Jews* 20.9.1.

727   *In tokne of tresoun and trey that they wroght.* Caiaphas, as head of the priests, is
           given primary responsibility for the death of Christ in the poem.

729–37   *By that was the day don . . . to cacchen hem reste.* As noted in the Introduction (pp. 11–
           13), these lines are almost assuredly influenced by *Destruction of Troy*, lines
           7348–56.

735   *Chosen chyventayns out.* The chieftains chosen before the Romans retire are the
           chiefs of the watch, a fact made clear in the next line, where mention is made of
           the "chekwecche": literally, the "check-watch," an officer whose duty is to check
           the status of the posted nightwatchmen.

745–64   *Waspasian bounys of bedde . . . with saphyres sett the sydes aboute.* The arming topos is a popular one in late medieval literature, perhaps made most famous by the extended arming of Sir Gawain in *Sir Gawain and the Green Knight*. For an overview, see Brewer, "The Arming of the Warrior."

757   *The glowes of gray steel, that were with gold hemmyd.* Oakden (*Alliterative Poetry in Middle English*, p. 100) notes that *Alliterative Morte Arthure*, line 912, might pick up this line from *Siege*: "His gloves gaylich gilt and graven at the hemmes."

760   *avental.* An aventail (from OF *esventail*), the "lower front piece of a helmet" or more simply "a vent or an air hole in a helmet" (*MED*). The *MED* also lists usage of the word to designate "a piece of chain mail protecting the lower face, neck, and part of the upper chest, later extending around the upper back." A "vent" in armor also appears, quite famously, in *Alliterative Morte Arthure*, lines 4249–51, where Arthur raises up Mordred's "fente" in order to kill him. Though most commentators have read this as the faceplate of the helm (in agreement with the *MED*), Sutton ("Mordred's End") has recently argued persuasively that the "*fente* is the cover protecting Mordred's backside." Though the context here makes such a reading unlikely, it is not entirely out of the realm of possibility.

770   *the bras rynges.* Not brass rings, but ringing brass; that is, the gates of the city are supposed to be made of brass. H speculates (p. 132) that, since a similar depiction of brazen gates appears in the Egerton *Mandeville's Travels*, "such architectural features may have [been] recognized as uniquely Palestinian."

774   *thogh ye fey worthe.* I have glossed this in the sense of "even if you are dying," but it is possible that it could be glossed as "though you work magic." In either case, the sense is clear: the Jews cannot get food or water through the siege.

777–80   *The pale that I pight have . . . in scholde ye tourne.* The syntax is difficult to follow here, but the sense is clear enough: Vespasian boasts that even if any of the Jews were to pass through the palisade that he has built to enclose the town and the odds were forty Romans against five hundred Jews and the Jews were all giants, *still* the Jews would be turned back.

786   *the devel have that recche.* This idiomatic, perhaps proverbial phrase means "may the devil take anyone who cares"; see *MED: recchen*, v. 2. K notes (p. 99) a correspondence with *Parlement of the Thre Ages*, line 447: "And he was dede of that dynt: the deuyll hafe that reche." The phrase also appears in *King Edward and the Shepherd*, line 312, and *Piers Plowman* A.7.112. It might be possible to read *recche* as "wretch" (deriving from OE *wrecca* rather than OE *reccan*) though the *MED* does not list the spelling as an alternative for the expected ME *wrecche*. And compare, for instance, this poem's own orthography in "wrecchys," line 302.

789–96   *By that a Jewe, Josophus, the gentyl clerke . . . water schold fayle.* The story of Josephus' clever attempts to convince the Romans that the siege is ineffective is actually, as K notes (pp. 99–100), a detail that ultimately derives from historical events at the siege of Jotapata; see Josephus, *Wars of the Jews* 3.7.10–20. Such ruses would be familiar to readers of many medieval romances, however. In *The Avowyng of Arthur*, lines 1051–1126, for example, Baldwin tells how he and his garrison, trapped by an opposing army, caused the siege to be lifted by putting out the last of their food and drink for a sumptuous feast attended by an emissary of the besiegers. Seeing such an abundance of supplies being so wantonly wasted, the emissary reported that the siege would never succeed; the invading army left.

822   *Fought right felly, foyned with speres.* Neilson ("*Huchown,*" p. 286) notes an echo of *Destruction of Troy*, line 10287 (compare also lines 4753 and 5795): "ffell was the fight foynyng of speires."

830   *as the storyj telleth.* The source referred to here is Higden's *Polychronicon*, though a number of different sources have been used in the compilation of the poem as a whole. See Introduction, pp. 21–23.

840   *archelers.* As K notes (p. 100), the term derives from Medieval Latin *archelharia*, meaning a type of balista.

841   *spryngoldes.* I.e., missiles (usually heavy stones) thrown from catapults (from AN *springalde*).

842   *Dryven dartes adoun, geven depe woundes.* Neilson ("*Huchown,*" p. 284) notes an echo of *Destruction of Troy*, line 4741: "Dryuen vp dartes, gyffen depe woundes." See the explanatory note to line 670, as well.

855–56 *Bot daunsyng and no deil with dynnyng of pipis / And the nakerer noyse alle the nyght-tyme.* Neilson ("*Huchown,*" p. 324) notes a possible echo of *Sir Gawain and the Green Knight*, line 118: "Nwe nakryn noyse with þe noble pipes."

856   *nakerer.* A kettledrum player (from OF *naquere*). A "naker" is a "type of kettledrum introduced into Europe by the crusaders, consisting, in varying sizes, of a hemispherical body of metal or wood with skin stretched tightly over the top" (Carter, *Dictionary of Middle English Musical Terms*, p. 317).

862   *That were freschere to fight than at the furst tyme.* H (p. 136) notes a parallel line in *Destruction of Troy*, line 9862.

881   *For ther as fayleth the fode ther is feynt strengthe.* Proverbial: Whiting F390.

882   *And ther as hunger is hote, hertes ben feble.* Proverbial: Whiting H645.

886   *masers.* A soldier equipped with a mace (from OF *massier*).

889   *we wol hunten at the hart.* As Lawton explains, the detail of the besiegers going hunting and hawking during the siege is true to conventions; see "Titus Goes Hunting and Hawking."

891   *Ride to the rever and rere up the foules.* Compare *Parlement of Thre Ages*, lines 208 and 217: "And ryde to a revere redily thereaftir . . . To the revere with thaire roddes to rere up the fewles." See explanatory note to line 889.

900   *Senek.* Nero ordered that Seneca, his tutor and advisor, kill himself on the accusation that Seneca had worked to replace him on the throne with Calpurnius Piso. Seneca loyally complied (a fate shared by Lucan). Subsequent medieval writers, drawn to Seneca's literary works, were quick to add the act to a long list of crimes

worthy of condemnation on Nero's part. Seneca is subsequently cited in *Mum and the Sothsegger* (a work reacting against Richard II's haughty treatment of advisors) as an example of right counsel (see lines 205 and 1212).

901   *His modire*. The murder of his mother Agrippina was a popular medieval image of Nero's brutality: he is said to have caused his mother's womb to be cut open and dissected so that he could see where he had come from — that she died in the process did not seem to disturb him. This terrible event was often used as an exemplum on why physicians should not perform dissection on human bodies.

   his mylde wif. Probably a reference to Nero's second wife, Poppaea Sabina. She pushed his first wife Octavia off of the throne, then (supposedly) encouraged Nero to kill his mother and Seneca (see explanatory notes to line 900 and 901, above). In AD 65, Nero kicked her to death while she was pregnant with their second child. Before becoming Nero's mistress and wife, Poppaea was married to the future emperor, Otho.

904   *To quelle the emperour quyk*. Nero died on 9 June 68, beginning the Year of Four Emperors in which civil wars led to the short terms of Galba, Otho, and Vitellius.

913   *with his teth he toggeth and byteth*. Though the *Siege*-poet is here relying heavily on the death of Nero in *Legenda aurea*, he has worked hard to paint Nero as a trapped animal. See the explanatory notes to lines 900 and 901.

926   *Gabba*. Servius Sulpicius Galba (r. 68–69). After Nero's suicide, Galba was quick to march on Rome (he had earlier in the year joined Julius Vindex in instigating a revolt against Nero) and proclaim himself the new Roman emperor. Like Nero, Galba is well known to the Middle Ages for his avarice. One of his early supporters, Otho, turned against him and gathered the support of the praetorians who ultimately murdered Galba (*OCD*). See the explanatory note to line 927.

927   *Othis Lucyus*. Marcus Salvius Otho (r. 69). Once a supporter of Galba's claim to the throne, Otho grew angry when Galba named Calpurnius as his successor. He pushed the praetorians to revolt against Galba, resulting in the emperor's murder (*OCD*). As K notes (p. xxi), the name "Otho Lucius" clearly marks this passage as indebted to Higden's *Polychronicon*. Otho's personal involvement in the death of his predecessor also makes this debt clear, since the other identified sources for the *Siege* make no mention of his presence at the murder. See the explanatory note to line 926.

938   *Vitel*. Aulus Vitellius (r. 69). After Otho's suicide, Vitellius was proclaimed emperor by his troops and made a march on Rome. He failed to gather the support of the eastern legions, however, who began to proclaim Vespasian as the new emperor. As prefect of Rome, Vespasian's eldest brother, Titus Flavius Sabinus, came into direct conflict with Vitellius and was killed. Ultimately, however, his forces defeated those soldiers loyal to Vitellius and the emperor "was dragged through the streets, humiliated, tortured, and killed" (*OCD*).

939   *Sire Sabyn*. The *Siege*-poet conflates two men with the name Sabinus. The historical Sabinus referred to here is Vespasian's eldest brother, Titus Flavius Sabinus, who was executed by Vitellius (see explanatory note to line 938). Elsewhere,

however, the poet refers to a Sir Sabinus of Syria, developed from a minor character who ultimately comes from Josephus' account (*Wars of the Jews* 6.1.6). This latter Sabinus was simply a warrior who defeats a number of Jews prior to his death on the walls and whose example spurs the Romans to conquer the Fortress Antonia. A similar story is told in this poem at lines 1197–1216.

943   *naked as an nedul.* See the explanatory note to line 365.

945   *his guttes alle.* Vitellius was a notorious glutton, a fact brought out by his murderers in the peculiarities of their butchery.

979   *And me the gates ben get and golden the keyes.* This line appears to be an echo of lines 398 and 575 in *Parlement of the Thre Ages*: "While hym the gatis were yete and yolden the keyes."

989–90 *who doth by another / Schal be soferayn hymself, sein in the werke.* The line seems to be proverbial, though nothing similar is attested in either Whiting or Tilley's *Dictionary of the Proverbs in England*. It certainly has the ring of a legal formulation: anyone who has another act on his behalf is fully responsible after the fact. See the explanatory note to lines 991–92, where this principle is given a concrete example.

991–92 *For as fers is the freke atte ferre ende / That of fleis the fel as he that foot holdeth.* The example (a proverb, see Whiting F112) is meant to prove the truth of the "legal judgment" in the previous two lines by pointing out that the man (*freke*) who stands apart from someone (*atte ferre ende*) and flays the flesh from their foot (usually using a leather whip of some kind) is just as fierce as the man who is holding them down for the torture (*he that foot holdeth*). H remarks (p. 142) that the "comparison, valorizing, not simply physical savagery, but psychological viciousness, seems stated in reverse," but the apparent reversal actually fits neatly with Sabinus' point. Even if Vespasian must return to Rome and act from afar, it is he who is truly responsible for what Sabinus and those on the ground in Jerusalem accomplish. Sabinus and the others might be the hands-on party (holding the foot, as it were), but the true ferocity of the Roman force will always be Vespasian. See the explanatory note to lines 989–90. H notes "the different discussion of counsel as a form of agency" in *Mum and the Sothsegger*, lines 743–50.

994   *Domyssian, his brother.* Titus Flavius Domitian (r. 81–96), a younger brother of Titus.

1006   *Made weys throw the walles for wenes and cartes.* Neilson ("*Huchown*," p. 286) notes an echo of *Wars of Alexander*, line 1324: "And makez a way wyde enogh waynez for to mete."

1013   *fayn as the foul of day.* Proverbial; see Whiting F561 and F566.

1047   *A man to the mody kyng that he moste hated.* The identity of the man whom Titus so passionately despises is not given. We might speculate that the man is Pilate — given Titus' visceral reaction to him and the overriding need to secure safe conduct for his transportation to and from the besieged city — but the episode ends with Titus forgiving the anonymous man. Given Titus' eventual actions toward

Pilate, this would be difficult to understand. The poet's primary source for this part of the poem, *Legenda aurea*, says that the unnamed man is a former servant of Titus that had been thrown in prison; Josephus sits the two men at table together after promises are given that no harm will come to the prisoner. Here, however, it is clear that the man is from the city, presumably a Jew.

1049–62   *Whan Tytus saw that segge . . . to go where he wolde.* Josephus' cure is in accordance with medieval humoral theory. Titus is suffering from a malady that makes him cold (line 1030) and lethargic (line 1032). At a humoral level, then, Titus' sorrow at his father's departure has caused him to grow phlegmatic: an overabundance of phlegm has caused him to become apathetic. Since phlegm is the cold and wet humor, Josephus' solution is to make Titus hot and dry by provoking him to anger, the sign of a choleric personality brought on by the production of yellow bile in the gall bladder. The blood grows hot in Titus, and his anger spurs him to break free from his apathy.

1078   *Ded as a dore-nayl.* Proverbial: Whiting D352. This half-line also occurs in *Parlement of the Thre Ages*, line 65.

1079   *as wolves they ferde.* The conditions within the city have reduced the Jews to the status of ravenous beasts.

1081–96   *On Marie, a myld wyf . . . and alle hire blode chaungeth.* The story of the mother driven so mad by hunger that she murders her infant son and eats him is a powerful one. Though the poet's direct source is surely *Legenda aurea*, the story ultimately derives from the account of Josephus (*Wars of the Jews* 6.3.4), who is probably adopting a story of a mother's cannibalism of her child during the siege of Samaria by Ben-hadad (told in 4 Kings [2 Kings] 6:28–29) by filtering it through the Lamentations of Jeremias (especially 2:20). The story is remarkably popular in the late Middle Ages. Merrall Llewelyn Price notes an "almost pathological proliferation of versions of the Maria story" at that time (p. 289). Sources of the story are as diverse as John of Salisbury's *Polycraticus*, Vincent of Beauvais' *Speculum historiale*, Boccaccio's *De casibus virorum illustrium*, and even Dante's depiction of the Gluttonous in *Purgatorio* 23.28–30: *Ecco / la gente che perdé Ierusalemme, / quando Maria nel figlio diè di becco* ["Behold the people who lost Jerusalem, when Mary plunged her beak into her son" — trans. Singleton]. Though she is unnamed in *Legenda aurea*, the mother is named Mary in most accounts of the story (including that of Josephus). Three manuscripts of the *beta* family of *Siege of Jerusalem*, including D, however, name her as Marion. The change of name is probably due to a desire to distance this mother from the Holy Mother. For more on the motif of mother-child cannibalism in the Vengeance of Our Lord tradition, and especially on the strong affinities between the Jewess and the Virgin Mary, see Price, "Imperial Violence and the Monstrous Mother." Price includes several manuscript illuminations of the incident from the fourteenth- and fifteenth-century accounts.

1093   *in a wode hunger.* It is possible that this phrase belongs to Mary's speech, but I have followed other editors (and the poet's source material) in attributing it to the narrator.

1101–04   *Than they demeden a dom . . . bot her stor mardyn.* The situation of the Jews is so desperate that they make the decision to kill all noncombatants in order to preserve resources. This is surely an embellishment on the part of the poet, and one that is not preserved in the sources. The only possible parallel, as K notes (p. 102), is a passage in *Vindicta Salvatoris* reporting that eleven thousand Jews killed themselves so that they would not fall prisoners to the Romans.

1107   *For he is wise that is war or hym wo hape.* Proverbial: Whiting W392.

1108   *And with falsede afere is fairest to dele.* The line seems to be proverbial, though nothing similar is attested in either Whiting or Tilley's *Dictionary of the Proverbs in England.*

1111   *With mynours and masouns myne they bygonne.* The Jews are not mining under the walls of the city (a counterproductive act in a siege) but mining under the walls that the Romans have erected to prevent both their escape and their procurement of supplies. As H observes (p. 146), the subsequent attack on Titus allows him "to participate in a scene of personal danger analogous to that faced by Vespasian at 815–18."

1118   *jepouns and jambers.* I.e., tunics and leg-guards. French terminology.

1126   *That the fure out flewe as of flynt-stonys.* K (p. 102) posits a potential echo of *Sir Gawain and the Green Knight*, line 459: "Þat þe fyr of þe flint flaȝe fro fole houes."

1137   *Jon the jenfulle, that the Jewes ladde.* Four manuscripts, all of the *beta* family (including D), name Josephus here, while the L text names the leader as John. Yet another text, that found in British Library, MS Cotton Caligula A.ii, Part I, reads *Iona.* John of Gischala is surely meant in these latter texts, as this is the name recorded in Josephus, *Wars of the Jews* 4.2.1. Higden, believed to be the *Siege*-poet's direct source for this portion of the poem, clearly reads *Johannes* (*Polychronicon*, book 4), though later scribes may simply have mistaken John to mean Josephus, whose name was more clearly associated with the Jewish defense of Judaea. See explanatory note to line 1138.

1138   *Symond.* Simon, son of Gioras. According to Josephus, John and Simon's mutual disdain placed the city in a state of near-constant civil war for the duration of the siege. Higden says that they had put their differences aside, however, in order to face the mutual enemy at full strength. Regardless, the *Siege*-poet has written any disagreements out of the story and thus follows Higden in portraying a more or less unified Jewish defense. See explanatory note to line 1137.

1143   *floryns.* As the currency of Florence, florins became the common currency of international trade in medieval Europe, akin to the euro today.

1157   *Josophus to preche.* According to Josephus' account, he agreed to try to convince John to move the fight from a siege to a battle on open ground once again as Titus was particularly concerned about causing damage to the Temple (*Wars of the Jews* 6.2.1). In that account, of course, Josephus had defected to the Roman side after the fall of Jotapata. The portrayal here is quite different, however, as Josephus is among the Jews in Jerusalem, ordering his people to surrender the city and submit to Titus, who has sworn to destroy the Temple. The conflation is roughly managed at best.

1173   *tille two yeres ende*. Another exaggeration, as the historic siege was a matter of months, not years. But the poet is here following *Legenda aurea*, which claims a far more drawn-out process.

1175   *Eleven hundred thousand Jewes*. The number of dead (1,100,000) is an exaggeration, but the point is surely to emphasize the enormous loss of life on the part of the Jews. See above, p. 5n14.

1195   *At eche kernel was cry and quasschyng of wepne*. Neilson ("*Huchown*," p. 287) notes an echo of *Destruction of Troy*, lines 4752 ("At yche cornell of þe castell was crusshyng of weppon") and 11090 ("Kene was the crie with crusshyng of weppyn"). See also the explanatory note to line 1198.

1198   *Leyth a ladder to the wal and alofte clymyth*. Neilson ("*Huchown*," p. 287) notes an echo of *Destruction of Troy*, line 4751: "Layn ladders alenght & oloft wonnen." See also the explanatory note to line 1195.

1203–04   *That the brayn out brast at both nosethrylles / And Sabyn, ded of the dynt, into the diche falleth*. Neilson ("*Huchown*," p. 287), noting that Sabinus had reached the wall via ladder, points out the echoes of *Destruction of Troy*, lines 4755–56: "Till þai lept of the ladder, light in the dyke, / The brayne out brast & the brethe leuyt."

1215   *this was the Paske-evene*. Although the historical events being described fall some months after Passover, the poet's sources have perhaps changed the chronology for a theological point: divine vengeance will no longer pass over the Jews, as they refused to recognize Christ.

1221–36   *Or the gates were yete . . . throw dynt of a slynge*. These portents do not take place over the course of the preceding year as indicated in line 1221; rather, they took place across the forty years in which vengeance was stayed (lines 19–24). The change is due to the poet's source, Higden's *Polychronicon*. On the abrupt introduction of these portents, Chism writes:

> These afterthoughts of portents emphatically separate the invaders from the victims by retroactively constructing a vulturelike signifier of Jewish doom. The sword and the army appear in the sky as divine retributions, looming above and beyond the city but themselves inaccessible and aloof. By situating these ancient portents unsequentially at the moment the walls of the city are finally broken and Romans are pouring in, the poem resists the disintegratory culmination toward which the battle fervor tends. It extracts the Romans from the danger presented by the breach of Jewish walls — the boundary that separates them — and transforms the vulnerable Roman army into an invulnerable heavenly one (Chism, "*The Siege of Jerusalem*: Liquidating Assets," p. 327).

Though Chism implies that the portents are a later part of the Vengeance of Our Lord tradition, or perhaps even from the hand of the *Siege*-poet alone, their source is none other than Josephus. And their appearance at this point in the story of the destruction of Jerusalem is not "unsequential" in the tradition by any means. In *Wars of the Jews* 6.5.3, in describing the conflagration of the Temple after the fall of the city to the Romans, Josephus describes a series of ill omens, what he terms "denunciations" of God, beginning with a "star resembling a sword, which stood over the city, and a comet, that continued a whole year"; there is uncertainty whether Josephus here means to indicate two phenomena (a star and a comet) or one (a star-like comet), but the fact that the comet is said to last one year is surely behind the later mistake that the omens lasted only the year of the siege itself. The other omens — an army in the clouds (lines 1225–26), a heifer birthing in the Temple (lines 1227–28), and a man who dies upon the wall proclaiming woe to Jerusalem — also originate in Josephus' *Wars of the Jews* 6.5.3.

1227   *A calf agen kynde calved in the Temple*. Numbers 19:1–10 describes the ritualized sacrifice of a red heifer as a purification offering, an act that would have been practiced in the Temple with some regularity. The omen is in Josephus' *Wars of the Jews* 6.5.3 (see explanatory note to lines 1221–36, above), but might have had additional significance for Christian exegetes (if not to Josephus himself): that the heifer calves just as the priests were preparing the sacrifice symbolizes that a New Law (the Lamb of Christ) has replaced the Old Law and thus the old ways of sacrifice. Paul makes explicit reference to this very exchange in Hebrews 9: 13–14, referring to the sacrifice of the heifers as "dead works" now that Christ has taken all sacrifices upon Himself:

> For if the blood of goats and of oxen, and the ashes of an heifer, being sprin- kled, sanctify such as are defiled, to the cleansing of the flesh: How much more shall the blood of Christ, who by the Holy Ghost offered himself unspotted unto God, cleanse our conscience from dead works, to serve the living God?

This miracle is clearly one more means for the *Siege*-poet, following his sources, to demonstrate the divine authority of Christ and the Christian Church as the new Israel, heirs to a new Jerusalem.

Of more contemporary note, Ultra-Orthodox Jews believe that the Temple destroyed by Titus and Vespasian cannot be rebuilt without the rite of pur- ification, a potential problem toward re-establishing the most holy of sites in Jerusalem since red cows are thought to have been extinct for centuries. One was born in Israel in 1997, however, raising fears that radical Israelis would use the heifer as an excuse to move violently against the Palestinians. One liberal news- paper wrote that the "potential harm from this heifer is far greater than the destructive properties of a terrorist bomb"; the editor recommended that the red cow, then a ten-month old calf named Melody, be shot at once. See Bronner, "Portent in a Pasture?"

1229   *a wye on the wal*. Though anonymous here, this figure is identified by Josephus (*Wars of the Jews* 6.5.3) as a certain Jesus ben Ananias. Josephus relates that during the Feast of Tabernacles, four years before the war against Rome began, Jesus began to cry out incessantly: "A voice from the east, a voice from the west, a voice from the four winds, a voice against Jerusalem and the holy house, a voice against the bridegrooms and the brides, and a voice against the whole people." When the Roman procurator Albinus had him beaten and flayed, his answer to every strike of the implements was, "Wo, wo to Jerusalem." For seven years and five months he would say little else. Then, during the siege of Jerusalem, he would go about the walls saying "Wo, wo to the city again, and to the people, and to the holy house." According to Josephus (and related in *Siege*, lines 1233–36), he added at one point "Wo, wo to myself also," and at that moment was struck and killed by a stone from one of the Roman siege engines.

The fact that the later traditions treat Jesus ben Ananias as an anonymous "voice of the people" — in *La Venjance Nostre Seigneur* (lines 1044–1110) the man is an idiot who has been proclaiming woe to Jerusalem for twenty years and whose death is caused by a random missile in an unsuccessful Roman attempt to breach the walls which is thenceforth regarded as an omen among the besieged Jews — might be due to the fact that his name was potentially discomforting or simply confusing. Perhaps, too, later exegetes felt that he was better nameless, when he could be thought to represent the sentinels said to be watching over the city and preparing for the ultimate salvation of Zion in Isaias 62:6: "Upon thy walls, O Jerusalem, I have appointed watchmen all the day, and all the night, they shall never hold their peace. You that are mindful of the Lord, hold not your peace." See the explanatory note to lines 1231–32.

1231–32 *Wo, wo, wo.* Though the pronouncement is made against Jerusalem and the Temple — the former in conjunction with the poet's source, Josephus' *Wars of the Jews* 6.5.3 — an exegetical connection was probably Apocalypse 8:13 (itself hearkening back to Jeremias 13:27): "And I beheld: and heard the voice of one eagle flying through the midst of heaven, saying with a loud voice: Woe, Woe, Woe to the inhabitants of the earth, by reason of the rest of the voices of the three angels, who are yet to sound the trumpet!" On this mysterious prophetic voice, see the explanatory note to line 1229.

1239 *the byschup, Seint Jame.* See explanatory note to line 724, above.

1242 *Without brunee and bright wede, in here bare chertes.* Forced into submission, the Jews come forth just as Vespasian requested when he first arrived at the gates (lines 349–54).

1251 *balies as barels.* Proverbial; see Whiting B53.

1263 *Out the tresour to take Tytus commaundyth.* Josephus' account claims that Titus tried to protect the Temple, but that it was destroyed by accident during an assault on a hard-line group of Jews — Titus only having glanced at its interior and only recovering Temple materials from surrendering priests. Regardless of the accuracy of Josephus' account, we know that Titus did, indeed, take possession of a number of Temple artifacts that were displayed when he returned to Rome in triumph. The Arch of Titus, commissioned to commemorate the event, depicts the Temple menorah among other items.

1268 *Bassynes of brend gold and other bryght gere.* Neilson ("*Huchown*," p. 287) notes an echo of *Destruction of Troy*, line 3169: "Bassons of bright gold, & oþer brode vessell." Oakden (*Alliterative Poetry in Middle English*, p. 100) records a similar line in *Cleanness*, line 1456: "For þer wer bassynes ful bryȝt of brende golde clere."

1281 *Now masouns and mynours han the molde soughte.* The historical destruction took place around 26 September 70, but the poem's timeline is far off from this.

Neilson ("*Huchown*," p. 287) notes an echo of *Destruction of Troy*, line 4774: "Mynours then mightely the moldes did serche."

1289–96   *Nas no ston in the stede stondande alofte . . . "Now is this stalwourthe stede distroied forevere."* The utter destruction of the Temple, in addition to the significance discussed in the Introduction, pp. 30–36, might also be intended to fulfill the prophecies of Jeremias 9:11 ("And I will make Jerusalem to be heaps of sand, and dens of dragons: and I will make the cities of Juda desolate, for want of an inhabitant") and 26:18 ("Sion shall be ploughed like a field, and Jerusalem shall be a heap of stones: and the mountain of the house the high places of woods"), the latter taken from Micheas 3:12.

1290   *Morter ne mude-walle bot alle to mulle fallen.* Neilson ("*Huchown*," p. 287) notes a distant echo of *Parlement of the Thre Ages*, line 433: "In manere of a mode walle that made were with hondes."

1292   *Bot doun betyn and brent into blake erthe.* Neilson ("*Huchown*," p. 287) notes an echo of *Destruction of Troy*, line 4777: "Betyn doun the buyldynges & brent into erthe."

1296   *distroied forevere.* The same half-line is used to describe the exploits of the dead Sir Gawain in *Alliterative Morte Arthure* (line 3873).

1301–34   *Pilat proffrith hym forth . . . corsedlich deied.* Pilate's life after the Crucifixion is shrouded in mystery, as no official records have survived. Though the *Siege*-poet is here following his primary sources in claiming that Pilate was still in Jerusalem at the time of the siege and taken into custody by Titus, such a scenario is historically unlikely. The idea that Pilate eventually committed suicide can be traced back to Eusebius of Caesarea, who cites unnamed records as showing that Pilate was forced to kill himself during the reign of Caligula, probably in the late 30s (*Ecclesiastical History* 2.7); still, there is no evidence that this is more than Christian revisionist history. For a fuller account of Pilate's later literary life, see Growth, "Pontius Pilate."

1312   This line, omitted in a number of manuscripts (including L) does not alliterate without emendation. In correcting the line I have followed H (p. 155), who also proposes another possible reconstruction:

> Perhaps a better line would see the initial conjunction (in L's usual form, *þey*) as the remnants of original *þof of*. . . . In this interpretation, the second word would have been lost in all mss. through haplography, to the great muddling of the construction; and the archetypal text would have read *had be fourmed.* . . . We would translate this reconstruction: "Although a hundred florins had been created from each farthing."

See also the textual note to this line.

1325   *Josophus, the gentile clerke.* The double meaning of *gentile* is clearly evident: Josephus is not just "noble," but also, perhaps, a "gentile," having forsaken his Jewish comrades in order to join the Romans.

1328   *Vienne.* L is alone in clearly giving Viterbo as the location of Pilate's imprisonment and death. Most copies in the *beta* family give the location as Vienne, a town in France's Rhone valley. Traditional accounts claim that Pilate's body was thrown into the Tiber after his death, but that evils plagued the area until the body was removed and placed elsewhere. According to one strand of legend, it was only in this second internment that Pilate was brought to Vienne and thrown into the Rhone (a Pilate's Tomb can still be seen in the area). Other legends place his final resting place as a lake near Lausanne or in a tomb beneath one of several mountains bearing the name Mt. Pilate.

1340   *Now rede us our Lorde*. This sort of conclusionary half-line is common to many alliterative poems. For example, one appears near the end of *Alliterative Morte Arthure* (line 3992).

TEXTUAL NOTES

ABBREVIATIONS: see Explanatory Notes, and the list of manuscripts on p. 40.

Minor orthographical differences have been disregarded in the construction of these notes, and the spelling provided follows either that of the first manuscript cited in a sequence or of the most common spelling in the sequence. It should also be noted that this is not a full accounting of textual variants between the many copies of the poem. Rather, these notes are an accounting of instances either where an alternative reading from the base text (L) has been adopted or where the text here presented differs from that of previous editors. Those students and scholars interested in accessing a fuller apparatus are encouraged to consult the edition of Hanna and Lawton (H), which greatly improves upon the readings provided in the earlier edition of Kölbing and Day (K).

1	Every effort has been made to place internal half-line separations in accordance with the scribe's punctus elevatus marking the same. Indents in the text correspond to large initials in L.
4	*Judeus londis.* So L, followed by K. D, E *Judees londe,* followed by H.
5	*Herodes.* So L, followed by K. U, C *Herode,* followed by H.
6	*was.* So L. P, A, U, D, E, C omit, followed by K, H.
10	*and.* So P, A, U, D, E, C, followed by H. L omits, followed by K.
11	*by-wente.* So L, U, D, E, C, followed by K. H emends to *vmbywente.*
12	*He.* So L, U, D, E, C, followed by K. P, A omit, followed by H.
	in. So P, A, U, D, E, C, followed by K, H. L: *on.*
13	*Hym.* So L, followed by K. P, A, U, D, E, C omit, followed by H.
	mannes. So L, followed by H. P, D: *men.* A, U: *mens,* followed by K.
14	*Hym$_1$.* So L, followed by K. P, A, U, D, E, C omit, followed by H.
16	*berne.* So P, A, U, D, followed by K, H. L, E, C: *man.*
	bolled. So L, followed by K. U, E: *bobbed,* followed by H.
17	*was.* So L, followed by K. H omits.
18	*Hym.* So L, A, followed by K. P omits, followed by H.
	a$_2$. So L, followed by K. P, A, U, D, E, C omit, followed by H.
23	*Fourty.* L: *XL.* I have expanded Roman numeration silently on all subsequent occasions.
	wynter as. So P, A, U, E, followed by K, H. L: *wynter was as.*
24	*Or.* So A, U, D, E, C, followed by K, H. L: *Our.*
25	*that.* So L, P, A, followed by K. U, D, E: *on,* followed by H.
26	*gate.* So P, A, U, D, E, C, followed by K, H. L: *gaten.*

27–28	The quatrain is broken in all extant copies. H assumes a loss of only two lines and numbers accordingly, a decision I have followed to facilitate cross-referencing between texts.
29	*noyet*. So L, followed by K. U: *neght*. P, A, D, C: *neʒet*, followed by H.
	hym in. So E, followed by K. L: *hym into*. P, U, D, C: *hym to in*, followed by H.
30	*inmyddis*. So P, U, D, C, followed by H. L: *amyd*. A: *in the myddis of*. E: *amyddis*, followed by K.
33	*is*. So L, followed by K. U, E, C omit. P, A, D: *a*, followed by H.
34	*in*. So P, A, U, D, E, C, followed by H. L: *on*, followed by K.
35	*upon*. So L, followed by K. P: *of*. A: *up heghe in*. U, D, C: *up in*, followed by H.
40	*For in*. So L, A, followed by K. P omits line. U, D, C: *Of*, followed by H. E omits.
43–44	The quatrain is broken in all extant copies. H assumes a loss of only two lines and numbers accordingly, a decision I have followed to facilitate cross-referencing between texts.
45	*Nathan*. So A, U, D, E, C, followed by K, H. L: *Nothan*. P: *Natan*.
	Grece. So P, A, U, D, E, followed by K. L: *Grecys*, followed by H.
48	a_2. So A, followed by D_{88}, H. L, P, U, D, E, D omit, followed by K.
49	*out*. So L, A, followed by K. P, U, D, E, C omit, followed by H.
55	*salt*. So P, A, U, D, E, C, followed by K, H. L: *wode*.
56	*dryveth*. So P, C, followed by H. L: *drof*, followed by K. A: *he drave*. U, E: *dryved*. D: *drivyn*.
	swythe. So P, U, D, E, C, followed by H. L: *faste*, followed by K. A: *full swythe*.
57	*wolcon*. So A, U, D, E, C, followed by K, H. L: *wolcom*.
58	*on loude*. So P. A: *one the lande*. L: *gon*, followed by K. H emends to *on lofte*.
59	*roos*. So L, A, U, D, E, C, followed by K. P: *roof*, followed by H.
61	*Hit*. So P, A, U, D, E, C, followed by H. L omits, followed by K.
62	*the*. So P, A, U, D, E, C, followed by K, D_{88}, H. L omits.
64	*hurtled*. So L, U, followed by K. P, A: *hurled*, followed by H. D, C: *hit hurlid*. E: *it hurtlyd*.
66	*worche*. So P, A, U, D, E, C, followed by H. L: *worthe*, followed by K.
	hem. So P, A, followed by H. L: *hit*, followed by K. U, D, E, C: *they*.
68	*uncouth costes*. So L, followed by K. P, A, U, D, E, C: *costes uncouth*, followed by H.
	kayrande on. So H. L: *kevereth*, followed by K. P: *yerne on*. A: *kayrande full*. U, D, C: *caried hem*. E: *caryed panne*.
69	*unradly*. So L, P, followed by K. A: *full rathely*. U, E, C: *ful redely*. D: *ful radly*. H emends to *on radly*.
72	*alle*. So L, A, followed by K. P: *he*. U: *she*. D, E, C: *hit*. H emends to *ʒo*.
74	*Stroke*. So L, followed by H. P: *Strake over þe*. A: *Starke*, followed by K. U, D, E, C omit line.
76	*byr*. So P, A, C, followed by K, H. L: *by*. U: *birth*. D, E: *breyd*.
78	*citezeins*. So P, A, U, D, C, followed by K, H. L: *suth*. E: *peple*.
	hem. So A, U, D, C, followed by K, D_{88}, H. L, P omit. E: *they*.
82	*hym*. So P. A, D, C: *hem*, followed by K, D_{88}, H. L, U omit.
84	L places the caesura prior to *sent*, though K's placement (followed by H) is far more reasonable.

seignour. So U, D, E, C, followed by K, H. L: *senatour.* P: *senur.* A: *senyȝoures.* Nero is clearly not a senator but the emperor of Rome.

86   *of the Jewen lawe.* So U, C, followed by D₈₈. L: *of Jewen lawe,* followed by K. P, A: *over þe Jewes alle,* followed by H. D, E omit line.

87   *lene.* So L, followed by H. P, A: *lenged,* followed by K. U, D, E, C omit line.

88   *God made.* So L, P, followed by K. A: *gome aughte,* followed by H. U, D, E, C omit line.

94   *that₂.* So L, E, followed by K. P, A, U, D, C: *as,* followed by H.

95   *worldlich.* So L. P, D, E, C: *worthy.* A: *wirchipfull.* U: *worthly.* K emends to *worlich,* followed by H.

101   *telle.* So P, A, U, D, E, C, followed by K, H. L: *sey.*

106   *ther.* So L, P, U, D, followed by K. A, C: *þat,* followed by H. E: *þere þat.*

  of. So A, followed by D₈₈, H. L, P, D, E omit, followed by K. U, C: *in.*

109   *taknyng.* So P, followed by H. L: *touche,* followed by K. A: *troche.* U, D, E, C: *trouth.*

117   *even.* So P, A, E, C, followed by H. L: *ever,* followed by K. U, D: *alle.*

118   *inwardly endeles.* So A, followed by H. So L: *endeles ever,* followed by K. P omits line. U, D, E, C omit.

  or. So U, D, E, C, followed by K, H. L: *byfor.* P omits line.

  erthe. So H. L, U, D: *world,* followed by K. P omits line. A omits. E: *wurld.* C: *worlde.*

  bygan. So H. L: *was bygonne,* followed by K. P omits line. A: *bygonnyne.* U, D, E, C: *was ever bygonne.*

120   *heye.* So D, E, followed by H. L, P, A, U, C omit, followed by K.

123   *And.* So L, A, E, followed by K. P, U, D, C omit, followed by H.

124   *ay.* So L, A, followed by K. P, U, D, E, C omit, followed by H.

125   *He wroght of water.* So L, followed by K. P, A, U, D, E, C: *of water he wroȝt,* followed by H.

127   *the palsy.* So P, U, D, C, followed by H. L: *piles,* with the *es* written over an erasure. A: *parilsye,* followed by K.

  hem. So P, A, followed by D₈₈, H. L omits, followed by K. U, D, E, C: *in.*

128   *ever ilke.* So A, followed by D₈₈. L, P, U, D, E: *eche,* followed by K. C: *yche a.* H emends to *ilka.*

131   *many.* So L. P, A, U, D, E, C omit, followed by K, H.

133   *ferly.* So P, A, U, D, E, followed by K, D₈₈, H. L: *ferre.* C: *mervayle.*

134   *berly.* So P, A, U, D, E, C, followed by D₈₈, H. L: *bere,* followed by K.

136   *brede.* So L, P, A, followed by K. U, D, E: *battes,* followed by H. C: *bettes.*

  bascketes. So L, U, followed by K. P: *berelepes,* followed by H. A, D, C: *basketes full.* E: *lepys ful.*

137   *of.* So P, A, U, D, E, C, followed by H. L: *out of,* followed by K.

  a. So P, A. L: *an,* followed by K. U, C: *one.* D, E: *o,* followed by H.

  sorte. So P, E, followed by H. L: *cite.* A: *sekte.* U, D: *sute,* followed by K. C: *assent.*

  seventy. So P, A, U, D, E, C, followed by K, H. L: *sixty.*

138   *hoten.* So L, followed by K. P, A, D, C: *chosen,* followed by H. U, E: *ichone.*

140   *were a-twynne.* So L, followed by K. A: *ware twelve makede.* U, C: *were dissevered.* D: *were all disseuered.* E: *alle departyd.* H emends to *atwynne.*

141   *of.* So P, A, U, D, E, C, followed by H. L: *out of,* followed by K.

  sorte. So P, D, E, followed by H. L: *cite,* followed by K. A: *soyte.* U: *sute.* C: *sent.*

143	*kaytefes*. So A, U, E, followed by K. L: *cayftes*. P omits. D: *chaytyfes*, followed by H. C: *pore kynreden*.
	His. So U, D, E, C, followed by D$_{86}$, H. L, P: *holy*, followed by K. A: *fro holy*.
144	*and*. So A, followed by D$_{88}$, H. L, P, U, D, E, C omit, followed by K.
146	*And*. So L, followed by K. P, A, U, D, E, C omit, followed by H.
147	*eke*. So L, P, followed by K. A: *then*. U, D, E, C: *after*, followed by H.
148	*that*. Added above the line in L.
151	*myche*. So L, followed by K. P, A, U, D, E, C: *after*, followed by H.
152	*Petrus*. So L, E, followed by K. P, A, U, D, C: *Petres*, followed by H.
154	*Crist*. So L, E, followed by K. P, A, U, D, C omit, followed by H.
157	*to Heven*. So U, D, C, followed by K. L: *heven*. P alters b-verse. A: *till heven*. E alters line. H emends to *hennes*.
162	*hadde Hym in hate*. So L, U, D, E, C, followed by K. P: *hatyd hym harde*. A: *hatede hym in herte*. H emends to *hatte in herte*.
165	*that*. So L, P, A, followed by K. U, D, E, C: *of whom*. H emends to *whom*.
	arst was. So L, followed K. P: *I are*. A, U, D, C: *I firste*. E: *Y arst*, followed by H.
	y-nempned. So L, followed by K. P, A: *nevende*. U, D, E, C: *tolde*. H emends to *nempned*.
167–248	C: missing folio.
167	*prively*. So L, P, U, followed by K. A: *prevaly*. D: *privily*. E alters a-verse. H emends to *purely*.
169	*on*. So P, A, D, followed by K, H. L, U, E: *in*.
	grounde. So P, A, D, followed by K, H. L, U: *erthe*. E: *wurld*.
172	*to helle*. So L. P: *it heles*. A: *thaym the hele*. U, D: *be hole*. K, H emend to *to hele*.
	an. So A, U, D, E, followed by K, H. L: *and*. P: *a*.
173	*A*. So P, A, followed by H. L, U, D, E: *At*, followed by K.
	renayed. So P, A, followed by H. L: *reyned þe emperour*, followed by K. U, E: *reyned*. D: *regnith*.
	the$_2$. So P, D. L omits, followed by K. A: *thou*. U: *a*, followed by H. E: *þat*.
	emperour. So P, A, U, D, E, followed by K, H. L: *þan*.
177	*were wonne*. So L, E, followed by H. P, D: *wer wele*, followed by K. A: *wele*. U: *weren al*.
181	*than*. So P, A, U, D, followed by K, H. L: *riche þan*.
182	*to telle*. So L, followed by K. P, A: *tille*, followed by H. U, D, E: *wille*.
183	*have don*. So L, followed by K. P, U, D, E: *don have*, followed by H. A: *dide*.
185	*bayne me*. So L, followed by H. P: *graunte me*. A: *be bayne to*, followed by K. U, D alter the line.
187	*forto*. So P, A, followed by D$_{88}$, H. L, U, D, E: *to*, followed by K.
197	*sought*. So A, followed by K, H. L: *þouȝt*. P, U, D, E: *sent*.
	unto. So P, U, followed by D$_{88}$. L, E: *to*, followed by K. A: *towarde*. D: *anone unto*.
202	*As*. So P, A, U, D, E, followed by K, H. L: *And*.
203	*afowe*. So P, U, D, E, followed by K, H. L, A: *afowne*.
207	*fele*. So K, H. L, P, A, U, D, E: *fast(e)*.
	of. So P, D, followed by K, H. L, A, U: *on*. E omits.
210	*he*. So P, A, D, E, followed by H. L, U omit, followed by K.
212	*come*. So P, U, D, followed by H. L, A: *was come*, followed by K.

215	*were.* So L, D, E, followed by K. P, A: *þat were,* followed by H. U: *ere.*
	kerchef. So P, A, U, followed by K, H. L: *clergyf.* D: *kerchifs.* E: *clooth.*
216	Editors have speculated that a section of text is missing from the poem after this line. At the very least there is a jump in the plot: the knights are sent out to seek the veil in line 216 only to return in the next line with both Veronica and her miraculous cloth. The following lines hearken the reader back to the refusal of the Jews to pay tribute to Rome (part of the reason for Nathan's journey in the first place) and seem to also imply disrespect on the part of the Jewish leadership toward the knights. The loss of text, as H notes (p. 104), is no doubt the result of eyeskip between *trewes* in the a-verse of line 216 and *trewes* in the a-verse of line 217.
217	*by.* So A, U, D, E, followed by H. L, P omit, followed by K.
	wayes. So P, A, U, followed by K, H. L: *wyes.* D: *dayes.* E: *weye.*
219	*and.* So P, A, U, E, followed by H. L: *þat,* followed by K. D: *þat,* above a canceled *and.*
220	*of.* So P, A, U, D, E, followed by K, H. L omits.
222	*Of.* So P, U, D, E, followed by K, H. L: *To.* A: *Byfore.*
228	*he.* So L, U, D, E, followed by K. P, A: *sho.* H emends to *ȝo.*
229	*he.* So P, A, U, D, followed by K, H. L: *þey.* E alters the line.
	warp. So P, A, followed by K, H. L: *warpen.* U, D: *warped.* E alters the line.
231	*To.* So P, U, D, E, followed by H. L: *Out of,* followed by K. A: *Towarde.*
	palace. So A, U, D, E, followed by H. L, P: *place,* followed by K.
	they. So L, A, followed by K. P omits, followed by H. U, D, E: *he.*
235	*Waspasian.* So L, P, A, E, followed by K. U, D: *Vaspasian,* followed by H.
243	*flambeth.* So L, followed by K. P, A: *flawe,* followed by H. U, D, E alter the line.
255	*wenten.* So L, A, followed by K. P: *wyten,* followed by H. U, D, E, C: *went al.*
256	*was lasar-liche.* So D, E, followed by H. L: *lasar was longe,* followed by K. P: *laythre was.* A: *lazare was laythe.* U: *was lazar ful leke.* C: *lazare was lyke.*
257	*departyng of stryf.* So P, followed by H. L: *his pyne was awey,* followed by K. A: *thay partede at the laste.* U, C: *partyng atte last.* D, E: *and partyng atte last.*
258	*this two.* So L, followed by K. P: *many.* A: *alle þo,* followed by H. U, D, C: *all the.* E: *of alle þat.*
259	*carieth.* So L, followed by K. P alters the line. A: *wente.* U: *cauth.* D: *caught.* E: *was takyn.* C: *kawȝte.* H emends to *aireth.*
	fram alle. So L, followed by K. P alters the line. A: *fro thaym alle.* U, D, C: *was hem fro.* E: *hem fro.* H emends to *fram hem alle.*
	eyr. So L, followed by H. P alters the line. U, D, E, C: *chirche.* K emends to *kirke.*
260	*symple pople.* So L, P, A, followed by H. U: *symple,* followed by K. D, E: *synful.* C: *somple.*
261	*Vernycle.* So P, A, U, D, E, C, followed by H. L: *veronycle,* followed by K.
	Waspasian. So L, P, E, followed by K. A, U, D, C: *Vaspasian,* followed by H.
264	*The Romaynes hit holdeth at Rome.* This half-line is almost surely in error as it stands in all extant manuscripts, and that error has, in turn, affected the b-verse. H has perhaps come closest to solving the problematic line by emending to *Þe Romaynes hit teldeþ a rome, / and for relyk holden* on the

supposition that the original line spoke of the building of a room to house the Vernicle and that "the scribes read the common noun as the name of the city and provided a preposition to smooth the construction" (p. 107). Still, the line is problematic enough to cast uncertainty on any explanation; I have opted to record L as it stands since it is clear in meaning even if faulty in meter.

	holden. So P, followed by D$_{86}$, H. L, A, U, D, E, C: *hit holden*, followed by K.
266	*withholde.* So L. P: *untane*. A: *tell*. U, D, *tynt*, followed by K. E: *nat payd*. C: *loste.* H emends to *withtane*.
267	*to holde.* The scribe has written *to take holde*, before canceling *take*.
280	*forwardis.* So L, followed by K. P, A, U, D, C: *forwarde*, followed by H. E: *avowes*.
281	*brynnyis.* So L. K reads *brynnyes*.
284	*gyng.* So U, D, C, followed by K, H. L: *kyng*. P: *gomes*. A: *gentills*. E alters the line.
	folwed. So L, followed by K. P, A, U, D, C: *after*, followed by H. E alters the line.
292	*Brayd.* So P, followed by H. L: *Sprad*. A: *Alle abowtte*. U, D, C: *The brede*, followed by K. E: *they spredde*.
293–369	A: missing folio.
293	*tal-sail.* So L, followed by K. P, U, D, C: *topsail*, followed by H. E: *her sail*.
296	*joyned.* So D, C, followed by K, H. L: *ryved*. P: *Rafe*. U: *Right*. E: *took londe*.
	up at. So L, followed by H. P: *at þe*. U: *unto*. D: *into*, followed by K. C: *to*.
	judeis. So L, followed by K. P: *þe Jues*. U: *Judee*. D, E: *Judees*, followed by H. C: *Judeus*.
	londys. So L, followed by K. P, U, D, E, C: *londe*, followed by H.
298	*moun.* So P, followed by K, H. L: *men*. U, E, C: *worthe*. D: *wroght*.
	wlonk. So U, D, followed by K, H. L: *blonk*. P: *walled*. E: *fayre*. C: *welthy*.
	tounnes. So L, followed by H. K misreads *tounes*.
299	*Syone.* So P, U, D, E, C, followed by K, H. L: *sene*.
300	*the$_2$.* So L, followed by K. P, U, D, E, C omit, followed by H.
304	*jouke.* So P, D, C, followed by K, H. L: *rouke*. U: *jouken*. E: *dwelle*.
	you. So U, D, E, C, followed by K, H. L: *ʒour*. P omits.
306	*ful.* So L, P, followed by H. U, D, C: *al*, followed by K. E alters the line.
307	*rich.* So L, followed by H. U, D, C: *reuth*, followed by K. E: *weepyng*.
313	*ther.* So P, U, D, E, C, followed by K, H. L: *þat*.
318	*comens.* So K, abbreviated *coes* in L. H expands to *comunes*.
319	*schacked.* So L, followed by K. P, U, D, E, C omit line. H emends to *samned*.
328	*torkeys.* So P, D, E, followed by K, H. L: *torken*. U: *turky*. C: *turcheyes*.
329	*Choppyn.* So D, followed by K, H. L: *Thoppyn*. P: *Chippen*. U: *Chopt*. E: *They settyn*. C: *They chopped*.
331	*grym.* So L, followed by K. P, U, D, E, C: *and grym*, followed by H.
332	*lyk to lyouns also.* So L, P, followed by K. D, E, C: *therto lyons two*. H emends to *to lyouns lyk*.
334	*stayned.* So D, followed by K, H. L: *strayned*. P, U, C: *and steynyd*.
335	*coloures.* So U, D, E, C, followed by H. L: *colour*, followed by K. P omits the line.

336	*on stage*. So L, followed by K. P omits the line. U, C: *in stage*. D: *on a stag*. H emends to *stage*.
343	*us*. So P, U, D, E, C, followed by K, H. L: *ȝou*.
343	*serchen*. So U, followed by D₈₈, H. L, P, D, C: *serche*, followed by K. E: *wetyn*.
344	*and what*. So P, U, followed by K, H. L: *ȝif*. D, E, C: *and what þat*.
347	*Gaf*. So L, followed by K. P omits. U: *Made*. D: *Garde*, followed by H. E: *And bad*. C: *They made*.
348	*come*. So U, D, followed by K, H. L: *coms*. P, E, C: *comyng*.
350	*mydday*. So U, D, E, C, followed by K, H. L, P: *undren of þe day*.
	moder-naked alle. So K, followed by H. L: *open-heded alle*. P: *uncled and nakyd*. U, D, C: *al modur-naked*. E: *to be clene nakyd*.
352	*whight*. So L, followed by K. P, U: *wye*, followed by H. D: *bierne*. E: *body*. C: *mon*.
353	*Crist*. So K. L: *Crist to take*. P, U, C omit, followed by H. D: *sake*. E alters the line.
354	*brynge Cayphas*. So P, U, D, C, followed by H. L: *make hem come*, followed by K. E: *bryngge also Cayphas*.
	Crist. So P, D, C, followed by H. L: *Jhesu Crist*, followed by K. U: *Jhesu*.
362	*alle twelf*. So L, followed by K. P, U, D: *hem als-tite*, followed by H. E: *anon*. C: *hem as sone*.
364	*flocken*. So L. P: *flowen*, followed by K, H. U, D: *flewen*. E, C alter half-line.
	fax. So P, U, D, C, followed by K, H. L: *face*. E: *fayr her*.
365	*Made him naked*. So L, followed by K. P: *Nackynde þaim*. U, D, E, C: *Als naked*. H emends to *Nakened*.
366	*visage*. So P, followed by H. L: *visages*, followed by K. U, D, E, C: *face*.
376	*scorned*. So L, followed by K. P, A omit line. U, C: *shamed*. D: *shamefully* (omits following *and*). E: *yschave*. H emends to *schorne*.
379	*myght*. So L, U, C, followed by K. P, A omit line. D: *mynt*, followed by H. E: *thretnyng*.
	maken. So D₈₈, followed by H. L, D: *make*, followed by K. P, A omit line. U: *recche*. E, C: *sette*.
384	*thee*. So L, followed by K. P, A, U, D, E add *to sey*, followed by H. C adds *and seyn*.
385	*wedande*. So L, followed by K. P: *wellande*, followed by H. A: *wylde and*. U, D, E, C: *wepand*.
390	*Bilt*. So L, C, followed by K. P: *Bellyd*. A: *Belde*. U, D: *Byggid*, followed by H. E: *Y-tymbryd*.
394	*gomes*. So L, P, A, followed by K. U, D: *the gomes*. E: *þe jewes*. C: *þe lordes*. H emends to *þe gollet*.
	to swelwe. So L, P, A, followed by K. U, D, E, C: *schewe*, followed by H.
398	*wlonfulle*. So L, followed by K. P: *wankyll*. A: *wankille*. U, D, C: *wanton*. E omits line. H emends to *wlonkfulle*.
	worlde. So A, followed by K. P: *folke*. U, D, C: *worme*. E omits line. H emends to *worde*.
399	*fauchoun*. So P, followed by K, H. L: *fauchouns*. A, D, U, C: *fawkon*. E omits line.
	thay. So A, followed by D₈₈. L, P omit, followed by K. U, D, C: *he*, followed by H. E omits line.

	hengede. So A. L, P: *hengeþ*, followed by K, H. U, D, C: *helde*. E omits line.
400	*swerd*. So L, P, A, followed by H. U, D, C: *werre*, followed by K. E omits line.
401	*A*. So L, P, A, followed by K. U, D, E, C: *On a*, followed by H.
	on sette. So L, P, A, followed by K. U, D, C: *assised*, followed by H. E: *y-fastnet*.
404	*al*. So L, P, A, followed by K. U, D, C: *it*. E alters line. H emends to *þat*.
405	*setlyng*. So L, followed by K. P, A, U, D: *saghtlyng*, followed by H. E: *acord*. C: *pece*.
407	*her*. So L, followed by K. P, U, D, C: *han*, followed by H. A: *hafe to*.
408	*burwe*. So P, A, U, D, C, followed by K, H. L: *toun*. E alters line.
409	*brad*. So K, H. L: *sprad*. A: *brighte*. P, U, D, E, C omit the line.
411	*runnen*. So L, followed by K. A: *range*. P, U, D, E, C omit the line. H emends to *ran*.
	ryngen. So D$_{88}$, followed by H. L, A: *rynge*, followed by K. P, U, D, E, C omit the line.
412	*a wap of the wynde*. So A, U, D, C, followed by H. L: *wynde of a wap*. P, E omit the line. K emends to *wap of a wynde*.
413	*bigly*. P, A, U, D, C, followed by H. L omits, followed by K. E alters the line.
415	*batail*. So L, followed by K. P, A, U, D, C: *beste*, followed by H. E: *dragun*.
	the. So L, followed by K. P, A, U, D, E, C: *his*, followed by H.
417	*And*. So L, followed by K. P, A, U, D, E, C omit, followed by H.
422	*Sixti*. So U, D, E, C, followed by H. L, P, A: *Sixtene*, followed by K.
423	*on*. So L, followed by H. P: *at*. A, U, D, C: *to*, followed by K. E: *abowte*.
426	After this line, L inserts an extra line, here omitted following K, H: *Right so in the cité they schapte hem therfore*.
427	*Armyng*. So P, A, U, D, E, C, followed by H. L: *With armyng*, followed by K.
429	*Waspasian*. So P, A, E, followed by K, H. L: *Waspasial*. U, D, C: *Vespasian*.
431	*Crist*. So L, followed by K. P, A, U, D, E, C omit, followed by H.
432	*biden*. So A, followed by D$_{86}$, D$_{88}$, H. L, E: *abide*, followed by K. P, D, C: *byde*. U: *abyden*.
434	*sixtene*. So P, U, E, C, followed by H. L: *six*, followed by K. A, D: *sexty*.
435	*as*. So P, A, U, D, E, C, followed by H. L omits, followed by K.
440	*helmes and harnays*. So L, followed by K. P, A, U, D, E, C: *an here with helmes*, followed by H.
442	*harmyng*. So L, followed by K. P, A, D, E, C: *harmes*, followed by H. U: *harme*.
444	*beden*. *b* written over an erasure in L.
452	*hundred*. So L, followed by K. P omits line. A: *hurdeschede*. U: *hurdist*. D: *hurdys*. E alters line. C: *hurdes*. H emends to *hurdised*.
454	*An*. So P, A, U, E, followed by K, H. L, C: *And*. D omits line.
	hundred. So U, E, C, followed by K. L: *hundred thousand*. P: *hundred houshid*. A: *hundred hosed*, followed by H.
464	*er*. So L, E, followed by K. P, A, U, D, C: *be*, followed by H.
	that. So L, followed by K. P, A, U, D, E, C: *þat þe*.
465	*at the laste*. So L, A, U, D, E, C, followed by K. P: *upon lofte*, followed by H.
466	*myd*. Added above the line in L.
467	*tabernacle*. L: *n* added above the line.
469	*was sett*. So A. L: *walynde*. P omits line. U, D, C: *walwed*, followed by H. E: *hanged*. K emends to *walwynde*.

471	*chosen.* So U, D, C, followed by K, H. L: *closen.* P, A omit line. E: *chose.*
	on. So L, followed by K. P, A omit line. U, E, C: *an,* followed by H. D: *wiþ.*
	charbokeles. So L, followed by K. P, A omit line. U, D, E, C: *chaundelers,* followed by H.
472	*bright.* So U, C. L: *barne.* P, A omit line. D: *brent.* E: *brende.* K emends to *barnd.* H emends to *bournde.*
473	*charbokles.* So D, E, C, followed by K, H. L: *chabokles.* P, A, U: *charbucle.*
474	*ther.* So L, P, A, U, D, C, followed by K. E alters line. H moves to the first word in line.
480	*Josue.* So A, U, D, E, followed by K, H. L, P, C: *Joseph.*
482	*rede water.* So U, D, followed by H. L: *rerewarde.* P: *brade water.* A: *rede waters,* followed by K. E, C: *red se.*
487	*that blased.* So L, followed by K. P: *and bemes.* A: *and beme wode.* U: *and bemewede.* D: *and bright wede.* E: *and pensellis.* C: *and trumpes.* H emends to *and beme-worde.*
488	*sonne.* So L, U, D, E, C, followed by K. P, C: *soyle.* A: *somme,* followed by H.
	uneth. So L, followed by H. P, A, U, D, E, C omit, followed by K.
489	*Waspasian.* So L, P, E, followed by K. A: *Than Waspasiane.* U, D, C: *Vaspasian,* followed by H.
	vale. So P, A, U, D, E, C, followed by K, H. L: *feld.*
490	*overbrad.* So K, H. L: *oversprad.* P: *brade.* A: *brode.* C: *ovurspradde.* U, D, E: *al oversprad.*
	wallis. So L, followed by K. P, A, U, D, E: *ʒatis.* C: *walle.*
493	*knyght.* So P, A, U, D, E, C, followed by K, H. L: *kynʒt.*
494	*bachelere.* So P, A, U, D, E, C, followed by H. L: *burges,* followed by K.
495	*come.* So P, A, U, D, followed by K, H. L: *comes.* E, C: *comyngge.*
498	*byndyng . . . betyng.* So P, U, D, E, C, followed by H. L transposes, followed by K. A: *buffettynge . . . betynge.*
	He on. So P, A, U, D, C, followed by K, H. L: *þe.* E: *he on his.*
501	*quycke-clayme.* So L, followed by K. P, A, U, D: *quyte-clayme,* followed by H. C: *voyde awey.*
504	*That.* So L, followed by K. P, A, U, D, C: *As,* followed by H. E omits line.
505	*mynde.* So L, followed by K. P, A: *mene.* U, D: *mynne,* followed by H. E omits line. C: *mynge.*
507	*That.* So L, followed by K. P, A, U, D: *His,* followed by H. E omits line. C: *The.*
	quik-cleyme. So L, followed by K. P, A, U, D: *quit-cleyme,* followed by H. E omits line. C alters line.
	whether. So P, A, followed by K, H. L: *for oþer.* U, D, C: *quite it where.* E omits line.
	he. So P, C, followed by H. L, A: *he ne,* followed by K. U, D: *him.* E omits line.
509	*mynde.* So L, P, A, followed by K. U, C: *mode,* followed by H. D, E omit line.
	us. So K. L omits, followed by H.
510	*realté.* So P, U, D, C, followed by D$_{88}$, H. L: *regnance,* followed by K. A: *rygalite.* E omits line.
511	*or ellys.* So L. P: *and oþer,* followed by H. A: *of all oþer landis.* U: *of erthe.* D, C: *on erthe,* followed by K. E omits line.
512	*lordschip.* So P, U, D, C, followed by K, H. L: *lord sup.* A: *the lordschipe.* E omits line.

513   *of.* So P, A, U, D, E, followed by K, D$_{88}$, H. L omits. C omits line.
517   *feynt.* So P, A, U, D, E, C, followed by K, H. L: *feyn.*
      fals. Corrected from *falf* in L.
518   *they wold.* So L. P omits line. A alters line. U, D, E, C: *þe world*, followed by
      K, H.
520   *storijs.* So L, P. A, D, E, C: *sternes*, followed H. U omits line. K emends to
      stourness.
522   *His.* So L, followed by K. A: *þyn*, followed by H. P, U, D, E C alter line.
526   *felde.* So L, P, A, followed by K. U, D, E: *stede*, followed by H. C: *place.*
      undere stele wedes. So U, D, E, followed by D$_{86}$. L: *stif steil undere*, followed by
      K, T. P: *stith steil undere.* A: *stuffed steil undere*, followed by H. C: *undur þe
      stele aray.*
529   *alle kyn.* So L, followed by K. P: *with cormous*, followed by H. A: *cormous.* D:
      cornmuse, followed by T. U, E, C: *curiouses.*
531   *schillande.* So L, followed by K, T. P omits line. A: *schakande.* U, C, C: *shrike
      in a.* E alters line. H emends to *schrikande.*
532   *wepith and waylith.* So D. L: *schal in a swem*, followed by K. P omits line. A:
      weltir solde in swoun. U: *shrillen on hye.* E: *wepeth an hey.* C: *wepyn on hyȝe.*
      T, H emend to *welter schal in swem.*
533   *Lacchen.* So L, P, followed by K, T. A, U, D, E, C add *Þey*, followed by H.
536   *throbolande.* So K, T, H. L: *þrowolande.* P: *and thrymbland.* A: *threpande.* U:
      thrilles. D: *þirled.* E: *hurleth.* C: *persheth.*
537   *here.* So P, U, D, E, C, followed by D$_{88}$, T, H. L omits, followed by K. A: *with.*
541   *to tolles.* L marks the caesura to come before *to.*
      beste. So P, A, U, D, E, C, followed by K, T, H. L: *bestes.*
542   *joynyng.* So P, A, U, D, E, C, followed by K, T, H. L: *joyned.*
544   *Tille.* So L, followed by K. P, A, U, D, E, C: *Þat*, followed by T, H.
545   *sore.* So L, U, D, E, C, followed by K, T. P, A: *sad*, followed by H.
551   *schyveryng.* So L, P, C. A, U, D, E: *schymeryng*, followed by K, T, H.
      scheldes. So P, A, U, D, E, C, followed by K, T, H. L: *schendes.*
552   *alle.* So L, followed by K. P, A, U, D, E, C omit, followed by T, H.
      fure. So P, A, U, followed by H. L, D, E, C: *a fure*, followed by K, T.
553   *Waspasian.* So L, P, A, E, followed by K, T. U, D, C: *Vaspasian*, followed by H.
555   *fals.* So A, D, E, C, followed by T, H. L: *fals men*, followed by K. P: *folke.* U:
      fals folk.
      forto. So P, A, D, followed by T, H. L, U, E: *to*, followed by K. C: *unto.*
556   *greved.* So L, followed by K. P: *þe grimly.* D, E: *wiþ grame*, followed by T. A, U,
      C: *grownde.* H emends to *gremed.*
      girden. So L, followed by K. P: *girden þey.* A, U, D, E, C: *þey girden*, followed
      by T, H.
559   *was.* So L, followed by H. P, A, U, D, E, C: *war*, followed by K, T.
562   *burnee.* So L, followed by H. P omits line. A: *those beryns.* U, D: *beerns*,
      followed by K. E, C emend line. D.
565   *hit.* L: added above the line.
571   *Rappis.* So L, followed by H. C: *Here ropes.* K, T emend to *Roppis.*
      rydders. So A, followed by K, T, H. L: *redles.* P omits line. U, D, C: *redely.* E
      alters line.

575   *in.* So P, A, U, D, E, C, followed by D$_{86}$, T, H. L: *in þe,* followed by K.

576   *That.* So P, A, U, D, E, C, followed by K, T, H. L: *Þe.*

579–80   Ordering of lines in L, followed by K. T, H invert line order.

579   *starke.* So P, U, D, E, C, followed by T, H. L: *storte,* corrected from *strrte,* followed by K. A: *stane.*

581   *dyed.* So U, D, E, followed by K. L: *doun diȝten.* P omits line. A, C: *diȝeden,* followed by H. T emends to *doun dyede.*

581   *in that stounde.* So U, followed by K. L: *hem sone.* P omits line. A: *full sone,* followed by T. D, E: *in a stounde.* C: *in a whyle.* H emends to *sone.*

583   *an anlepy.* So A, followed by K, T, H. L: *olepy.* P: *anely ane.* U, D: *an.* E, C: *on.*

584   *a.* So U, D, C, followed by D$_{88}$, H. L, P, A omit, followed by K, T. E: *þe.*

586   *made.* So L, A, U, D, C, followed by K, T. P: *ma,* followed by H. E omits.

589   *a.* So P, U, E, C, followed by D$_{88}$, T, H. L omits, followed by K. A: *ane.* D: *þe.*

590   *ilka.* So A, followed by D$_{88}$, H. L, U, D: *eche,* followed by K. P, E, C: *iche a,* followed by T.

591   *to the berfray.* So P, A, U, D, E, followed by K, T, H. L: *þe bischup.* C: *to þe bastyle.*

         and. So L. P, A, U, D, E, C omit, followed by K, T, H.

         the$_2$. So P, U, D, E, C, followed by T, H. L: *his.* A: *those,* followed by K.

595   *redde on.* So P, A, U, D, E, C, followed by K, T, H. L: *redden.*

599   *Fele of.* So L, D. P: *Felles þe.* A: *He fellide.* U: *Felde of,* followed by K, T, H. C: *And felde.* E alters line.

608   *mart.* So L, followed by T, H, though *red* has been added above the line by a later hand. P: *morte.* A: *merrede full.* U, D, E, C: *marred,* followed by K.

610   *Unriven.* So A, followed by K, T, H. L: Ronnen over. P omits line. U, D, C: *Wele-arayed.*

614   *or the fight ended.* So L. K emends to *that no freke skapide,* H emends to *and noȝt a freke skaped,* both from variants of P, A, U, D, E, C.

616   *wynnen.* So K. L: *wynmen.* P, U, D: *wan.* A: *wane.* E omits. C: *wanne.* T, H emend to *wonnen.*

620   *pile.* So L, followed by K. P: *pynnes.* A, U, C: *pyne,* followed by T. D, E: *pinne,* followed by H.

623   *manye.* So L, followed by K. P, A, U, D, E, C: *þykke,* followed by T, H.

626   *Quarten.* So L. P: *Whappen,* followed by T, H. A: *Warppis.* D: E *Quattid.* C: *They shette.* K emends to *quarren.*

         out querels. So A, D, E, C, followed by T, H. L inverts, followed by K. P: *doune querels.*

         quarters. So L, P, A, D, E, C, followed by T. K emends to *quartotes.* H emends to *quartes.*

630   *The.* So L, followed by H. P, A, U, D, E, C: *For þe,* followed by K, T.

632   *Wanted.* So P, A, followed by K, T, H. L: *Wounded.* U, D: *Wanted hem.* E: *lakkyd hym.* C: *They wanted.*

636   *thus.* So P, A, U, D, E, C, followed by T, H. L: *so,* followed by K.

637   *As rathe.* So D, followed by T. L, A: *Sone.* P: *Onone.* U: *Alsone.* E, C: *As sone.* H emends to *Rathe.*

637   *ros yn.* So D. L: *rosen.* P, E, C: *rose on,* followed by K, T, H. A: *and rase one.* U: *gan rise on.*

638   This line added in the margin of L by the same hand.

       on brode. So P, A, C, followed by T, H. L: *anon*, followed by K. U: *her bemes*.
           C: *on brode and*. E: *up*.

       ryse. So A, D, followed by T, H. L, C: *aryse*, followed by K. P, U, E: *rayse*.

641   *spare*. So L, P, A, U, D, E, C, followed by K, T. H emends to *sparen*.

644   *manye*. So L, followed by K. P, U, D, C: *noble*, followed by T, H. A: *full nobylle*.
           E alters line.

646   *Made wayes full wide*. So A, U, D, followed by T. L: *Made wide weyes*, followed
           by K. P: *Weyes made they wide*, followed by H. E alters line. C: *They made
           wayes full wide*.

652   *Greided*. So P, U, D, followed by T, H. L: *Groded*, followed by K. A, C: *Getyn*.
           E: *Deepe ypyȝt*.

653   *Hit*. So P, A, U, D, E, C, followed by K, T, H. L: *he*.

655   *hyghte*. So P, A, followed by T, H. L: *haste*, followed by K. U, D, E: *hye*. C:
           hyed.

658   *unarwely*. So A, followed by K, T, H. L: *arwely*. P: *egrely*. D: *ful hastily*. C: *full
           smertelye*.

661   *beldes*. So A, D, followed by T, H. L: *þat bilde was*, followed by K. P: *bretage*. U,
           E omit line. C: *byggynges*.

       full. So A, followed by T. L: *wel*, followed by H. P omits. D, C: *so*. U, E omit
           line.

665   *and brode*. So L, followed by K. P omits. A: *and bare*. U, D, C: *at a bir*, followed
           by T, H. E omits line.

667   *above*. So L, followed by H. P: *aboune*. A, U, D, C: *abowte*, followed by K, T.

       halves. So P, A, D, C, followed by T, H. L: *sydes*, followed by K. U alters line.
           E omits line.

674   *playande*. So P, A, followed by K, T, H. L: *blowande*. U, D, C: *boyland*. E omits.

675   *Brennande*. So P, A, U, D, E, C, followed by K, T, H. L: *Brennen*.

       many. So U, D, C, followed by H. L, P, A omit, followed by K, T. E alters line.

       barels. So L, P, A, followed by K, T. U, D, C: *barel*, followed by H.

683   L omits line. Supplied from P, following K, T, H.

       freke. So P, followed by T, H. A: *unfongede*. U omits. D: *found*. E: *fonde*,
           followed by K. C: *out wente*.

       fele harmes. So P, followed by T. A: *feþer-hames*, followed by K, H. U, D, E, C:
           fressh harmes.

684   *Ne*. So P, A, U, D, followed by K, T, H. L: *Þat*. E alters line. C: *Nor*.

686   *kirnels*. So L, followed by K, T. P: *kyrnels*. A: *kirnells*. U, D, E: *corners*. C:
           cornerers. H emends to *kirneles*.

       alle. So U. L, P, A, D, E, C omit, followed by K, T, H.

687   *stewe*. So P, A, C, followed by T, H. L, U: *steem*, followed by K. D, E: *stench*.

689   *to toun*. So L, followed by H. P, A, U, E, C: *to þe toune*, followed by K, T. D:
           þe wellis.

690   *strande*. So A, followed by K, T, H. L, P: *strem*. U: *cours*. D, E, C: *spryng*.

695   *What*. So P, U, D, E, C, followed by K, T, H. L: *With*. A: *Whatekyns*.

697   *deyes*. So P, A, D, E, followed by K, T, H. L, C: *deþes*. U: *dayes*.

699   *Firste*. So P, A, D, C, followed by T, H. L: *Þen*, followed by K. U: *And than*. E:
           Bot feerst.

702	*half*. So P, A, U, D, followed by K, T, H. L, E: *side*. C: *parte*.
704	*kagged*. So K, H. L: *kagges*. P: *cacchyd*, followed by T. A: *chachede*. U: *catched*. D: *cacchid*. E: *bounde*. C: *were kawȝte*.
708	*sett*. So P, A, U, C, followed by T. L: *souȝt*, followed by L. D: *syed*, followed by H. E alters line.
	the₂. So P, A, U, D, C, followed by D₈₈, T. L omits, followed by K. E alters line.
709	*men*. So L, A, E, C, followed by K, T. P, U, D: *ledes*, followed by H.
710	*topsailes*. So D₈₈, H. L: *topsail*, followed by K, T. P, C: *topsayle*. A: *topsaile*. U, D: *and topsaile*. E: *topseyl*.
715	*here*. So L, P, followed by K, T. A: *hem by þe*, followed by H. U, D, E, C: *hemself by the*.
716	*doun*. So P, A, U, D, E, C, followed by K, T, H. L omits.
	daschen. So P, followed by H. L: *daschande*. A, U, D, E, C: *daschede*, followed by K, T.
718–24	As H (pp. 130–31) was the first to realize, these lines are a direct quotation of Vespasian's orders concerning the dead prisoners. This construction has only survived in pieces throughout the manuscript record, requiring "extensive, although minimalist, surgery" to be reclaimed.
719	*alle*. So P, A, U, C, followed by T, H. L: *twelf*, followed by K. E: *caste*. D *cursid*.
720	*brennen*. So H. L: *brenten*, followed by K, T. P: *brynd*. A: *brynte*. U, D, E, C: *brent*.
	browne. So P, A, E, C, followed by T, H. L, U, E: *þe browne*, followed by K.
721	*wende*. So H. L, P, U, D: *went*, followed by K, T. A, E, C: *wente*.
722	*blowen*. So P, followed by H. L, D, E: *blewen*, followed by K, T. A, U: *blewe thay*. C: *þey blewen*.
723	*for*. So L, P, followed by T, H. A, U, D, E, C: *to*, followed by K.
	doun. So L, followed by H. P, A, U, D, E, C: *duke*, followed by K, T.
724	*bidde*. So H. L, A: *bade*, followed by K, T. P, U, D, E: *bad*. C: *badde*.
	bischop. So P, A, U, followed by D₈₆, T, H. L, E, C: *bischopes*, followed by K. D: *bisshops*.
725	*twelf*. So P, U, D, E, C, followed by T, H. L, A: *alle*, followed by K.
727	*they*. So A, U, D, E, C, followed by T, H. L: *he*, followed by K. P omits line.
728	*here*. So P, A, U, D, E, C, followed by T, H. L: *his*, followed by K.
729	*dymmed*. So D, followed by K, H. L: *dymned*. P: *and dryven*. A: *and dynnede*. U: *and dymmed*. C: *& þenne dymmedde*.
730	*montayns*. So L, followed by H. U, D: *the montayns*, followed by K.
731	*rysten*. So P, A, followed by K, H. L: *rusken*. U, D, C: *to reste*. E omits line.
733	*aboute betyn abrode*. So L, followed by K. P, A: *on brade bette*. U: *al obrode is brent*. D: *and brood ar bette*. E: omits line. C: *and brode were made*. H emends to *abrode betyn*.
741	*schadewes*. So L, followed by K. P, A, U, D, E: *schadew*, followed by H. C alters line.
742	*lyften*. So P, U, E, followed by K, H. L: *lyfteneþ*. A: *to newen*. D: *lyft up*. C: *sone leften up*.
743	*full*. So U, D, followed by D₈₈, H. L, P omit, followed by K. A: *one*. E, C alter line.
746	*face*. So P. L, U: *fote*, followed by K. D, E, C: *foote*. A: *fourche*. H emends to *fronte*.

747   *pallen.* So A, D, followed by K, H. L, P: *pale.* U, E omit line. C: *gay.*

749   *The grate.* So U, D, C, followed by H. L: *Grayþed.* P: *Þe grace.* A: *The grate was,* followed by K. E: *With a grate.*

750   *colour.* So L, followed by H. P: *to couer.* A: *colourede,* followed by K. U, D, C: *of colour.* E: *with colours.*

754   *polisched.* So P, A, U, D, E, C, followed by H. L: *purged,* followed by K.

756   *above.* So L, followed by H. A: *abowte,* followed by K. U: *al about.* D: *cast about.* E alters line. C: *aboven.*

758   *hanleth.* So L, followed by H. A: *Than hendely.* K emends to *hauleþ over.*

760   *avental.* So P, A, U, D, E, C omit, followed by H. L: *with avental,* followed by K.

767   *sewen.* So L, followed by H. P, C: *saw.* A: *seese.* U: *syen.* D: *seyen,* followed by K. E: *seen.*

770   *Bet.* So P, followed by H. L: *Betynge,* followed by K. A alters line. U, D, E: *And bet.* C: *And beteth.*

      that all. So P. L: *on,* followed by K. A alters line. U, D, C: *þat,* followed by H. E alters line.

773   *walle.* So L, followed by K. P, A: *walles,* followed by H. U, D, E, C omit line.

775   *hit never.* So P, A, followed by H. L: *noȝt o droppe.* U, D: *never.* E alters line. C: *maye nevur.*

776   *O droppe.* So P, U, D, C, followed by H. L omits, followed by K. A: *A dope.* E: *for o droppe.*

      dey scholde. So P, A, U, D, C, followed by H. L: *deþ scholde dey,* followed by K. E alters line.

778   *hath.* þ written over an erasure in L.

779   *defenden.* So P, followed by H. L, C: *fyȝten.* A, U, D: *fende off,* followed by K. E: *defende and hold of.*

780   *ye tourne.* So P, A, U, D, C, followed by K, H. L: *we wende,* with *we* inserted above the line. E: *ȝe nevere.*

781   *manschyp.* So L, D, followed by K. P, A: *menske,* followed by H. U, C: *wirship.* E: *wysdom.*

      were hit. So P. L: *were hit ȝit,* followed by K, H. U, D: *it is.* E, C: *hit were.*

      to. So P, A, U, D, E, C, followed by H. L omits, followed by K.

784   *any.* So A, U, D, C, followed by K, H. L omits. P omits line. E alters line.

      stray. So A, U, D, C, followed by K, H. L: *stay.* P omits line. E alters line.

789   *gentyl.* So L, A, E, C, followed by K. P: *gynnes.* U, D: *gynful,* followed by H.

793   *and dryen.* So D. L: *deyed.* P: *dryen.* A: *and dryede.* U, C: *and dried.* E alters line. K emends to *dryed.* H emends to *dryeden.*

797   *Bot.* So P, A, U, D, E, C, followed by H. L omits, followed by K.

801   The caesura is marked following *nothyng* in L.

      note newe. So P, A, U, D, C, followed by D$_{86}$. L: *anewe note,* followed by K. E: *newe werk.*

808   *dyt.* So L, followed by H. P, A, U, D, C: *dyn,* followed by K. E: *noyse.*

811   *the.* Added above the line in L.

814   *Brente.* So P, A, followed by K, H. L: *Brenten.* U, D: *men he brent.* E alters line. C: *he hem brente.*

820   *habiden.* So A, U, D, E, C, followed by H. L: *habben,* followed by K. P *hab.*

821	*braydyn*. So A, U, D, E, C, followed by H. P: *brayed þan*. L: *bowyn*, followed by K.
	bekered. L: *b* corrected from *k*.
822	*felly*. So L, D, E, C, followed by K. P, A: *felony*. U: *felonsly*, followed by H.
823	*Jokken*. So K. L: *Jolken*. P: *Jugkyn*. A: *Thay jusken at those*. U: *And the*. D: *Jollid*. E: *And beryn*. C: *Ther þey jolledde*. H emends to *Iouken*.
829	*a*. So L, D, followed by K. P, A, U, C omit, followed by H. E alters line.
	bely. So P, U, C: *bely*, followed by H. L, A, D: *body*, followed by K. E alters line.
830	*a*. So P, A, U, D, E, C, followed by H. L: *þe*, followed by K.
	of. So H. L, P, A, C: *on*, followed by K. U: *out of*. D, E: *in*.
	stayre. So P, A, C, followed by H. L: *staf*. U: *toure*. D, E: *stound*. K emends to *staf-slyng*.
832	*And was*. So L, followed by K. P, U, D, E omit, followed by H. A, C: *And*.
840	*archelers*. So K, D$_{88}$, H. L, U, D: *archers*. P: *aschelers*. E: *achillers*. C: *asshelers*.
843	*by resting*. So P, A, U, D, E, C, followed by K, H. L: *reste*.
	sonne. So P, D, followed by H. L: *þat synne*. A, U, E, C: *the sonne*, followed by K.
844	*toles*. So P, followed by H. L: *ton*, followed by K. A: *toose*. U, D, E, C alter line.
857	*doun*. So L, followed by K. H reads *don*.
	sprongen. So P, A, C, followed by K, H. L: *spryngen*. U, D, E omit line.
858	Caesura unmarked in L.
863	*on ernest*. So L, followed by K. P, C: *firste*. A: *in haste*. U, D, E omit. H emends to *ȝernest*.
864	*specke*. So L, followed by K. P, A, U, D, C: *schewe*, followed by H. E alters line.
866	*torfere*. So P, A, followed by K, H. L: *torsom*. U, D: *tray*. E alters line. C: *tormente*.
867	*graunten*. So A, followed by H. L: *scheweth*, followed by K. P, U, D, E, C: *grauntede*.
870	*lese folke*. So A, followed by K. L: *lesne*. P, U: *ledes*. D: *losse*. C: *folk*. E alters line.
878	*marden*. So A, followed by K, H. L, P: *maden*. U, E: *spende*. D: *spendid*. C: *have spended*.
879	*hunger*. So P, A, D, E, C, followed by K, H. L omits. U omits line.
880	L, P omit line. Supplied from A, following K, H.
883	*sege*. So P, A, U, D, E, C, followed by K, H. L: *cite*.
886	*and masers*. So A, U, followed by H. L: *maser*. D: *and marcers*. E: *and masons*. C: *and bedelles*. K emends to *masers*.
	The caesura is marked following *men* in L.
	he. So A, U, C, followed by H. L: *he to*, followed by K. P omits line. D, E alter line.
887	*chefly*. So A, followed by K. L: *chersly*, followed by H. P omits. U: *ful styfly*. C: *styfely*. D, E alter line.
891	*the*. Added above the line in L.
892	*fele*. So L, followed by H. K reads *fole*.
893	*lyked*. So L, followed by K. P: *lykeþ*, followed by H. A: *wolde*. U, D, E alter line. C: *beste pleseth*.

895   *Torneien.* So K, H. L: *Tornen.* P alters line. A: *With tournaye and.* U, D: *And turnyd with.* E: *And wente withowte.* C alters line.

       the. So A, U, D, E, C, followed by K, H. L: *þe þe.*

896   *oure Lord.* So P, A, C, followed by H. L: *and God.* U, D: *and Lord*, followed by K. E alters line.

       grace. So L, followed by K. P, U, D: *joye*, followed by H. A: *heven.* E, C alter line.

899   *bothe.* So P, followed by H. L omits. A omits line. U, D, E: *yit therto.* C: *also*, followed by K.

901   *mylde.* So P, A, D, C, followed by K, H. L, U, E: *myde.*

903   *this.* So P, A, D, E, C, followed by K, H. L: *þus.* U: *the.*

906   *brytten.* So P, A, D, followed by K, H. L: *brenten.* U: *birten.* E: *cacche.* C: *murder.*

910   *privé.* So P, A, U, D, E, C, followed by H. L: *þore*, followed by K.

914   *a prikkes.* So A, U, D, followed by H. L: *a pokes*, followed by K. P: *pryk.* E alters line. C: *a prikke.*

919   *stryketh.* So L, followed by K. P: *styked.* A: *stekide.* U: *strike.* D: *stikyd.* E alters line. C: *smote.* H emends to *stykeþ.*

923   *mynden.* So D$_{88}$, H. L: *mynde*, followed by K. P: *mene.* A: *menyn.* U: *mynne.* D: *myn.* E alters line. C omits line.

925   *togedres gan.* So H. L: *togedres þan*, followed by K. P: *togeder er gone.* A: *gadirde þam togedire and.* U: *togeder gan gone to.* D, E: *gan togidir gon.* C: *gedered togydur and.*

       geten. So P, U, D, followed by K, H. L, E: *chossen.* A, C: *gatt.*

927   *Lucyus.* So A, U, D, E, C, followed by K, H. L: *lyous.* P: *Lustius.*

928   *lord.* So L, D, E, C. P, A, U: *lede*, followed by K, H.

929   *they.* So P, A, U, D, E, C, followed by K, H. L: *þe.*

       metten. So P, A, U, D, C, followed by D$_{88}$, H. L, E: *mette*, followed by K.

931   *more.* So L, P, D, E, followed by H. A, U, C: *no more*, followed by K.

932   *and.* So P, A, E, followed by D$_{86}$, H. L, C: *and þe*, followed by K. U: *and his.* D: *þe.*

933   *And whan.* So L, followed by K. P, U, D, E, C: *Whan*, followed by H. A: *Than when.*

934   *on ernest.* So L, followed by K. P: *in.* A: *in areste.* U, D: *in ernest.* E omits. C: *aftur.* H emends to *ȝernest.*

935   *That.* So P, A, U, D, C, followed by H. L: *Þe*, followed by K. E alters line.

936   *Than.* So L, followed by K. P, A, U, D, E: *An*, followed by H. C: *He.*

       he heldeth. So L, followed by K. P, A, U, D, E, C: *ȝelde.* H emends to *ȝeldeþ.*

937   *raisen.* So P, U, D, followed by H. L: *risen up*, followed by K. A, C: *rayssede.* E: *resyn þo.*

938   An unknown number of lines appear to have been lost at this point. For more on the loss of text here and after line 942, see H (pp. 139–40).

939   *that.* So P, A, U, D, C, followed by K, H. L omits. E alters line.

941   *Waspasian.* So L, P, E, followed by K. A omits line. U, D, C: *Vaspasian*, followed by H.

942   *Sent.* So P, U, D, E, followed by K, H. L: *Souȝt.* A: *Sendis.* C: *He sente.*

943   *as$_1$.* So P, D, E, followed by K, H. L: *is.* A, C omit. U: *al.*

944   *drowe.* So U, D, E, followed by H. L: *drowe hym*, followed by L. P: *was drawen.* A alters line. C: *drawen.*

945	*gome.* So L, P, U, D, followed by K. A: *gome hymselfe.* E: *gorel*, followed by H. C: *prince.*
946	*boweled.* So P, C, followed by K, H. L: *bowewed.* A: *boluede.* U, D, E alter line.
947	*yermande.* So K, H. L: *ȝernande.* P: *heledand.* A: *ȝarande.* U: *yemerand.* D alters line. E: *stumbling.* C: *gronynge.*
948	*they.* So P, A, U, D, E, C, followed by K, H. L omits.
949	*segge.* So P, U, D, followed by K, H. L, C: *man.* A alters line. E: *Vitayl.*
955	*men.* So L, A, U, C, followed by K. P, D, E omit, followed by H.
956	*of the burwe so bold was.* So P, A, U, D, C, followed by H. L: *was so bold þe bruwe for*, followed by K. E: *was so boold out of þe town.*
959	*and₂.* So A, C, followed by H. L, P, U, D, E omit, followed by K.
960	*and.* Added above the line in L, followed by H. K omits.
963	*for.* So P, A, U, C, followed by H. L, D, E: *her*, followed by K.
973	*broght of blys.* So V, followed by H. L, P, A, U, C: *of blys broȝt.* D omits line. E alters line.
974	*lond.* So L, U, E, C, followed by K. A, V: *lede*, followed by H. P, D omit line.
976	*and I so.* L reads *& so & I so*, with the initial *& so* marked for deletion.
978–79	K inverts these lines following P, A, V, U, C, then reinstates the first word of each line so that they read *Tille me the gates . . . / And I this toured toun . . . .* H follows L.
978	*toun.* So P, A, V, U, D, E, C, followed by K, H. L: *doun.*
	have. So P, U, D, E, C, followed by K, H. L: *han.* A, V omit.
	my. So A, V, U, D, E, C, followed by H. L, P omit, followed by K.
981	*Brosten and betyn.* So L, followed by K. P: *brayde and brosten.* A, V: *Betyn and brosten*, followed by H. U: *Brent and brusten.* D: *Broke and brusten.* E: *Bete and brusten.* C: *And beten and breken.*
983	*thy.* So P, A, V, U, D, followed by K, H. L: *þe.* K's emendation. E alters line. C omits line.
	this. So L, followed by K. P, A, V, U, D: *þe*, followed by H. E alters line. C omits line.
988	*doun.* So L. H reads *don.*
989	*who.* So A, V, followed by D₈₆, H. L, U, C: *whoso*, followed by K. P: *þat who.* D: *þat whoso.* E omits line.
990	*sein.* So P, A, V, followed by K, H. L: *seint.* U: *yseyn.* D: *set.* E omits line. C omits.
992	*of.* So P, A, C, Ex, followed by K, H. L: *ofte.* V omits. U, D, E omit line.
999	*the.* So P, A, V, U, D, E, Ex, followed by H. L, C: *þy*, followed by K.
1001	*lote.* So L, P, A, followed by H. V, U, D, E, C: *look.* K emends to *loke.*
	his. So P, A, V, U, D, E, C, followed by H. L: *þe*, followed by K.
1004	*burnes.* So U, D, followed by K, H. L, P: *burne.* A, V, C omit. E alters line.
1005	*I.* So P, A, V, U, D, E, Ex, followed by H. L: *And I*, followed by K. C: *For I.*
1006	*the walles.* So P, A, E, followed by K, H. L omits. V, D, C: *þe wall.* U: *wal.*
1007	*hap.* So P, A, V, U, E, followed by H. L: *þe happis.* D: *hele.* K emends to *þe happe.*
1008	*be to-hewen.* So L, followed by K. P, Ex: *tohewen be*, followed by H. A: *hewen forto be.* V: *hewen be.* U, C: *hewen to be.* D: *britnyd to be.* E: *deed forto be.*
1010	*Alle.* So L, P, followed by K. A, V, U, D, Ex omit, followed by H.
	to. So A, C, U, D, C, followed by K, H. L, Ex omit. E: *on.*

1018   *upon grounde*. So L, followed by K. P, A, V, D, C: *under God*, followed by H. U, E: *under the cope*.

1019   *Ne*. So P, A, V, U, D, E, followed by K, H. L: *Be*. C: *Nor*.

        stondande. So P, A, V, U, D, C, followed by K, H L: *stonden*. E: *laft*.

1021   *he*. So P, V, followed by H. L: *his*. A, C: *he his*, followed by K. U, D: *the kyng*. E: *Waspasyan*.

1023   *God*. So P, V, U, D, E, C, followed by K, H. L omits. A: *to God*.

        forto. So A, U, followed by H. L, P, V, D, C: *to*, followed by K. E omits.

1024   *hertis*. So A, V, D, E, C. L, P: *herte*, followed by K, H.

1025   *the*. So P, A, V, U, D, E, C, followed by H. L omits, followed by K.

1027   *hath*. So A, V, U, D, C, followed by K, H. L: *han*. P alters line. E omits.

        so. So A, V, U, C, followed by K, H. L omits. P alters line. D, E: *such*.

1033   *He*. So P, A, V, U, D, E, C, followed by K. L: *Ben*. H emends to *Be-*.

        woxen. So L, followed by H. P: *waxen*. A, V, C: *wexe*, followed by K (*woxe*). U: *waxeth*. D: *wexid*. E omits.

1034   *And*. So L, followed by K. P, A, V, U, D, E omit, followed by H. C alters.

1035   *sente*. So P, A, V, U, D, E, C, followed by H. L: *wende*. K emends to *sende*.

1036   *condit*. So P, A, followed by K, H. L: *condis*. V, U, E: *condit hym*. D: *conduyt þei*. C: *a condyte*.

1038   *freke*. So P, A, V, U, D, followed by K, H. L, C: *man*.

1040   *with a goode wylle*. So L, P, A, V, C, followed by K. U, D, E: *þe gome forto hele*, followed by H.

1051   *with the hete*. So P, A, V, C. L: *to sprede*. D alters. K, H emend to *to brede*.

        to brede. So P, A, V, U, C. L: *abrode*, followed by K, H. D: *to blede*. E: *to wurche*.

1052   *resorte*. So L, followed by H. P, A: *to resorte*, followed by K. V, C: *to comforte*. U, D, E: *to restore*.

1061   *saghtles*. So P, D, followed by H. L: *satles*, followed by K. V, A, U: *saughtled*. E: *acordyd*. C: *sawe how*.

1062   *ther*. So L, followed by K. A, V, U, D, E, C omit, followed by H.

        he. So L, C, followed by K. P, A: *hym beste*. V: *hym*, followed by H. U, D: *him gode*. E: *þat he*.

        wolde. So L, E, C, followed by K. P, A, V, U, D: *lykede*, followed by H.

1067   *And*. So P, A, U, D, E, followed by K, H. L: *Now*. V omits. C: *Thanne*.

1069   *Now*. So A, V, E, followed by K, H. L: *And*. U, D, C omit.

        tore. So P (?), followed by K, H. L: *hard*. A, U, D, E, C: *tym*. V omits.

1071   *fourty*. So D, E, followed by H. L, A, V, U, C: *four*, followed by K.

1077   *flatte*. So U, D, E, followed by K, H. L: *platte*. P: *faste*. V: *fellen*.

1080   *wyght*. So A, U, D, followed by K, H. L: *wye*. E: *grete*. C: *feble*.

1082   *ho brad*. So L, followed by K. P: *brynt it*. A: *Made brede*. V: *brad hit*. U: *braid*. D: *brad*, followed by H. E: *leyde*. C: *leyde hit*.

1086   *hunger*. So A, V, U, D, E, followed by K, H. L: *hingur*. C: *honger is*.

1088   *And entre*. So L, followed by K. A, V, U, D, C: *entre*, followed by H. P, E alter line.

        cam out. So L, E, followed by K. A, V, U, D, C: *out cam*, followed by H. P, E alter line.

1089   *smel*. So L, V, E, followed by K. A, U, D, C: *smelle*. H emends to *rich*.

        into. So U, D, E, followed by H. L: *to*, followed by K. P, A, V, C: *in*.

        strete. So P, A, V, U, D, E, C, followed by H. L: *walles*, followed by K.

1090	*felden.* So V, followed by D$_{88}$, H. L, P, U, E: *felde,* followed by K. A: *felide.* C: *þer felede.*
1092	*layned.* So P, A, V, followed by H. L: *loyned,* followed by K. U, D, C: *ykept.*
1095	*forth.* So L, P, followed by K. A, V, U, D, C omit, followed by H.
1097	*Away.* So L, followed by K. P alters line. A: *And furthe.* V, U, D, E, C: *Forþ,* followed by H.
	wepyng. So L, D, E, followed by K. P alters line. A, V, U: *wepande,* followed by H. C: *wepynge.*
	ech one. So L, followed by K. P alters line. A, U, D, E, C: *full sore.* V: *sore,* followed by H.
1100	*fyne.* So L, followed by H. A, V, U, D: *pyne,* followed by K. E, C: *peyne.*
1103	*olde age.* So L, followed by K. A, V, C: *elde,* followed by H. U, D: *grete elde.* E: *gret age.*
1104	*That.* So A, V, U, D, followed by H. L omits, followed by K. E: *Þo þat.* C: *And.*
1105	*to$_1$.* So L, followed by H. A: *thay,* followed by K. V, U, D, E omit.
1109	*wayes.* So A, V, U, D, E, C, followed by K, H. L: *wyes.*
1112	*on.* So L, followed by H. P, A: *in,* followed by K. V, U, D, E, C: *undir.*
1113	*after.* So L, followed by H. A, V, D, E: *after one,* followed by K. U, C: *on.*
	redeth. So L, followed by H. D: *ridis.* C: *rode.* K emends to *rideþ.*
1117	*and.* So L, followed by H. A, V, U, E omit, followed by K.
1122	L omits line. supplied from A, following K, H.
	And. So P, A, followed by K. V, U, D, E, C omit, followed by H.
	scharpe. So V, U, D, C, Ex, followed by K, H. A: *scharpere.* E: *wol scharpe.*
1123	*wede.* So L, U, D, C, followed by K. P, V: *yren,* followed by H. A: *iryns.*
1125	*hetter.* So A, followed by H. L, D: *herty,* followed by K. P: *hetty.* V: *hettill.* U, E: *hertly.* C: *byttur.* Ex: *herter.*
1126	*the.* So P, A, V, U, D, E, C, followed by H. L omits, followed by K.
	flewe. So P (?), A, V, U, D, E, C. L: *flowen.* K, H emend to *flowe.*
1130	*issed.* So U, D, E, followed by K. L: *dissed.* P: *hyes.* A: *faste hyes.* V: *issues.* C: *hovede.*
1132	*holpen.* Corrected from *helpen* in L.
1134	*mynours.* So A, V, U, D, E, C, followed by K, H. L: *mynour.* P: *mason.*
	forto. So P, A, V, U, D, E, Ex, followed by D$_{88}$, H. L, C: *to,* followed by K.
1138	*forsoken.* So V, U, E, followed by D$_{88}$, H. L, A, D, C, Ex: *forsoke,* followed by K.
1139	*that.* So P, A, V, U, D, C, followed by H. L: *þis,* followed by K.
1140	*rejoyced.* So D, followed by K, H. L: *joyced.* A: *rewede of.* V, C: *shulde rejoisse of.* U, E: *renewed.*
1141	*by.* So P, A, V, U, D, E, C, followed by H. L: *with,* followed by L.
1145	*for.* So A, V, U, D, E, C, followed by K, H. L: *fro.*
1146	*gyven.* So A, V, D, C, followed by K. L: *ȝoven.*
	erthe. So A, V, U, D, E, C, followed by K, H. L: *lyve.*
1149	*Swounen.* So L, followed by H. A, E: *Some,* followed by K. V: *Sum men.* U: *Swollyng.* C: *Swonyng.*
	and. So A, V, U, D, E, C, followed by D$_{88}$, H. L omits, followed by K.
1150	*lanterne.* So A, V, U, D, E, C, followed by K, H. L: *laterne.*
1153	*hem overe.* So V, U, D, C, followed by K, D$_{88}$, H. L: *evere.* A: *þam alle over.*

1154   *diche*. So U, D, E, C, followed by K, H. L: *diche depe*. A: *dikis*. V: *dyke*.

1156   *had*. So A, V, C, followed by H. L: *hadde*, followed by K. D, E: *he had*.

1157   *he*. So A, V, C, followed by K, H. L: *he he hadde Josophus*. U, D, E: *He bad*.

         to enforme. So A, U, C, followed by K, H. L omits by mislineation, placing the phrase at the head of the following line. V: *and hem forto lerne*. D, E: *enfourme*.

1158   *Forto save*. So A, V, C, followed by K, H. L: *Enforme hem to save*. U, D, E: *In savying of*.

1167   *ilka*. So U, followed by H. L: *eche*, followed by K. A: *iche a*. D, C: *eche a*. V alters line.

1170   *Withouten*. So A, U, D, followed by K, H. L: *Souȝten*.

1171   *Goren*. So K, H. L: *Toren*. A: *Thay gorrede*. U: *Thei gored*. D: *They gorid*. C: *Ther þet gorede*. V: *Þey slitten*.

1172   *Fayner*. So V, U, D, followed by K, H. L, C: *Fayn*. A: *And faynere*.

         than of. So A, V, U, D, followed by K, D$_{88}$, H. L: *were*. C: *and þenne of*.

1174   *sought*. So V, followed by K, H. L: *þouȝt*. A: *bysoughte*. U: *setten*. D, C: *set*. E: *laste*.

         cité. So A, V, U, D, E, C, followed by K, H. L: *toun*.

1178   *wyse*. So A, V, C, followed by K, H. L: *side*. U: *half*. D: *way*.

1181   *Armen*. So L, followed by H. A: *Than thay armede*. V, U, E, D: *Þey armed*. D: *Þan armyd*. K emends to *Þei armen*.

1187   *fyghtyng men*. So A, followed by K, H. L: *men*. V, C: *of fyghtande men*. U: *of men*. D, E: *of folk*.

         ilka. So U, followed by H. L, E, C: *eche*, followed by K. A, V: *aythir*. D: *eche a*.

1190   *mynours*. So A, V, U, D, C, followed by K, H. L: *mynour*.

         myne. So A, V, U, D, E, C, followed by K, H. L: *mynde*.

1192   *brenyed*. So A, V, followed by H. L, D, E: *brayned*, followed by K. C: *armedde*.

1196   *brayned*. So L, U, E, followed by K. A: *birssede*. V: *brusshed*. D: *braynid*. C: *fell*. Ex: *brusyd*. H emends to *brosed*.

1199   *Wendeth*. So L, followed by K. A, V: *wane up*. U: *He wynnes*. D: *Wynneþ*, followed by H. C: *And wanne up*.

1200   *for ston*. So L, followed by H. A: *for stones*, followed by K. V, C: *on þe walle*. U: *on stone*. D, E: *on a stone*.

         ware. So U, followed by H. L, A: *gere*, followed by K. V, D, E: *weede*.

1205   *tyme*. So L, C, followed by K. A, V, U, D, E: *stounde*, followed by H.

1209   *Than*. So A, V, U, D, E, C, followed by H. L omits, followed by K.

1211   *hit*. So V, U, D, followed by H. L: *he*, followed by K. A: *scho*. E alters line.

1216   *to*. So A, V, U, D, E, C. L omits, followed by K, H.

1218   *the$_1$*. So A, V, D, C, followed by H. L: *ȝour*, followed by K. U, E: *this*.

1219   *agenes*. So D$_{88}$, H. V: *agains*. U: *ageyns*. D, C: *aȝens*. E: *al aȝens*. L: *aȝen*, followed by K. A: *mawgrethe*.

1220   *ben*. So L, followed by H. K emends to *be*.

1221   *yete*. So A, followed by H. L, U, D: *ȝolden*, followed by K. V: *unshette*. C: *geten*.

         al the yeres tyme. So V, followed by D$_{88}$, H. L: *thre ȝer byfore*, followed by K. A: *was all þe ȝeres tyme*. U, D: *thre ȝer aforne*. E alters line. C: *al þe thre ȝeres tyme*.

1223   *brennyng*. So A, V, U, D, E, C, followed by K, H. L: *brendyng*.

1224	*hond*. So L, followed by K. A, V, U: *hold*, followed by H. D, E, C: *holdyng*.
	of. So A, U, D, E, C, followed by K, H. L: *þe*. V omits.
1228	*the*. So A, V, U, E, C, followed by K, D$_{88}$, H. L, D omit.
1230	*voys$_{2,3}$*. So A, V, followed by H. L: *and . . . and*, followed by K.
1233	L, U, D, E omit line, followed by K. Supplied from V, following H.
	taken and wonnen. So H. A: *wonnen and tane*. V: *taken and graunted*. C: *taken and ʒolden*.
1234	*Yit*. So L, A, V, U, D, C, followed by K. H moves to head of b-verse.
	another. So C. L: *o*, followed by K, H. A: *a*. V: *one*. U: *thyes*. D: *þis ilk*.
1235	*worldly*. So L, followed by K. A: *worþly*, followed by H. V, U, D, E: *worthy*. C: *wordy*.
1236	*a*. So A, V, U, D, E, C, followed by L, D$_{88}$, H. L omits.
1237	*the vilayns*. So H. L, E: *þey*, followed by K. U: *thei*. D: *þei*.
1241	*and*. So L, followed by H. A, V, C: *anone thay*. E: *þanne and*. K emends to *þey*.
1244	*evere*. So D, C. L, A omit, followed by K. V, U, E: *ay*, followed by H.
1246	*stande*. So A. L: *stoken*. U, D: *stynt*. A: *stande*. V, C: *stonde*. K emends to *steken*. H emends to *styken*.
	on. So L, followed by H. A, V, U, D, C: *in*, followed by K.
1248	*enfamyned*. So V, U, followed by K, H. L: *enfamyed*. A: *enfameschede*. D: *with famyne*. C: *famyssched*.
	and defeted. L, A: *for defaute*, followed by K. V: *for faute*. U: *and defete*, followed by H. D: *defetid*. C: *þe for defaute*.
1256	*flikreth*. So H. L: *stikeþ*. A, U: *strykes*. V: *flikeþ*. D: *strikis*. E: *striketh*, followed by K. C: *ryche*.
1259–60	Order of lines as given by L, followed by K. A, V, U, D, E invert order, followed by H.
1259	*kende*. So H. V, D: *kindelled*. U: *kynde*, followed by K. L: *tende*. E: *lyʒt*. K emends to *kynde*. A, C alter line.
1260	*So were they*. So L, followed by K. A: *Þat one ane*. V: *Þat ay*, followed by H. U: *That over*. D: *Þat evere with*. E: *And ever more*. C: *That evur*.
	and. So L, C, followed by K. A, V, U, D, E omit, followed by H.
1262	*perische*. So A, V, U, D, E, C, followed by H. L: *persche*, followed by K.
	for. So V, U, D, E, C, followed by H. L, A: *for here*, followed by K.
1267	*pulisched*. So D$_{88}$. L: *pulsched*, followed by K, H. A, V: *and poleschede*. U, D, E: *ypolsched*.
1269	*metalles*. So V, followed by H. L: *metals*, followed by K. A, U, D, C: *metalle*. E: *marbul*.
1270	*copper*. So A, V, followed by K, H. L: *coppe*. U, D, E, C: *Cuppes*.
1271	*with*. So A, V, U, D, E, C, followed by K, H. L: *as*.
	over. So V, U, D, E, C, followed by H. L: *was over*, followed by K.
1274	The caesura is marked following *tresours* in L.
	they. So A, U, D, E, C, followed by H. L: *þey þer*, followed by K. V: *þe*.
1275	*and jemewes*. So U, D, E, C, followed by H. L: *jewels*. A: *and gemmys*. V: *gemmys*. K emends to *iemewes*.
1276	*fyne*. So V, U, D, E, C, followed by K, H. L: *rede*. A: *full fyne*.
	ther. So H. L, A, V, U, D, C omit, followed by K. E: *ywis*.
1277	*Riche*. So L, A, V, followed by K. U, E: *Ne*. D, C: *Ne riche*, followed by H.

1280   *wale*. So L. A: *wele*. V: *chese*. U, D: *welde*. E *hadde*. C: *toke*. K emends to *waleþ*.

1283   *hurled*. So U, followed by H. L: *hadde*, followed by K. A, C: *and had*. V: *and drof*. D: *hurtlid*. E: *and hurlyd*.

1286   *Tille*. So D, E, followed by H. L, A, V, U: *Tille alle*, followed by K.

1287   *a*. So A, followed by K, H. L: *þe*. V, U, D, E alter line. C omits line.

1290   *mude*. So A, V, E, followed by K, H. L, D: *made*. U, C omit line.

1293   *overtilt*. So U, D, followed by H. L: *overtourned*, followed by K. A: *overtytt*. V: *overtekte*. E: *overthrowe*. C: *overkaste*.

1295   *they*. So A, V, followed by H. L, U, D, E, C omit, followed by K.

        seiden. So V, U, followed by D$_{88}$, H. L, A, D, E, C: *seide*, followed by K.

1298   *Alle the*. So E. L: *As iuge*, followed by K. A: *To iuggen thase*. V: *To iuge þe*. U: *Os alle the*. D: *And al þe*. C: *To iuge the*. H emends to *Alle*.

        as. So A, D, C, followed by H. L, U omit, followed by K. V: *a*. E alters.

1299   *Criours*. So V, U, D, C, followed by K, H. L: *Crioure*. A: *And bedells*. E: *And*.

1304   *hethyng*. So V, U, D, followed by K, H. L: *hevyng*. A: *hethynges*. E: *betyng*. C: *rebukynge*.

        After this line, L inserts the following line (omitted from all other MSS): *And of þe tene þat hym tidde   tell hym þe soþe*.

1309   *acate*. So U, followed by H. L: *cate*, followed by K. A: *bargaun*. V: *achat*. E: *acade*. C: *countes*.

1312   L, U, D, E omit line. Supplied from A, following H. See explanatory note.

        fourmed. So H. A: *bene*. V, C: *ben worth*. K emends to *bene ful*.

1317   *the myddis*. So A, D. L: *myddel*, followed by K. V, C: *myddes*, followed by H. E: *þe mydde*.

        of the. So A, D, E, followed by K. L: *of*. C, V: *þe*, followed by H.

1322   *on*. So V, C, followed by K, H. L: *out of*. A: *of*. D: *in*. E omits.

1325   *ajorned*. So U, D, E, C, followed by H. L: *aiorneyd*, followed by K. A: *aioynede*. V: *ioyned*.

1327   *put*. So A, U, D, E, C, followed by H. L: *do*, followed by K. V omits.

        pynen. So A, followed by D$_{88}$, H, L, V, U, D, E, C: *pyne*, followed by K.

1328   *Vienne*. So U, D, E, C, followed by H. L: *Viterbo*, followed by K. A: *Vittern*. V: *Vettury*.

        he. So U, D, C, followed by H. L, V place before *venjaunce*, followed by K.

1334   *the*. So L, followed by K. H omits. A, V, U, D, E, C omit line.

1335–36   The quatrain is broken in L, the only extant copy. H assumes a loss of only two lines and numbers accordingly, a decision I have followed to facilitate cross-referencing between texts.

1337   *don*. So A, V, U, D, E, C, followed by K, H. L: *dempte*.

        drowen. So V, U, followed by D$_{88}$, H, L, D: *drow*, followed by K. A: *tuke*. E, C: *drewe*.

❧ BIBLIOGRAPHY

Alliterative Morte Arthure. In *King Arthur's Death: The Middle English Stanzaic Morte Arthur and Alliterative Morte Arthure*. Ed. Larry D. Benson, rev. Edward E. Foster. Kalamazoo, MI: Medieval Institute Publications, 1994. [See also *Morte Arthure*.]

Aquinas, Thomas. *Catena aurea: Commentary on the Four Gospels, Collected out of the Works of the Fathers by S. Thomas Aquinas*. Trans. Mark Pattison, J. D. Dalgrins, and T. D. Ryder. Oxford: John Henry Parker, 1841–45.

Aston, Margaret. "The Impeachment of Bishop Despenser." *Bulletin of the Institute of Historical Research* 38 (1965), 127–48.

Augustine, bishop of Hippo. *The Confessions and Letters of St. Augustin*. In Schaff, *A Select Library*, vol. 1.

———. *St. Augustin's City of God and Christian Doctrine*. In Schaff, *A Select Library*, vol. 2.

———. *St. Augustin: Homilies on the Gospel of John; Homilies on the First Epistle of John; Soliloquies*. In Schaff, *A Select Library*, vol. 7.

———. *Saint Augustin: Expositions on the Book of Psalms*. In Schaff, *A Select Library*, vol. 8.

The Avowyng of Arthur. In *Sir Gawain: Eleven Romances and Tales*. Ed. Thomas Hahn. Kalamazoo, MI: Medieval Institute Publications, 1995.

Barnie, John. *War in Medieval Society: Social Values and the Hundred Years' War, 1337–99*. London: Wiedenfield and Nicolson, 1974.

Bell, David N. *A Cloud of Witnesses: An Introductory History of the Development of Christian Doctrine*. Kalamazoo, MI: Cistercian Institute Publications, 1989.

———. *Many Mansions: An Introduction to the Development and Diversity of Medieval Theology*. Kalamazoo, MI: Cistercian Institute Publications, 1996.

Benson, C. David. "A Chaucerian Allusion and the Date of the Alliterative 'Destruction of Troy.'" *Notes and Queries* 219 (1974), 207.

Benson, Larry D. "The 'Rede Wynde' in 'The Siege of Jerusalem.'" *Notes and Queries* 205 (1960), 363–64.

Bernard, of Clairvaux. *The Works of Bernard of Clairvaux*. Vol. 7: *Treatises III*. Trans. Conrad Greenia. Kalamazoo, MI: Cistercian Publications, 1977.

Boethius. *The Consolation of Philosophy*. In *Boethius*. Ed. and trans. H. F. Stewart, E. K. Rand, and S. J. Tester. Loeb Classical Library 74. Cambridge, MA: Harvard University Press, 1973.

Brandon, S. G. F. *The Fall of Jerusalem and the Christian Church: A Study of the Effects of the Jewish Overthrow of A. D. 70 on Christianity*. London: S. P. C. K., 1951.

Breisach, Ernst. *Historiography: Ancient, Medieval, and Modern*. Second edition. Chicago: University of Chicago Press, 1994.

Brewer, Derek. "The Arming of the Warrior in European Literature and Chaucer." In *Chaucerian Problems and Perspectives*. Ed. Edward Vasta and Zacharias P. Thundy. Notre Dame: University of Notre Dame Press, 1979. Pp. 221–43.

Bronner, Ethan. "Portent in a Pasture? Appearance of Rare Heifer in Israel Spurs Hopes, Fears." *Boston Globe*. Sunday, April 6, 1997. Pp. A1, A22.

Brown, Carleton, and Rossell Hope Robbins, eds. *The Index of Middle English Verse*. New York: Columbia University Press, 1943.

Carter, Henry Holland. *A Dictionary of Middle English Musical Terms*. Indiana University Humanities Series 45. Bloomington, IN: Indiana University Press, 1961.

Chaucer, Geoffrey. *The Complete Works of Geoffrey Chaucer*. Ed. W. W. Skeat. Second edition. Oxford: University Press, 1899.

———. *The Riverside Chaucer*. Third edition. Gen. ed. Larry D. Benson. Boston, MA: Houghton Mifflin, 1987.

The Chester Mystery Cycle. Ed. R. M. Lumiansky and David Mills. 2 vols. EETS s.s. 3, 9. London: Oxford University Press, 1974–86.

Chism, Christine. "*The Siege of Jerusalem*: Liquidating Assets." *Journal of Medieval and Early Modern Studies* 28 (1998), 309–40.

———. *Alliterative Revivals*. Philadelphia: University of Pennsylvania Press, 2002. [See chapter 5: "Profiting from Precursors in *The Siege of Jerusalem*."]

Cleanness. In *The Poems of the Pearl Manuscript: Pearl, Cleanness, Patience, Sir Gawain and the Green Knight*. Ed. Malcolm Andrew and Ronald Waldron. Rev. ed. Exeter: Exeter University Press, 1996.

Conzelmann, Hans. *History of Primitive Christianity*. Nashville: Abingdon Press, 1973.

Cursor mundi: A Northumbrian Poem of the XIVth Century in Four Versions. Ed. Richard Morris, et al. EETS 57, 59, 62, 66, 68, 99, 101. London: Oxford University Press, 1961–66.

Cutler, John L., and Rossell Hope Robbins, eds. *Supplement to the Index of Middle English Verse*. Lexington: University of Kentucky Press, 1965.

Dante Alighieri. *The Divine Comedy*. Trans., with commentary, Charles S. Singleton. 2nd ed. 3 vols. Bollingen Series 80. Princeton, NJ: Princeton University Press, 1977.

Davis, Paul K. *Besieged: An Encyclopedia of Great Sieges from Ancient Times to the Present*. Santa Barbara, CA: ABC-CLIO, 2001.

Day, Mabel. "Strophic Division in Middle English Alliterative Verse." *Englische Studien* 66 (1931), 245–48.

Dean, James M., ed. *Medieval English Political Writings*. Kalamazoo, MI: Medieval Institute Publications, 1996.

Delany, Sheila. Review of Bonnie Millar, *The Siege of Jerusalem in its Physical, Literary and Historical Contexts*. *Speculum* 76 (2001), 1081–82.

Destruction of Troy. See *The "Gest hystoriale."*

Duggan, Hoyt N. "Strophic Patterns in Middle English Alliterative Poetry." *Modern Philology* 74 (1977), 223–47.

———. "The Shape of the B-Verse in Middle English Alliterative Poetry." *Speculum* 61 (1986), 564–92. [Argues for a strict ME form of the b-verse.]

———. "The Authenticity of the Z-text of *Piers Plowman*: Further Notes on Metrical Evidence." *Medium Ævum* 56 (1987), 25–45.

———. "Final *-e* and the Rhythmic Structure of the B-Verse in Middle English Alliterative Poetry." *Modern Philology* 86 (1988), 119–45.

Eusebius, of Caeserea. *Ecclesiastical History*. Ed. and trans. Kirsopp Lake. Loeb Classical Library 153. Cambridge, MA: Harvard University Press, 1964.

Everett, Dorothy. "The Alliterative Revival." In *Essays on Middle English Literature*. Ed. Patricia Kean. Oxford: Clarendon Press, 1955. Pp. 46–96.

Finlayson, John. "*Morte Arthure*: The Date and a Source for the Contemporary References." *Speculum* 42 (1967), 624–38.

Florence de Rome. Ed. A. Wallensköld. 2 vols. SATF 98–99. Paris, 1907.

Furneaux, Rupert. *The Roman Siege of Jerusalem*. New York: D. McKay Co., 1972.

The "Gest hystoriale" of the Destruction of Troy: An Alliterative Romance Translated from Guido de Colonna's "Hystoria Troiana" Edited from the Unique Manuscript in the Hunterian Museum, University of Glasgow. Ed. George A. Panton and David Donaldson. EETS o.s. 39, 56. London: N. Trübner, 1869–74.

Gospel of Nicodemus. In *The Middle-English Harrowing of Hell and Gospel of Nicodemus*. Ed. William Henry Hulme. EETS e.s. 100. London: Oxford University Press, 1907.

Gower, John. *Confessio Amantis*. Ed. Russell A. Peck, with Latin translations by Andrew Galloway. Kalamazoo, MI: Medieval Institute Publications, 2000–04.

Gransden, Antonia. *Historical Writing in England II: C.1307 to the Early Sixteenth Century*. London: Routledge & Kegan Paul, 1982.

Growth, Peter. "Pontius Pilate." In *A Dictionary of Biblical Tradition in English Literature*. Gen. ed. David Lyle Jeffrey. Grand Rapids, MI: William B. Eerdmans, 1992. Pp. 622–24.

Guddat-Figge, Gisela. *Catalogue of the Manuscripts Containing Middle English Romances*. Munich: W. Fink, 1976.

Hall, Thomas N. "Medieval Traditions about the Site of Judgment." *Essays in Medieval Studies* 10 (1993), 79–97.

Hamel, Mary. "*The Siege of Jerusalem* as a Crusading Poem." In *Journeys toward God: Pilgrimage and Crusade*. Ed. Barbara N. Sargent-Baur. Kalamazoo, MI: Medieval Institute Publications, 1992. Pp. 177–94.

Hanna, Ralph, III. "Contextualising *The Siege of Jerusalem*." *Yearbook of Langland Studies* 6 (1992), 109–21.

———. *Pursuing History: Middle English Manuscripts and Their Texts*. Stanford: Stanford University Press, 1996. [See chapter 5: "On Stemmatics."]

———, and David Lawton. See *Siege of Jerusalem*.

Hebron, Malcolm. *The Medieval Siege: Theme and Image in Middle English Romance*. Oxford: Clarendon Press, 1997. [See chapter 5: "The Siege of Jerusalem."]

Higden, Ranulf. *Polychronicon Ranulphi Higden monachi Cestrensis; Together with the English Translations of John Trevisa and of an Unknown Writer of the Fifteenth Century*. Ed. Joseph Rawson Lumby. Rerum Britannicarum medii aevi scriptores (Rolls Series) 41. 9 vols. London: Longman & Co., 1865–86.

Hornstein, Lillian Herlands. "Miscellaneous Romances." In *A Manual of the Writings in Middle English 1050–1500*. Ed. J. Burke Severs and Albert E. Hartung. 10 vols. to date. New Haven: Connecticut Academy of Arts and Sciences, 1967–.

Hulbert, J. R. "The Text of *The Siege of Jerusalem*." *Studies in Philology* 28 (1930), 602–12.

Jacobs, Nicholas. "Alliterative Storms: A Topos in Middle English." *Speculum* 47 (1972), 695–719.

Jacobus de Voragine. *Legenda aurea*. Ed. Johan Georg Theodor Grässe. Dresden: Impensis Librariae Arnoldianae, 1846.

———. *The Golden Legend*. Trans. Granger Ryan and Helmut Ripperger. New York: Arno Press, 1969.

———. *Legenda aurea: Edizione critica*. Ed. Giovanni Paolo Maggioni. 2 vols. Rev. ed. Millennio Medievale 6, Testi 3. Florence: SISMEL, Edizioni del Galluzzo, 1998.

Josephus, Flavius. *The Works of Flavius Josephus*. Trans. William Whiston. Baltimore: Armstrong and Plaskitt, 1830.

Kaluza, Max. "Strophische Gliederung in der mittelenglischen rein alliterirenden Dichtung." *Englische Studien* 16 (1892), 169–80.

Keen, Maurice H. *The Laws of War in the Late Middle Ages*. London: Routledge and Kegan Paul, 1965.

Keiser, George R. "Edward III and the Alliterative *Morte Arthure*." *Speculum* 48 (1973), 37–51.

King Edward and the Shepherd. In *Middle English Metrical Romances*. Eds. Walter Hoyt French and Charles Brockway Hale. New York: Prentice-Hall, 1930.

Knighton, Henry. *Knighton's Chronicle, 1337–1396*. Ed. and trans. Geoffrey Howard Martin. Oxford: Clarendon Press, 1995.

Kölbing, Eugen, and Mabel Day. See *Siege of Jerusalem*.

Langland, William. *Piers Plowman: The A Version, Will's Visions of Piers Plowman and Do-Well*. Ed. George Kane. London: Athlone Press, 1960.

Large, David Clay. *Between Two Fires: Europe's Path in the 1930s*. New York and London: W. W. Norton, 1990.

Lawton, David. "Titus Goes Hunting and Hawking: The Poetics of Recreation and Revenge in *The Siege of Jerusalem*." In *Individuality and Achievement in Middle English Poetry*. Ed. O. S. Pickering. Woodbridge, UK: D. S. Brewer, 1997.

———. "Sacrilege and Theatricality: The Croxton *Play of the Sacrament*." *Journal of Medieval and Early Modern Studies* 33 (2003), 281–309.

Lindberg, Carter. *The European Reformations*. Oxford: Blackwell, 1996.

Livingston, Michael. "The Seven: Hebrews, Hellenists, and Heptines." *Journal of Higher Criticism* 6 (1999), 32–63.

Maidstone, Richard. *Richard Maidstone's Penitential Psalms: Ed. from Bodl. MS Rawlinson A 389.* Ed. Valerie Edden. Middle English Texts 22. Heidelberg: C. Winter Universitäts-verlag, 1990.

———. *Concordia (The Reconciliation of Richard II with London).* Ed. David R. Carlson, with verse translation by A. G. Rigg. Kalamazoo, MI: Medieval Institute Publications, 2003.

Mandeville, John. *The Defective Version of Mandeville's Travels.* Ed. M. C. Seymour. EETS o.s. 319. Oxford: Oxford University Press, 2002.

Matthews, William. *The Tragedy of Arthur: A Study of the Alliterative "Morte Arthure."* Berkeley: University of California Press, 1960.

McIntosh, Angus, M. L. Samuels, and Michael Benskin, eds., with the assistance of Margaret Laing and Keith Williamson. *A Linguistic Atlas of Late Mediaeval English.* 4 vols. Aberdeen: Aberdeen University Press, 1986.

Mézières, Philippe de. *Letter to King Richard II: A Plea made in 1395 for Peace between England and France.* Ed. and trans. G. W. Coopland. Liverpool: Liverpool University Press, 1975.

Middle English Dictionary. Gen. eds. Hans Kurath and Sherman M. Kuhn. Ann Arbor: University of Michigan Press, 1952–2003.

The Middle English Prose Translation of Roger d'Argenteuil's Bible en françois: Edited from Cleveland Public Library, MS Wq091.92–C.468. Ed. Phyllis Moe. Middle English Texts 6. Heidelberg: Winter, 1977.

Millar, Bonnie. "The Role of Prophecy in the *Siege of Jerusalem* and Its Analogues." *Yearbook of Langland Studies* 13 (1999), 153–78.

———. *The Siege of Jerusalem in Its Physical, Literary and Historical Contexts.* Dublin: Four Courts Press, 2000.

Mercer Dictionary of the Bible. Gen. ed. Watson E. Mills. Macon, GA: Mercer University Press, 1990.

Moe, Phyllis. "The French Source of the Alliterative Siege of Jerusalem." *Medium Ævum* 39 (1970), 147–54.

Morey, James. *Book and Verse: A Guide to Middle English Biblical Literature.* Urbana: University of Illinois Press, 2000.

Morte Arthure: A Critical Edition. Ed. Mary Hamel. Garland Medieval Texts 9. New York: Garland Publishing, 1984. [Discusses the dating of the *Siege* and its relationship to the *Alliterative Morte Arthure*, pp. 46–58. See also *Alliterative Morte Arthure.*]

Mum and the Sothsegger. In *Richard the Redeless and Mum and the Sothsegger.* Ed. James M. Dean. Kalamazoo, MI: Medieval Institute Publications, 2000.

Neilson, George. *"Huchown of the Awle Ryale," the Alliterative Poet.* Glasgow: James MacLehose & Sons, 1902.

Nicholson, Roger. "Haunted Itineraries: Reading the *Siege of Jerusalem.*" *Exemplaria* 14 (2002), 447–84.

Oakden, J. P., with Elizabeth R. Innes. *Alliterative Poetry in Middle English: A Survey of the Traditions.* Manchester: Manchester University Press, 1935. [See pp. 44–46 and 85–111.]

Oxford Classical Dictionary. Third edition. Ed. Simon Hornblower and Antony Spawforth. Oxford: Oxford University Press, 1996.

Oxford English Dictionary. Second edition. Ed. J. A. Simpson and E. S. C. Weiner. Oxford: Clarendon Press, 1989.

Palmer, J. J. N. *England, France and Christendom, 1377–99.* Chapel Hill: University of North Carolina Press, 1972.

Parlement of the Thre Ages. In *Wynnere and Wastoure and The Parlement of the Thre Ages.* Ed. Warren Ginsburg. Kalamazoo, MI: Medieval Institute Publications, 1992.

Patience. See *Cleanness.*

Pearsall, Derek. *Old English and Middle English Poetry.* London: Routledge and K. Paul, 1977.

Peck, Russell A. "Willfulness and Wonders: Boethian Tragedy in the *Alliterative Morte Arthure.*" In *The Alliterative Tradition in the Fourteenth Century.* Ed. Bernard S. Levy and Paul E. Szarmach. Kent, OH: The Kent State University Press, 1981. Pp. 153–82.

———. "Social Conscience and the Poets." In *Social Unrest in the Late Middle Ages.* Ed. Francis X. Newman. Medieval & Renaissance Texts & Studies 39. Binghamton, NY: Medieval & Renaissance Texts & Studies, 1986. Pp. 113–48.

Perroy, Édouard. *L'Angleterre et le Grand Schisme d'Occident: Étude sur la Politique Religieuse de l'Angleterre sous Richard II (1378–99)*. Paris: J. Monnier, 1933.

Pollard, Alfred W., and G. R. Redgrave. *A Short-Title Catalogue of Books Printed in England, Scotland, and Ireland and of English Books Printed Abroad, 1475–1640*. Second ed., rev. and enlarged. 3 vols. London: Bibliographical Society, 1976–91.

Pratt, John H. *Chaucer and War*. Lanham, MD: University Press of America, 2000.

Price, Merrall Llewelyn. "Imperial Violence and the Monstrous Mother: Cannibalism at the Siege of Jerusalem." In *Domestic Violence in Medieval Texts*. Ed. Eve Salisbury, Georgiana Donavin, and Merrall Llewelyn Price. Gainesville: University Press of Florida, 2002. Pp. 272–98.

Price, Patricia. "Integrating Time and Space: The Literary Geography of *Patience, Cleanness, The Siege of Jerusalem*, and *St. Erkenwald*." *Medieval Perspectives* 11 (1996), 234–50.

Rhoads, David M. *Israel in Revolution, 6–74 C. E.: A Political History Based on the Writings of Josephus*. Philadelphia: Fortress Press, 1976.

Saul, Nigel. *Richard II*. New Haven, CT: Yale University Press, 1997.

Scattergood, V. J. "Chaucer and the French War: *Sir Thopas* and *Melibee*." In *Court and Poet: Selected Proceedings of the International Courtly Literature Society [Liverpool 1980]*. Ed. Glyn S. Burgess. Liverpool: Francis Cairns, 1981. Pp. 287–96.

Schaff, Philip, et al., ed. *A Select Library of the Nicene and Post-Nicene Fathers of the Christian Church*. 14 vols. New York: Christian Literature, 1886–90; rpt. Edinburgh: T&T Clark, 1991–97.

Schermann, Theodorus. *Prophetarum Vitae Fabulosae: Indices Apostolorum Discipulorumque*. Leipzig: Teubneri, 1907.

The Siege of Jerusalem. Ed. Eugen Kölbing and Mabel Day. EETS o.s. 188. London: Oxford University Press, 1932. [Based on copy L.]

———. Ed. Thorlac Turville-Petre. In *Alliterative Poetry of the Later Middle Ages: An Anthology*. Washington, DC: Catholic University of America Press, 1989. Pp. 158–69. [Based on copy D, but limited to lines 521–724.]

———. Ed. Ralph Hanna and David Lawton. EETS o.s. 320. Oxford: Oxford University Press, 2003. [Based on copy L.]

The Siege of Jerusalem in Prose. Ed. Auvo Kurvinen. Mémoires de la Société Néophilologique de Helsinki 34. Helsinki: Société Néophilologique, 1969.

Sir Gawain and the Green Knight. See *Cleanness*.

Sir Perceval of Galles. In *Sir Perceval of Galles and Ywain and Gawain*. Ed. Mary Flowers Braswell. Kalamazoo, MI: Medieval Institute Publications, 1995.

Spearing, A. C. *Readings in Medieval Poetry*. Cambridge, UK: Cambridge University Press, 1987.

Stillwell, Gardiner. "*Wynnere and Wastoure* and the Hundred Years' War." *English Literary History* 8 (1941), 241–47.

———. "The Political Meaning of Chaucer's Tale of Melibee." *Speculum* 19 (1944), 433–44.

Sumption, Jonathan. *Pilgrimage: An Image of Mediaeval Religion*. Totowa, NJ: Rowman and Littlefield, 1975.

Sundwall, McKay. "The *Destruction of Troy*, Chaucer's *Troilus and Criseyde*, and Lydgate's *Troy Book*." *Review of English Studies*, n.s. 26 (1975), 313–17.

Sutton, John William. "Mordred's End: A Reevaluation of Mordred's Death Scene in the Alliterative *Morte Arthure*." *Chaucer Review* 37 (2003), 280–85.

Taylor, John. *The "Universal Chronicle" of Ranulf Higden*. Oxford: Clarendon Press, 1966.

Tilley, Morris Palmer. *A Dictionary of the Proverbs in England in the Sixteenth and Seventeenth Centuries*. Ann Arbor: University of Michigan Press, 1950.

Tipton, Charles. "The English at Nicopolis." *Speculum* 37 (1962), 528–40.

Titus and Vespasian, or, the Destruction of Jerusalem in Rhymed Couplets. Ed. John Alexander Herbert. Roxburghe Club 146. London: The Roxburghe Club, 1905.

The Towneley Plays: Re-edited from the Unique MS. Ed. George England. EETS e.s. 71. London: Oxford University Press, 1897; rpt. 1952.

Turville-Petre, Thorlac. *The Alliterative Revival*. Cambridge, UK: D. S. Brewer, 1977.

Usk, Adam. *The Chronicle of Adam Usk, 1377–1421*. Ed. and trans. C. Given-Wilson. Oxford: Clarendon Press, 1997.

Van Court, Elisa Narin. "*The Siege of Jerusalem* and Augustinian Historians: Writing about Jews in Fourteenth-Century England." *Chaucer Review* 29 (1995), 227–48.

La Vengeance de Nostre-Seigneur: The Old and Middle French Prose Versions. Ed. Alvin E. Ford. 2 vols. Studies and Texts 63, 115. Toronto: Pontifical Institute of Mediaeval Studies, 1984–1993. [The first volume discusses and edits families A and B of the French tradition; the second volume completes the study by discussing and editing families C to I.]

La Venjance Nostre Seigneur: The Oldest Version of the Twelfth-century Poem. Ed. Loyal A. T. Gryting. Contributions in Modern Philology 19. Ann Arbor: University of Michigan Press, 1952.

Vindicta salvatoris. In *Evangelia apocrypha*. Ed. Constantine Tischendorf. Leipzig: H. Mendelssohn, 1876. [This edition includes the Latin text based on London, British Library MS Harley 495, pp. 471–86.]

The Wakefield Pageants in the Towneley Cycle. Ed. A. C. Cawley. Old and Middle English Texts 1. Manchester, UK: Manchester University Press, 1958.

Waldron, Ronald A. "Oral-Formulaic Technique and Middle English Alliterative Poetry." *Speculum* 32 (1957), 792–804.

The Wars of Alexander: An Alliterative Romance Translated Chiefly from the Historia Alexandri Magni de preliis; Re-edited from Ms. Ashmole 44, in the Bodleian Library, Oxford, and Ms. D.4.12, in the Library of Trinity College, Dublin. Ed. Walter W. Skeat. EETS e.s. 47. London: N. Trübner, 1886.

———. Ed. Hoyt N. Duggan and Thorlac Turville-Petre. EETS s.s. 10. Oxford: Oxford University Press, 1989.

Whiting, Bartlett Jere, with the collaboration of Helen Wescott Whiting. *Proverbs, Sentences, and Proverbial Phrases from English Writings Mainly before 1500*. Cambridge, MA: The Belknap Press of Harvard University Press, 1968.

Wright, Stephen K. *The Vengeance of Our Lord: Medieval Dramatizations of the Destruction of Jerusalem*. Studies and Texts 89. Toronto: Pontifical Institute of Mediaeval Studies, 1989.

Wynnere and Wastoure. See *The Parlement of the Thre Ages*.

Yeager, R. F. "*Pax Poetica*: On the Pacifism of Chaucer and Gower." *Studies in the Age of Chaucer* 9 (1987), 97–121.

The York Plays: The Plays Performed by the Crafts or Mysteries of York on the Day of Corpus Christi in the 14th, 15th, and 16th Centuries. Ed. Lucy Toulmin Smith. New York: Russell & Russell, 1963.

MIDDLE ENGLISH TEXTS SERIES

Richard Maidstone, *Concordia (The Reconciliation of Richard II with London)*, edited by David R. Carlson, with a verse translation by A. G. Rigg (2003)

Three Purgatory Poems: The Gast of Gy, Sir Owain, and The Vision of Tundale, edited by Edward E. Foster (2004)

William Dunbar, *The Complete Works*, edited by John Conlee (2004)

Chaucerian Dream Visions and Complaints, edited by Dana M. Symons (2004)

Stanzaic Guy of Warwick, edited by Alison Wiggins (2004)

DOCUMENTS OF PRACTICE SERIES

Love and Marriage in Late Medieval London, selected, translated, and introduced by Shannon McSheffrey (1995)

Sources for the History of Medicine in Late Medieval England, selected, introduced, and translated by Carole Rawcliffe (1995)

A Slice of Life: Selected Documents of Medieval English Peasant Experience, edited, translated, and with an introduction by Edwin Brezette DeWindt (1996)

Regular Life: Monastic, Canonical, and Mendicant Rules, selected with an introduction by Douglas J. McMillan and Kathryn Smith Fladenmuller (1997); second edition, selected and introduced by Daniel Marcel La Corte and Douglas J. McMillan (2004)

Women and Monasticism in Medieval Europe: Sisters and Patrons of the Cistercian Reform, selected, translated, and with an introduction by Constance H. Berman (2002)

Medieval Notaries and Their Acts: The 1327–1328 Register of Jean Holanie, introduced, edited, and translated by Kathryn L. Reyerson and Debra A. Salata (2004)

COMMENTARY SERIES

Commentary on the Book of Jonah, Haimo of Auxerre, translated with an introduction by Deborah Everhart (1993)

Medieval Exegesis in Translation: Commentaries on the Book of Ruth, translated with an introduction by Lesley Smith (1996)

Nicholas of Lyra's Apocalypse Commentary, translated with an introduction and notes by Philip D. W. Krey (1997)

Rabbi Ezra Ben Solomon of Gerona: Commentary on the Song of Songs and Other Kabbalistic Commentaries, selected, translated, and annotated by Seth Brody (1999)

John Wyclif: On the Truth of Holy Scripture, translated with an introduction and notes by Ian Christopher Levy (2001)

Second Thessalonians: Two Early Medieval Apocalyptic Commentaries, translated with an introduction by Steven R. Cartwright and Kevin L. Hughes (2001)

The Glossa Ordinaria on the Song of Songs, translated with an introduction and notes by Mary Dove (2004)

MEDIEVAL GERMAN TEXTS IN BILINGUAL EDITIONS SERIES

Sovereignty and Salvation in the Vernacular, 1050–1150, introduction, translations, and notes by James A. Schultz (2000)

Ava's New Testament Narratives: "When the Old Law Passed Away," introduction, translations, and notes by James A. Rushing, Jr. (2003)

History as Literature: German World Chronicles of the Thirteenth Century in Verse, introduction, translations, and notes by R. Graeme Dunphy (2003)

TO ORDER PLEASE CONTACT:

Medieval Institute Publications
Western Michigan University
Kalamazoo, MI 49008-5432
Phone (269) 387-8755
FAX (269) 387-8750

http://www.wmich.edu/medieval/mip/index.html

Medieval Institute Publications is a program
of The Medieval Institute, College of Arts
and Sciences, Western Michigan University

Typeset in 10/13 New Baskerville
with Golden Cockerel Ornaments display
Designed by Linda K. Judy
Composed by Michael Livingston and Julie Scrivener
Manufactured by McNaughton & Gunn, Inc., Saline, Michigan

Medieval Institute Publications
College of Arts and Sciences
Western Michigan University
1903 W. Michigan Avenue
Kalamazoo, MI 49008-5432
http://www.wmich.edu/medieval/mip

 WESTERN MICHIGAN UNIVERSITY